BEATING THEM AT THEIR OWN GAME

First published in 2006 by
Liberties Press
Guinness Enterprise Centre | Taylor's Lane | Dublin 8 | Ireland
www.LibertiesPress.com
General and sales enquiries: +353 (1) 415 1224 | peter@libertiespress.com
Editorial: +353 (1) 402 0805 | sean@libertiespress.com
Liberties Press is a member of Clé, the Irish Book Publishers' Association

Trade enquiries to CMD Distribution
55A Spruce Avenue | Stillorgan Industrial Park | Blackrock | County Dublin
Tel: +353 (1) 294 2560 | Fax: +353 (1) 294 2564

ISBN 10: 1–905483–10–4
ISBN 13: 978–1–905483–10–5

2 4 6 8 10 9 7 5 3 1

A CIP record for this title is available from the British Library

Set in Garamond
Printed in Ireland by Colour Books
Unit 105 | Baldoyle Industrial Estate | Dublin 13

BEATING THEM AT THEIR OWN GAME

HOW THE IRISH CONQUERED ENGLISH SOCCER

PATRICK WEST

For Conor and Patrick

CONTENTS

FOREWORD

'Seville where they get the oranges – but for us only the bitter lemon.' Thus Philip Greene signed off after the Republic had lost to Spain in that lovely city in the heart of Andalusia.

And after another away defeat by Spain there was a headline in the *Evening Press* that said 'SEÑORS AND JUNIORS'.

Those rather pithy comments were typical of the mood among the Republic's football folk a generation ago.

Even though we had twice come close to qualifying for the World Cup Finals in that era of moral victories and gallant defeats, Stuttgart in the midsummer of 1988 will forever be seen as a timemark.

I was on the terrace to the left of England's goal when Tony Galvin set off on a run down the far wing. Little danger was apparent: all the English defenders were present and correct.

He got to within about fifteen yards of the corner flag and sent over a cross parallel to the end line. It went about ten yards beyond the far post.

Kenny Sansom, the tidiest left-back in England or anywhere, mis-kicked. The ball went up in an arc.

John Aldridge won the first jump. His header went to Ray Houghton. He nodded the ball tantalisingly away from Peter Shilton and inside the far post.

All heaven broke loose. The remaining eighty-three minutes was played in an atmosphere made up of rejoicing and apprehension.

That period gave all of the Green Army an intimation of infinity, not to mention eternity.

Packie Bonner was like the boy on the burning deck or Cuchulainn at the ford, or the Spartans at Thermopylae.

At last normal time (only it seemed very far from normal) was up and we began to breathe with some ease.

Then all kinds of watches, not to mention clocks, were being consulted in Stuttgart and in Knocknagoshel, and Boston and Kilburn. Our hearts almost stopped.

That brilliant leprechaun named Peter Beardsley broke through the middle and shot from the edge of the box. I saw the net tremble. The ball grazed over the bar.

That night in the hotel in the mountains we experienced jubilation unrestricted.

About midnight I managed to find a quiet corner, kind of. I was joined by Kevin Moran, who said: 'I'd give anything to be down in Ballybunion tonight.'

My room was on the ground floor; about three o'clock I had to give up my bed to two lasses from Aer Lingus whose hotel was miles away.

I sat on a low branch of a mighty oak and cobbled my piece for the *Evening Press*.

I was joined by Liam Brady. He had missed out on the greatest occasion in the Republic's football history – nor was he ever to play in the Finals of the World Cup or the European Championship.

*

We will move the calendar back now to a night in Heysel Stadium in Brussels in the March of 1981.

It was a night of heavy rain and with thunder and lightning for bad measure.

It was an occasion for survival. The Republic seemed home but not dry with five minutes to go.

Then Steve Heighway seemed to have fouled a Belgian midfielder twenty yards from the end line and halfway to the Republic's left.

Seamus McDonagh was blatantly obstructed as he went for the ball as it dipped under the bar. Thus Belgium scored the only goal of the game.

The loss of that point was to prove very costly. Eoin Hand had already suffered a stroke of extremely bad luck.

The Republic had got a bad result in Cyprus – they won only 2–3. France won there 0–7. Eoin inherited that bad result.

Thus France got to the Spanish Finals on goal difference. It was of little consolation that the Belgian who had dived that night in Brussels confessed his crime a few years later.

Eoin Hand's first stewardship produced the best football in the history of the Republic.

It involved a famous 3–2 victory over France in a World Cup game at Lansdowne Road.

Fortune didn't ride shotgun with him. At the end of his stewardship we had cause to appreciate an old German two-liner: 'When Lady Good Luck comes to your bedside, she kisses you on the cheek and flits away; when Lady Bad Luck comes, she sits down and takes out her knitting.'

I have been at all of our games against England since 1957 – alas, I missed the most sensational meeting of all.

That was in Goodison Park in September 1949. It was a friendly – if you could imagine such between those two countries.

England were preparing for the World Cup; they fielded their best eleven. You could back the Republic at ten to one.

The game resembled that in Stuttgart almost forty years later: it was a siege. England attacked in waves.

Tommy Godwin emulated Packie Bonner before Packie was born. We scored twice in breakaways.

Con Martin scored a penalty. Peter Farrell got a late second goal.

There was little celebration: Con Martin, then playing with Aston Villa, got a lift back to Birmingham.

The two League of Ireland players, Tommy Godwin and Tommy O'Connor, came back on the Liverpool ferry.

A few friends met them at the North Wall; perhaps they all went to an early pub – I don't know.

In time I became acquainted with Con Martin and Peter Farrell and Tommy O'Connor. It was a privilege to know great men with no airs and many graces.

You can read all about the modest heroes of 1949 and many more in this enthralling book.

Con Houlihan, Autumn 2006

9

PROLOGUE

England were beaten by a bunch of boyos from their own backyard.

THE *SUN*, JUNE 1988

As an Englishman, I must confess that one of my most traumatic teenage memories was that goal by Ray Houghton in Stuttgart in 1988. His header, which gave Ireland a 1–0 win over England that year, thoroughly rattled us Sassenachs. Many of my compatriots will agree. No one likes losing to local rivals – rivals whom you consider inferior to yourselves, and indeed have spent eight hundred years feeling superior to. We had long got used to succumbing to South Americans, Germans, Italians and a multitude of others – but the Irish? After all, we invented the game, and as accustomed as we had become to losing to countries that had embraced soccer, it seemed perverse, even unfair, to be beaten by a nation that we all thought didn't actually like the game, that had positively disdained it for so long.

The ordeal of that 1–0 scoreline was exacerbated by the fact that my mother is Irish: I was annoyed that I had been forced into a conflict of loyalties that made me realise that, no matter how hard I tried, I didn't feel Irish: no matter how hard I had tried to resist it, I realised I was a chauvinist, Little Englander. My reaction, and that of my compatriots, was one of humiliation. Little did I fully appreciate at the time the jubilation that the result had generated on the other side of the Irish Sea – a result that made grown men weep. We had always seen ourselves as superior to the Irish, especially as, during the late 1980s, we were undergoing an economic renaissance just as Ireland was suffering another of its periodic downturns.

Of course, the Irish are said to have been beating the English at their

11

own game in a different manner for decades now, as my cousins, aunts and uncles in Dublin would persistently remind me when I holidayed there as a boy: the Irish speak the English language better than the English themselves, they would say. As well as being constantly mocked for my lazy Cockney glottal-stops and for employing the term 'Aren't I?' instead of the more grammatically correct 'Amn't I?', I was informed that the finest and most inventive writers of English were Irish. As I grew older, I became accustomed to being ribbed that, while all the English did was read the *Sun* and watch *EastEnders,* the Irish were busy venturing off to summer schools to discuss the merits of Wilde, Joyce and Yeats.

Many cultural commentators have perceived the intention of these writers – particularly Joyce, with his ability to master (and then mangle, and thereby mock) the English language – to be to exact post-imperial revenge. The Irish, so long derided as mentally inferior to the English, sought to show up their neighbours by proving that they were in fact superior to them. In retrospect, Houghton's goal was similar, and the manner in which the Irish have embraced the game, particularly by taking it back to the imperial bosom, may be seen as an example of the so-called servant teaching the master a lesson.

Beating Them at Their Own Game: How the Irish Conquered English Soccer is the story of rise of soccer in Ireland since 1945, and the enormous, disproportionate contribution Irish footballers have made to the English game in England. To employ the term 'conquered' may seem hyperbole, but considering the sheer number of top-class footballers from a nation of five million who have succeeded in a nation of forty-five million, I think it appropriate. It is also apposite when taking into consideration the fact that, although soccer has always been played in Ireland, it never used to be a national sport. Quite the contrary: it was regarded as a 'foreign game' and was often frowned upon as being 'un-Irish' – a sport for 'West Brits' played only in the Protestant North and among the undesirable elements of the poor working classes in Dublin, Cork and Limerick.

This is the story of the men who flocked to England in the postwar era as the game blossomed in popularity from the 1940s onwards, and of the children of the diaspora who have also made the game their own. It tells of their struggles, triumphs and disappointments. It is about the men who have become heroes in Ireland, and in England, through beating the English at their own game.

And it is a story worth telling, because it is an often-neglected one. As the *Sunday Tribune*'s Dave Hannigan lamented a few years ago, the role played by the Irish in helping the matches between the top English clubs become some of – if not *the* – most exciting and popular sporting spectacles in the world is frequently ignored. In December 2002, as the English Football Museum in Preston formally inducted twenty-three players and six managers into its inaugural Hall of Fame, Hannigan noted that not a single one of the twenty-nine men hailed from the Republic of Ireland. There were Scots, like Kenny Dalglish, and players from the North, such as George Best, but the South was conspicuous by its absence. 'What sort of a distorted version of the game's history is the museum passing on if there isn't one person from the Republic of Ireland reckoned good enough for induction at this stage?' he asked. 'Do the names Johnny Carey, Liam Whelan, Liam Brady, Johnny Giles and Paul McGrath mean anything to these people? What about Denis Irwin and Roy Keane?'[1] *Beating Them at Their Own Game* hopes to do justice to all of these players, and more. It does not pretend to be a comprehensive study: to chart intimately the lives and careers of every Irishman who has made it in English soccer would take not one book but a shelf-full of them.

Moreover, this book is about the changing relationship between England and Ireland, and the way in which Ireland has changed in the last sixty years. By embracing soccer, Ireland has demonstrated that it no longer has an inferiority complex in regard to England: it no longer feels that it has to protect Gaelic games, those signifiers of 'pure Irishness', against the behemoth across the water. Indeed, it is worth noting that soccer's ascendancy has not seen the popularity of hurling or football diminish. Quite the reverse, in fact: Gaelic games have never been so popular. It also mirrors the end of a deeper insularity that is characterised by the era of Éamon de Valera or John Charles McQuaid, in that Ireland has embraced what has become the world's game. Some say that the decline of the Catholic Church, or the rise of the Celtic Tiger economy, or the transformation of the country into a liberal, multiracial, multicultural place represent the coming of modernity to Ireland; a good argument could be made for the fact that the country has taken to its heart a sport that was invented by twelve men in a London pub in 1863.

*

My thanks to Seán O'Keeffe and to Peter O'Connell, for their help and patience, to Carlos and Louise Kenny, to Richard West, and most of all to Mary Kenny, Ed West and Mark Scully, without whom this book would not have been possible.

A NOTE ON THE TEXT

Fans of Celtic or Rangers, or indeed detractors of either club, will notice that this book is about the relationship between England and Ireland, not *Britain* and Ireland. Thus the story of Irish players in Scotland is omitted from the book. The relationship between England, Scotland and Ireland in terms of football warrants a study in itself. Apologies are therefore due to fans of Bertie Peacock, Sean Fallon, Packie Bonner, Paul Byrne, Neil Lennon and others who have made it in Scotland. Apologies, too, to supporters of Shamrock Rovers, Bohemians, Sligo Rovers, Derry City, Linfield, Glentoran and every other team on the island of Ireland, as this book concerns the travails and exploits of Irish players in England.

On the other hand, Ulster Protestant footballers are included in a separate chapter not out of any sectarian sensibilities, but because soccer has always been intrinsic to Ulster Protestant culture in a way that it has not amongst Irish Catholics. And while English–Ulster Protestant relations have been marked by ambivalence on both sides, Ulster Protestant culture has historically been more Anglophile than Southern Catholic culture. Likewise, second-generation Irish footballers warrant their own chapter not necessarily because they are 'less Irish' than native Irishmen, but because they have often been deemed so, and thus their experiences have been different.

Owing to the restructurings in English football that took place in 1992 and 2004, the top tier of English football will be referred to as 'the First Division' in relation to events before 1992, and as 'the Premiership' thereafter. Likewise, 'the Second Division' became 'the First Division in the 1992–93 season, and 'the Championship' in 2004–05. For the sake of brevity and clarity, where necessary I have used the terms 'first tier of English football' and 'second tier of English football'. Similarly, as the

15

League Cup has gone through many incarnations over the years – the Milk Cup, the Littlewoods Cup, the Rumbelows Cup, the Coca-Cola Cup, the Worthington Cup and the Carling Cup – it is referred to throughout simply as 'the League Cup'.

1

ALBION'S SEED

A BRIEF HISTORY OF THE ENGLISH GAME

England invented football and, like the English language, football has colonised the world. This may sound like something of an exaggeration, or perhaps an example of typical Anglo-Saxon jingoism. But it is largely true; more to the point, it is a widely held perception – both among Englishmen and, for a long time, many Irishmen. There have been myriad forms of football played in different cultures and at different times, but the one that the English codified is the one that conquered the world: it is the only remaining variant of the game that we can describe as truly global.

Today, the word 'football' – or 'futebol', 'fotboll', 'futbol' or 'fußball' – is invariably used as shorthand for the sport that the English invented. That its name is variously spelt in a corrupted anglophone manner bears testament to the fact that the game was spread by the English. What else could explain the fact that Juventus play in the same colours as Notts County, an English club who donated spare kits to the English-run Italian club in 1903? There are Argentinian teams called Racing Club, River Plate and Newell's Old Boys – and for good reason. It is no accident that AC Milan are not called 'Milano', or that the club, established by English expatriates, to this day bears the Cross of St George on its badge.

No wonder then that, in Ireland, the word 'football' was guarded so jealously, to refer to the indigenous fifteen-a-side pursuit, rather than to the eleven-a-side game that came from across the sea. It was as though the English had taken so much away from Irish culture that the retention of the name 'football' became a form of cultural resistance. Similarly, and not by coincidence, only in Australia and the United States – both also former British colonies – is 'the beautiful game' known as soccer, in opposition to the home-grown forms of football played in those two countries.

Like religion or music, the urge to play a sport in which opposing participants seek to gain possession of a ball and conquer territory with it seems to be a universal human impulse. Football of a sort was played during the Han dynasty in ancient China, during the second century BC: the game called 'Tsu Chu' which emerged during that era involved kicking a ball stuffed with leather. It is said that even Chinese emperors took part in this game. The Greeks and Romans had variants of the sport, as did the Egyptians, Polynesians, Japanese, Inuit and Aztecs. (In the Aztec form of the game, the captain of the losing side was ritually sacrificed.)

In Europe, by the Middle Ages variants of footballs were being played in many parts of the continent. In fourteenth-century Florence 'calico', a twenty-seven-a-side game with six umpires, developed. Various forms sprang up in England in the twelfth century: matches often resembled mass brawls between entire villages, with goals frequently a mile or more apart. Concurrently, a form of football emerged in Ireland along similar lines: it too usually involved inter-village competitions between large numbers of men, in which the intention was to get the ball across a boundary line separating two villages.

In 1331, Edward III tried to ban football, fearing that its popularity was distracting the masses from the vital, martial pursuit of archery. He and many subsequent English monarchs were also concerned – probably with justification – that playing football promoted lawlessness. Centuries before Johnny Giles and Roy Keane ventured to England, there was particular concern about the Irish being especially violent when it came to the game. One fourteenth-century report reads: 'On Monday, March 25, 1303, Thomas of Salisbury, a student at Oxford University, found his brother Adam dead, and it was alleged that he was killed by Irish students, whilst playing the ball in the High Street towards Eastgate.'[1] Indeed, the Irish were considered to be vicious footballers on account of their custom of deliberately kicking people in the head. In his play *The White Devil (1612)*, the dramatist John Webster had one of his characters say: 'Like the wild Irish, I'le nere thinke thee dead, Til I can play at footeball with thy head'.[2] The English were initially lenient about the playing of the game in Ireland, with the 1527 Statute of Galway permitting the playing of 'foot balle', but they did forbid hurling because it was a game of the native Irish. In 1695, however, the Sunday Observance Act proscribed the playing of any type of sport on the island, with anyone caught doing so fined a shilling, a substantial sum of money at that time.

Football in England and Ireland continued nonetheless in the ensuing centuries, with various forms of the game being codified in public schools in England during the eighteenth century, and many clubs emerging independently outside educational establishments. But there remained confusion when such teams played each other. Apart from prosaic matters such as the size of the pitch and the goal size, how throw-ins should be taken, and so on, there were fierce disagreements as to whether handling of the ball – not to mention passing, 'shinning' (deliberately kicking opponents' shins) hacking, tripping, charging, barging and wrestling – should be permitted. Only in October 1863, when a dozen of England's biggest clubs convened at the Freemasons' Tavern in Great Queen Street, London, was a set of rules established, and association football (so called due to the fact that an association of clubs codified the game) or soccer, was born. 'By it,' said the historian A. J. P. Taylor of that meeting, 'the mark of England may well remain in the world when the rest of her influence has vanished.'[3]

Just as a form of football had emerged in Ireland at the same time as it had done so in England in the Middle Ages, so by the late nineteenth century football in Ireland was also in the process of establishing a common code, reducing the number of players, and standardising the game. This was not just in order to rationalise Gaelic football – which then had two codes, one, a field game, and the other a cross-country pursuit that lasted an entire day – but also constituted a reaction to the growing popularity of the English sports of rugby and soccer, which had become very popular in Dublin and were also being played beyond the Pale, while hurling was becoming nearly extinct.

The establishment of the Gaelic Athletic Association in 1884 was ostensibly a reactive move against the further Anglicisation of the country but, in fact, the codification of Gaelic football involved a great deal of imitation of the British codification of football: the rectangular, clearly delineated pitch; the rational, angular goalposts (to replace, in the case of Gaelic football, the boughs of two trees); the differentiation between teams by the wearing of different colours, and the transformation of the game from a mass free-for-all into one played with a select few men –

with the reduction of the number of players per team from twenty-one (in 1884) to seventeen (in 1892) and finally to fifteen (in 1913). In the opinion of one prominent sports writer: 'Gaelic football is as traditional as the bicycle pump'.[4]

Whereas the codification (or, if you must, creation) of Gaelic football was an overtly nationalistic measure, enacted in a period of 'cultural reawakening' and during agitation for Home Rule, the establishment of soccer in England was only implicitly political. Rather than viewing it as a quintessentially national sport, the English regarded soccer as a servant of Empire: it was designed to make young Englishmen sturdy, competitive, disciplined and co-operative, and to prevent them growing up frail or effeminate – or, worse, idle – one of the great fears of the Victorians was what boys might do with their idle hands.

The English exported the game via their servicemen, their businessmen and colonial servants, and were eager, global proselytisers of the sport. Cricket, on the other hand, was regarded as strictly a game for the Englishman and his imperial subjects, a sentiment embodied by the Reverend James Pycroft, who, in writing the first history of cricket in 1851, noted that 'none but an orderly and sensible race of people would so amuse themselves' and that, while 'English settlers everywhere play cricket', there was no cricket club that 'dieted either on frogs, sauerkraut or macaroni.'[5]

Certainly, to begin with, football spread as local English businessmen, settled in Italy, Argentina and elsewhere, established their own athletic clubs and old boys' clubs. But the locals got interested, and either joined such establishments or, having watched this Saxon sport from the touchlines, started to play it themselves. In Dublin and other garrison cities in Ireland, young men likewise watched British soldiers play this game and began to mimic it. The fact, however, that they learnt this sport not from watching businessmen on their weekends off at an old boys' club, but from the enforcers of imperial occupation, was significant: Ireland is unique in that it is the only country in the world that tried to resist the onset of the game for political reasons, the only country where soccer was derided specifically because it came from another country.

2

IRELAND SAYS 'NO'

In my childhood in a small western town the local soccer club had the status of an illegal organisation.

JOHN WATERS, *MAGILL*, JULY 2002

The burgeoning game of association football had begun to appear in Ireland in the 1860s, principally in the North, but it was not until 1880 that an Irish Football Association was formed. Within a decade, a league and cup had also been established, and by 1883 the game had spread to Dublin, with the formation of the Dublin Association Football Club. The Irish Fotball Association was formed in 1880; by 1890, the Irish League had been established. association football faced competition from the tellingly entitled Gaelic Athletic Association for the Preservation and Cultivation of National Pastimes – later just the Gaelic Athletic Association – which was formed in 1884.

The long history of the GAA's hostility towards soccer, and its ban on members attending or playing that or any other 'foreign game', is well-documented. Such measures were partly proactive, in that the GAA saw them as a means of protecting the sport as a signifier of Ireland's cultural identity, but also part reactive, as the British perceived well the role of Gaelic football in the nationalist movement. From the outset, members of the Royal Irish Constabulary kept a sharp eye on the GAA as it became infiltrated by the Irish Republic Brotherhood. The ban on British soldiers or policemen from the Royal Ulster Constabulary joining the GAA was not merely a gesture against British rule: it was a measure designed to keep spies out of the GAA.

The moment when the GAA and the nationalist–republican movement coalesced, in opposition to British rule and English cultural and sporting influence, came on Bloody Sunday, 21 November 1920, when the Black and Tans burst into a Gaelic-football match between Dublin and Tipperary at Croke Park and shot into the crowd, leaving thirteen dead. Some died of gunshot wounds, others in the resulting stampede. Although soccer would survive in the south, it remained at worst stigmatised, and at best regarded as a pursuit that was somehow not completely Irish. The creation in 1921 of the Football Assocation of the Irish Free State (later to become the Football Association of Ireland) as a body separate from the Irish Football Association in Belfast, only aggravated matters, leading to accusations from the GAA that the IFA was a partitionist organisation.

The existence of the GAA's notorious Vigilance Committees is testament to the zeal with which the association sought to keep Ireland uncontaminated by foreign – that is, English – influence. Their members would clandestinely attend soccer matches and report back on any GAA members who they say watching the game. Con Martin, who went on to play for Aston Villa, was such a casualty. In 1941, he won a Leinster football championship medal with Dublin: he could have been on the same Leinster side that went on to win the All-Ireland title that year, but he was spotted at a soccer match at Drumcondra in the interim and duly expelled from the GAA. The renowned Limerick hurler Mick Mickay also enjoyed watching rugby and soccer, but the Limerick County Board, in the realisation that his talents were too great to lose, appointed him to their Vigilance Committee so that he could go to soccer matches, ostensibly to 'spy' on spectators! Even Douglas Hyde, who was a patron of the GAA, was blackballed for attending an international soccer match in his capacity as President of Ireland.[1]

The accusation that soccer was 'un-Irish' or unpatriotic was a source of great irritation to those who defended the game. As Minister for Education Donough O'Malley put it in 1968: 'Rugby and soccer people are sick and tired of having the finger pointed at [them] as if they were any worse Irishmen for playing these games. When Ireland was asked for sons to call to the colours, we were there and were not asked what shape of a ball we used.' Condemnation of soccer as 'foreign' also flew in the face of reality: it was not the game of the Ascendancy but one played by the common man in the street – or in the park. It required no crossbar, and no hurley stick – merely a ball and a set of jumpers for goalposts – and as a result remained the sport of the common man. As Osmonde Esmonde TD told Dáil Éireann in June 1931: 'The Soccer Association, which previously was looked upon as somewhat of an English and shoneen association, because of the fact that it was an English game in those days, and was played by the British Army, is now largely played by the very poor working classes of the towns. People would hardly accuse the people of Ringsend and that section of Dublin, who are amongst the most enthusiastic supporters of the Rovers and the Shelbournes, of being snobbish.'[2]

In fact, the GAA was hostile towards soccer for most of the early twentieth century for the same reason that the Church habitually denounced cinema and British tabloid newspapers: precisely because they were so popular in Ireland, and thus were deemed to be a threat. In Dublin, at least, soccer has since independence always been a sport of the people and not of the moneyed classes. Those who went to games saw no contradiction between playing this game and being patriots. John Joseph Byrne told the Dáil as much in June 1941: 'At any time in Dalymount Park or any of the principal parks in this city, you will see thirty thousand people at these matches – members of the National Army, members of the Old IRA and followers of certain forms of sport who are not supposed to be there, according to their rules, but are there all the same. The Irish government should face up to their responsibility. I can assure them that it was a sight worth seeing when thirty thousand – on one occasion thirty-two thousand – were at a football match, and when the National Anthem of this country was played they stood with their hats off and most of them joined in it themselves. We have ministers of state who enjoy these soccer matches. The government should, once and for all, in case there is any prejudice against it, face the fact that the country as a whole desires no prejudices so far as the sport of the country is concerned.'[3]

The difference between then and now is that of scale and geography. Soccer had yet to become a truly national sport throughout the country and, correspondingly, Ireland did not produce in sufficient quantity and quality players who would ply their trade on the other side of the Irish Sea. This transformation can be gauged by listening to how the Irish international team speaks. As recently as the 1980s, one would mostly hear Scouse, Cockney, Glaswegian and Mancunian accents – from players of Hiberno-English lineage who represented Ireland on account of their ancestry. By contrast, Ireland's international team of 2006 is overwhelmingly home-grown, reflecting the manner in which the game has taken root in the country even in the last twenty years.

In the prewar era, there were of course Irishmen who went to England to play professional soccer, but none became household names. No one achieved the status of the likes of Dixie Dean, Ted Drake, Alex James or Stanley Matthews. There was no equivalent then of a Danny Blanchflower, George Best, Pat Jennings, Niall Quinn or Roy Keane. John Carey at Manchester United comes close, as he began his career in England in 1936, but he only really made his name after the Second World War.

There were some prewar Irishmen worthy of mention, such as Dubliner Patrick O'Connell, who, after beginning his career at Belfast Celtic, joined Sheffield Wednesday in 1908 and then, after a spell at Hull City, moved to Old Trafford, captaining Manchester United in the 1914–15 season. But the First World War interrupted his career, and his place in footballing history owes more to his time as a manager in Spain than to his prowess as a player. He ended up coaching Real Betis, leading them to their first and only La Liga title in 1935. Moving to Catalonia, as manager of Barcelona 'Patricio' O'Connell, as he was now dubbed, helped the side to two cup finals and the Catalonian Championships twice. He so impressed the IFA, who had an unwritten rule only to select Protestants, that he was not only chosen to play for Ireland, but captained them.

Another prewar Irishman who deserves a footnote in English football is Ulsterman Billy McCracken. He won three FA Cups with Newcastle United and is credited with single-handedly forcing a change in the offside rule. Prior to 1925, a player needed three opponents ahead of him to remain onside. During the early 1920s, McCracken, alongside fellow defender Frank Hudspeth, had mastered the art of catching players offside. McCracken's ploy, which frustrated the opposition and annoyed the supporters, was mimicked by other teams, so that by the mid-1920s English football had become boring to the point of being unwatchable, with as many as forty offside decisions per game. In 1925, the FA finally took action: after organising a trial game between Amateurs and Professionals at Highbury, which was played requiring only two opponents in front of the attacking player, it duly revised the law along these lines.

(Newcastle United has a long tradition of signing Irishmen, although the results have not always been harmonious. After one game in 1938, Dominic Kelly, a centre-half who was a staunch Catholic, was found brawling on the dressing-room floor with outside-right Jock Park, a Scots Protestant. Kelly had his hand around Park's throat, roaring 'Say "God Bless the Pope!"', to which Park bellowed back: 'God Bless King Billy!' The two men were eventually prized apart by their team-mate Harry Clifton; the directors subsequently banned any talk of religion for the rest of the season.[4])

Until the postwar era, however, first-class football in England was overwhelmingly played by Englishmen (with a small number of Scots and Welshmen). So what changed things? Why did the Irish start to come over in increasing numbers in the ensuing years? First of all, the 1940s and 1950s saw greater interaction between the populaces of Britain and Ireland, with a hundred thousand Irishmen from both sides of the border enlisting in British forces during the Second World War.[5] Britain was also short of civilian manpower during the conflict and in the decades of rebuilding that followed it. There were therefore employment opportunities in England – and, particularly in the 1950s, a severe lack of such opportunities in Ireland. As a result, between 1953 and 1962, sixty thousand Irish people per year migrated to Britain from their home country.[6] As a result, many Irishmen, and their children, became familiar with English customs and pastimes. Indeed, becoming a professional football was one way of escaping the poverty of 1950s Ireland. Certainly, the family of Sunderland's Charlie Hurley, as well as Everton's Tommy Eglington and Manchester United's Roy Keane, were driven to England by economic considerations; Martin O'Neill was a promising Gaelic footballer but opted for soccer because he knew that it would provide financial security; and Pat Jennings's decision to sign up to become a professional footballer in England was partly to help support his large, poor family.

Another spur, for the generation that arrived at English clubs in the 1970s and 1980s, was technological: BBC radio transmissions began bringing the game to Irish ears from the 1930s onwards, while BBC television brought images of English football from the 1960s onwards, especially in the form of *Match of the Day*. Even RTÉ catered for – and thus stoked up – interest in the game, broadcasting English First Division games on television (a luxury not afforded to English people at the time). Likewise, the introduction across Ireland in 1992 of Sky Sports television, and the ensuing extensive live coverage of games in homes and pubs throughout Ireland, has been in part responsible for the current crop of Irish-born professional footballers.

These media meant that the 1966 World Cup was the first in the tournament's history to be a truly global event, followed in real time. As Con Houlihan remembers: 'It was the first World Cup to be broadcast on television in this country – we have never been the same since.'[7] Recently, one correspondent to the *Irish Independent* recalled: 'For me, and, I'm sure, many others in this country, 1966 was the year when we learnt, courtesy of the extensive televising of football's showpiece, that a whole big world of sport was out there to be explored. . . . I can recall the joy of listening to the sports show, each Saturday, on BBC Radio 3 . . . The '66 World Cup did a powerful PR job for the game in this country, rural areas particularly, which was, I believe, destined to be a contributing factor to the momentous happenings in the summers of 1988 and 1990.'[8]

There were underlying cultural factors too, principally the gradual liberalisation and modernisation of Irish society that began in the 1960s, and a reaction to the hegemony of the GAA, Fianna Fáil and the Catholic Church – that 'triple-headed monster', as one commentator has called it[9] – which saw itself as the guardian and custodian of 'authentic Irishness'. While soccer had, for the urban working classes, simply been a game, for the children of the middle classes, playing the 'foreign game' became an act of subversion. 'There was a sense that soccer provided a form of liberation from the weight of authority represented by GAA leaders, clergy and teachers,' remembers the writer John Waters. 'We gravitated voluntarily towards soccer because, perhaps, in descending order: it was an international game, which enabled us to feel connected with the outside world; it was subversive of that which, however much we felt drawn to it in one sense, undoubtedly oppressed us in another; and it belonged to that forbidden place, England.'

In short, economics, migration, technology, globalisation and the changing face of Irish society ensured that the English game was taken up in Ireland, and lay the conditions for Ireland, in due course, to take it back to England.

3

THE IRISH INVASION

The years immediately following the cessation of hostilities in 1945 saw the popularity of soccer in England at an all-time high, with a record forty-one million people passing through the turnstiles during the 1948–49 season. It also witnessed the beginning of a record number of Irishmen passing through the docks of Dun Laoghaire and Dublin Port to make their way to the ports of Holyhead and Liverpool in order to make a new life for themselves in Britain. It was inevitable, then, that a good number of these émigrés would leave the country in order to make a living playing England's national sport.

The names of these men are etched in the minds of all good Irish soccer fans today: Carey, Best, Dunne, Stapleton, Brady, O'Leary, Keane and Keane. Overwhelmingly, Irish footballers have made names for themselves with three clubs – Arsenal, Manchester United and Liverpool – but many others have proverbially flown the Tricolour for sides throughout England. I will look at the careers of a number of these men.

CON MARTIN

I shook hands with General Franco, or he shook hands with me.

CON MARTIN[1]

Alongside his childhood companion John Carey (see Chapter 4), Con Martin was one of the most recognisable Irishmen in English soccer during the 1940s. Alas, his career was also mired in controversy. Martin had the unfortunate distinction of not only being a victim of the GAA's war on soccer but also becoming entangled in the struggle between the IFA and the FAI, and the conflict between club and country. To compound this, he was also caught up in the sectarian cauldron that was 1940s Belfast. Unfortunately for him, being an unwilling pawn in other people's squabbles rather detracted from his substantial footballing feats.

To call Martin an all-rounder, or simply a utility player, would be something of an understatement. He began his international career as a goalkeeper, switched to centre-half at Aston Villa, was periodically employed to play as centre-half and then centre-forward, before being moved back into goal again. Martin captained both the Northern-based Ireland team and the Southern-based Éire (as it was then known), and was capped in five different positions. He was an accomplished Gaelic footballer and also played golf, was invited by an English cricket team to turn out for them one summer, and was a basketball player of some note, once taking on the Americans at their own game.

Cornelius Martin hailed from Rush in County Dublin; by the age of eighteen he was playing senior football for Dublin, having bypassed the minor game. As a boy he would cycle in the morning to play soccer at Drumcondra, then cycle to Skerries to play Gaelic football in the afternoon, before returning to Rush in the evening. Gaelic had been his first love, but circumstances dictated that he would not be able to pursue it, and follow Dublin to the 1942 All-Ireland final. 'My family were very upset about it,' recalls Con of his ejection from the GAA. 'They were all big followers of GAA. I didn't mind so much. I was young.'[2] Undaunted, he sustained an interest in other athletic activities: having joined the Air Corps as a mechanic, he represented them at basketball against the American Forces.

Upon demobilisation in 1946, Martin joined the Belfast club Glentoran, earning his first international call-up later that year. He joined the southern Ireland team as reserve goalkeeper on its tour of Iberia the same year: he made his debut as a substitute against Portugal and played well in Ireland's remarkable 1–0 win over Spain. Jackie Carey drew Matt Busby's attention to Martin, and Busby was so impressed that he offered him a contract – to play in goal. But Martin wanted to play as an outfielder, and turned down the offer. Leeds United soon offered him a contract as an outfield player.

Martin's first season at Elland Road was catastrophic. In 1946–47, the first season since the war had stopped league football in 1939, Leeds ended rock bottom of the First Division with a meagre eighteen points. The next campaign almost saw them only narrowly avoid dropping out of the Second Division. Martin, a talent too good to waste in England's second tier, was subsequently signed by Aston Villa.

Villa, still trying to recapture their glory days before the First World War – days that still haunt them – were a useful side in the early 1950s and they, and Martin, enjoyed some exciting Cup runs. At that time, Manchester United emerged as a real force in English football. It was thus ironic that Martin ended up playing in goal for Villa – the very reason he had spurned United in the first place. In the 1951–52 season, the Aston Villa manage, George Martin, established him as the first-choice keeper. 'Last season I noticed that after practice matches he would go into goal and invite the lads to shoot at him,' said the manager, upon announcing the decision. 'He obviously revelled in it and it struck me more and more forcibly that he was a natural. Then when I watched him playing cricket, I noticed that he sighted a ball very quickly. It all helped to build up the idea in my mind that he was a natural goalkeeper.'[3] Warwickshire also noticed his ball-catching skills and asked him to play cricket for them in the summer, but he wanted to return to Dublin for the break. Still, he continued to play cricket for Rush: on one occasion he hit four sixes and two fours in an over.[4]

His lack of silverware did not deter Ireland selectors, and he won thirty caps, scoring six goals. His international career was fraught with controversy, however. Just as the governments in Stormont and Leinster House had, prior to the declaration of the republic in 1948 and the signing of the Ireland Act the following year, remained undecided as to whether Partition was a temporary or a permanent measure, the relationship between the IFA and the FAI was ambiguous – but they too would in the 1950s reach a final divorce, with Con Martin being one of the casualties.

Martin had first been made aware of the role that politics played in football when he was playing for a Protestant team in Belfast. He recalled 'being heckled for playing for Glentoran when I was up the Falls Road.' Contrarily, he wasn't subject to prejudice from Protestants at Glentoran. 'No, it wasn't a big deal,' he remembered. 'I never sensed anything at all. It never dawned on me that this situation would become violent.'[5]

Relations between the IFA and the FAI had been genial since the formation of the latter in 1924; each organisation could choose players from the whole of the island to appear at international level. Four months after making his southern Ireland debut against Portugal, Martin made his debut for northern Ireland debut as a wing-half. 'I can remember playing for northern Ireland at Windsor Park on a Saturday and the south of Ireland on a Monday at Dalymount Park'[6]

Matters came to a head in March 1950 when he was selected, alongside Jackie Carey, to play for the North against Wales. His loyalties, he says, were 'half and half really; I'd great respect for the people of the North and the Association [the IFA].'[7] Manchester United, however, were pushing for the title, and Busby refused to release Carey, as they had an important game – against Aston Villa! Manchester United won the game 6–0. The next day, Con was called into the office by the Villa chairman, who showed him the various letters he had received from the Republic labelling him 'Judas' and warning him that he would not be welcome home unless he desisted from playing for the North. The director refused to let him play for the IFA's Ireland. 'I had to do it for the club that paid my wages, not that I wanted to. It was very sad. I had lots of friends there. I was sorry that I had to make that decision.'[8] Many more Southerners were likewise forbidden from playing for northern Ireland, while others were intimidated into following the lead of these players.[9] It was a sorry ending for Martin – and a sorry beginning for the permanent separation of soccer in Ireland. It was also shabby treatment of a player who, while playing for the south, had helped to beat England on their own soil only the year before (see Chapter 9).

Although he never won a League or Cup medal, and was the victim of inter- and intra-sporting squabbling, Con Martin remembers his time as both a footballer and a Gaelic footballer with affection: 'I had twenty years playing as a professional footballer and as a sportsman, and I enjoyed every minute of it.'[10] His only regret is that he never played in an All-Ireland final. He remained playing between the sticks for Villa – his natural position, and his unwanted calling – until 1953, and quit domestic and international football in 1956, the year before Villa would win the FA Cup with Peter McParland.

On his return to Waterford, Con played soccer for Waterford, and played golf with his friends Tommy Eglington and Peter Farrell. He has since spawned a soccer dynasty: his son Mick went on to play for Manchester United, Newcastle United and the Republic of Ireland, while his grandson Owen Garvan currently plays for Ipswich Town.

Thirty years after being deprived of his membership of the GAA, when Rule 42 was lifted he was presented with his Leinster winners' medal. It was a fitting end to a career that spanned both Gaelic football and soccer.

PETER FARRELL AND TOMMY EGLINGTON

HOLIDAY FOOTBALL FORM? NO SUCH THING

HEADLINE IN THE *LIVERPOOL DAILY POST,* 28 DECEMBER 1955
EVERTON WERE BEATEN 6–2 BY BIRMINGHAM ON 26 DECEMBER –
AND THEN BEAT THE SAME CLUB 5–1 THE NEXT DAY

Today, the Merseyside club that is perceived to be the most Irish is Liverpool – something that seems to be confirmed by the proliferation of Tricolours spotted on the Kop and the abundance of red replica kits seen on the streets of Irish cities and towns. Conversely, Everton muster minimal support in the Republic: they are perceived as being more of a team for born-and-bred Scousers, or it is even thought that, as they play in the same colours as Glasgow Rangers, they are in some way a 'Loyalist' team.

It was not always so; in fact, the reverse was true. In the 1940s and 1950s, Everton were one of the most Irish outfits in England. More than half of the first team in that era were Irish, with the Toffees fielding no fewer than five Southern Irish internationals: Jimmy O'Neill, Don Donovan, Tommy Clinton, Peter Farrell and Tommy Eglington. The last two, both Dubliners, were to form one of the most effective and enduring partnership in the history of English football, a partnership that they maintained at four different clubs.

While Peter Farrell was born in south Dublin, Tommy 'Eggo' Eglington was a northsider. Nonetheless, the 'Berlin Wall' of the Liffey did not prevent them from forming an enduring friendship. Eglington was a fine hurler and Gaelic footballer at Scoil Muire in Marino, and helped to establish a soccer team called Grace Park, which in its first season won a local schoolboy league-and-cup double. From there, he moved on to join Munster Victoria, Distillery of the Leinster League, before being signed by Shamrock Rovers.

Farrell and Eglington met when they were signed by Rovers on the same day in June 1946. In three seasons the pair made three FAI Cup final appearances: they were denied a hat-trick of Cup wins when they succumbed to Drumcondra in 1956. Farrell was unusual for a wing-wizard in that he was not afraid of using his physical strength against his opponents and putting in hard work. Eglington was known for his precision passing and acceleration – his fitness owed a great deal to a disciplined training regimen that meant that he suffered no serious injury at any time in his career – and he and Farrell's performance in southern Ireland's shock defeat of Spain in 1946 brought him to the attention of Everton.

The Toffees sought to bring over Farrell and Eglington as a pair for a combined fee of £20,000. But despite being given the chance to appear on a bigger stage, where they could play alongside and against some of the greatest names in football, they were reluctant to go. 'There was a lot of deprivation in England, and coming from Dublin, where there was plenty of food available, we didn't fancy the idea of rations,' Eggo remembered.[11] The two were leant on by the chairwoman of Rovers, Mrs Mai Cunningham, who was eager for the transfer money but also, looking out for the boys, was keen to convey to them that this really was an opportunity of a lifetime for them. It took the two a fortnight to mull over the offer before they realised that it was one they could not refuse.

In 394 league appearances, Eglington netted seventy-six goals; Farrell scored seventeen times in 453 games. In a display of characteristic dedication, the pair even remained with Everton when the club was relegated to the Second Division in 1951. Farrell was captain for seven seasons, and helped to lead the Toffees to promotion out of the Second Division in 1953–54. During that season, Eggo did his bit by scoring five goals in one game against Doncaster Rovers.

A charismatic wit, Eggo was a gentleman on the pitch. Before his death in February 2004, he would often recall one particular game between Everton and Blackpool in which the Toffees were so fearful of the danger posed by Stanley Matthews that he brought Eggo back to help bolster the defence. After he had been pestering Eglington for some time, Matthews tapped Eglington on the shoulder and said: 'Tommo, you'll not score too many goals playing back here.'

'True enough,' he replied, 'but then you won't be troubling our goalkeeper too often either.'[12]

Eglington, with Farrell, later departed Merseyside, but they continued their partnership on the other side of the Mersey, playing for Tranmere Rovers. Eglington netted five times for Tranmere. Farrell made six appearances for northern Ireland and twenty-four for the south, although, much to his chagrin and regret, Eggo was not selected for the 1949 game against England, held at Goodison Park – a game which southern Ireland won 2–0. He was, however, in the line-up that exacted revenge over the Austrians at Dalymount Park in March 1953: Austria, who had dispatched southern Ireland 6–0 the previous year, were the subject of a 4–0 drubbing, with Eglington getting one of the goals. Similarly, Farrell was capped by both Irelands, with his most celebrated appearance coming for the South in the 1949 game at Goodison Park, where he added to Con Martin's strike towards the death to give Ireland the victory.

One of Eglington's appearances for northern Ireland was memorable for a performance – or, one might say, an instant of insane courage – from another Irishman. When that Ireland team came to face England at Goodison in 1947, Eglington's team-mate on the left was Peter Doherty. Doherty went to meet a cross, fearlessly keeping his eye on the ball as England's colossus of a goalkeeper, Frank Swift, came out to challenge him. Doherty woke up in the dressing room fifteen minutes later, having been knocked unconscious, to be told that his goal had secured the Irish a 2–2 draw.

Peter Farrell left Tranmere in 1960 to manage the Welsh side Holyhead Town, and then Sligo Rovers. Eglington returned to Ireland the following year, and played the game well into his forties, finishing his career with Cork Hibernians. He was a golfer of some repute, and became a butcher. In gratitude to their long service to Merseyside, the municipal authorities decided to name two streets after the late footballers – something that is, to my knowledge, unique in British footballing history. Today, one can still visit Eglington Avenue and Farrell Close in Liverpool.

CHARLIE HURLEY

Carved from the finest mahogany, gifted on the ground and supreme in
the air, his presence could paralyse the opposition before he touched the
ball. When Sunderland won a corner, Hurley would commence his rum-
ble towards the penalty area. If he felt like intimidating the opponents
he might stroll rather than jog. When he arrived, we could begin.
Indicating with an upraised arm the point to which he wished the ball
delivered, he bounced on the balls of both feet like a gymnast contem-
plating a vault, and the crowd chanted 'Charlie, Charlie' in ecstasy. . . .
The ball would come over . . . there would be an apocalyptic crack as
ball met polished hardwood brow. Charlie would smile as the net bulged,
wave to the crowd, and trot sedately back to his place at the heart of the
defence. I adored him . . . he was the greatest of them all.

GRAHAM BRACK, SUNDERLAND FAN[13]

Known to Black Cat fans simply as 'The King', Charlie Hurley was a legend at Sunderland before Niall Quinn was born. The Corkman was
blessed with a vast physique, and was held in due reverence on account
not only of his manifest confidence, level-headness and leadership ability but also – paradoxically, for someone regarded as honorary royalty at
Roker Park – for his common touch. Some contend that, at his peak, he
was the finest centre-half in England. Such qualities saw to it that Hurley,
a genial, gentle giant, was eventually voted by Sunderland supporters as
their player of the century.

This was quite an accolade coming from fans of a north-east club
who have always had a particular dislike of Londoners and Essexmen, for
'Big Charlie' spoke in a Cockney drawl. When he was a youth at the end
of the Second World War, his parents, desperate to find work, had migrated to England. His father found work at Ford's Dagenham plant, and
Hurley junior was soon spotted by a scout for Third Division Millwall
playing football in Essex; in 1953 he signed for the club on a professional basis.

Hurley made more than a hundred appearances for the London club,
where he became something of a cult hero, but Sunderland, struggling in
the lower reaches of the First Division, secured his services in 1957.

Quite how bad Sunderland were at the time was made abundantly clear on his debut in September that year, when the Black Cats were thrashed 7–0, with Hurley himself adding to the score with an own goal. Relegation to the Second Division followed in 1958.

Charlie would be a constant in the ensuing seasons in the second tier: Sunderland twice narrowly missed out on a return to the First Division in 1962 and 1963, ending each campaign in a frustrating third place. The disappointment of 1962–63 was particularly acute. Sunderland, bolstered by the new signings of George Mulhall, Johnny Crossan and Brian Clough up front, were title favourites, and indeed finished only a point behind the Second Division winners Stoke, being pipped by Chelsea on goal average. The loss of Clough midway through the season proved fatal. In a Boxing Day clash against Bury, after Hurley had missed a penalty, Clough, who had scored twenty-eight goals in twenty-eight games, charged in for a tackle and damaged his cruciate ligament. The injury kept him out of the game and would eventually end his career.

Sunderland had enjoyed some decent Cup runs: they reached the quarter-finals in 1960–61 and again in 1963–64, when, with six minutes remaining, they led the holders Manchester United 3–1. But a Cup upset was averted as United hit back twice, going on to take the tie. 'It was a terrible feeling, the biggest regret of my playing career,' Hurley recalled.[14]

Even so, he was compensated by Sunderland's outstanding league campaign that season: in 1964, at the third time of asking, Sunderland finally returned to the First Division. Such was Hurley's preeminence on the pitch that season that, despite the fact that he was a Second Division player, he finished runner-up to Bobby Moore as 1964 Footballer of the Year. At Roker Park, the supporters' reaction to securing promotion was cathartic – a mixture of relief and ecstasy. 'We did a lap of honour and went inside, but they were chanting for us to go out again,' he remembers. 'We were shaking hands with big miners and big shipbuilders who were crying their eyes out. That is how important it was.'[15]

Charlie had from the outset enjoyed an intimate rapport with the fans. After taking his pre-match lunch at the Roker Hotel, he would make his way by foot to the players' entrance at the stadium, stopping to chat with the team's fans. 'I used to get coal miners coming up to shake my hand, the black dust from the pit ingrained in their palms and fingers. I was so proud they had the same respect for me playing football for a living as I had for them doing the tough jobs they did.'[16] In 401 appearances for the Black Cats, he scored twenty-six goals, mostly from set-piece headers. Not that he was always keen to use his bonce: Hurley, a man who liked to keep dapper, turned down heading practice the day Ireland played England in 1957. As he said: 'I'm not going to head any of those balls because otherwise I'll have to shampoo my hair and get my hairdryers out and everything. I did my hair this morning and I don't intend doing it again.'[17] His appeal went beyond Wearside. Across the water a little boy from Kilrea, County Derry, used to listen to Hurley's exploits via the wireless. While his eight other siblings were mad about Celtic, Hurley's feats turned the young Martin O'Neill into an avid Sunderland fan.

Although he was an Essexman by upbringing, Charlie Hurley doesn't consider himself to be an Englishman. 'If the rules were the same when I was playing as they are now, I'd probably have qualified for England, but I'd never have done it,' he said two years ago.[18] He has returned to Cork on occasions, once to look for the house in which he was born – only to find that it had been demolished. Although his name suggests an ancestral link to the Gaelic game, he confesses that he has never seen a hurling match and until recently didn't know that it was played with a stick called a hurley.

He was thus proud to be picked to play for his native country against his adopted one in 1957: he made his debut against England at Dalymount Park in May 1957. For the first of his forty appearances for the Republic, he pulled on the green jersey a mere twenty-four hours after playing in a league game, and after enduring a miserable overnight ferry crossing. His appearance in that famous game, which ended 1–1, with England scoring a controversial ninety-third minute equaliser, made his old man even prouder. It was 'the greatest kick in my father's life,' Charlie said.

His passion, self-assurance and gift for leadership were the principal reasons why he was appointed acting coach of the national side in 1968, a year before he made his final international appearance. In 1969, after twelve years with Sunderland, he left the club – much to sorrow of the fans, who paid their respect by holding an 'Abdication Party' for 'the King' at the town's Mecca Ballroom. After a period at Bolton Wanderers, he went on to manage Reading, who in 1973 were drawn against Sunderland in the FA Cup fourth round. Hurley made his old team sweat it out, taking the Black Cats to a replay at Elm Park after a 1–1 draw. In many respects, it would have been a pity if the Royals had overcome the Black Cats, as Sunderland – Hurley's team in his heart – went on to win the FA Cup that year, their first major trophy win since 1937.

Hurley retains a close connection with Sunderland. In 1997, he was selected to move the centre spot from Roker Park to the club's new Stadium of Light, and almost forty years after he last played for them, his name is still revered and he still receives fan mail – even from people who never saw him play. In 1979, the year of the club's centenary, Sunderland were in the doldrums in the Second Division, with crowds dwindling. It was not really the time for celebrations, so the Supporters Assocation held a vote for 'Player of the Century'. The King was duly chosen.

JOHN GILES

Take the piss out of me or Leeds United again, I'll break your f—king
leg for you.

JOHNNY GILES TO FRANK WORTHINGTON,
AFTER HAVING HAD A BALL LOBBED OVER HIM[19]

The 1960s and 1970s was a golden age for soccer-hardmen in England,
with characters such as Norman 'Bite Yer Legs' Hunter, Ron 'Chopper'
Harris, and Ireland's own bruiser, John Giles. But whereas his leg-crunch-
ing contemporaries will forever be principally remembered for their
rough-and-ready approach – their names are today still seldom printed
without those middle-name monikers in inverted commas – Giles is
known for much more, in that he became one of the most proficient
practitioners of the midfield game and an inspiration for his country.
Twice English First Division winner, twice victor in European competition, and bearer of two FA Cup winners' medals, John Giles did much
more than just put himself about.

Giles is understandably still irked that the label of the hard-hitting
troublemaker has stuck to him, long after his playing days have ended. 'I
slightly resent it when people say I was just a hard man. The '60s were a
hard time, and as a little guy and a creative player I tended to get singled
out, so I quickly learned that I had to stick up for myself.'[20] In many
respects, the hard-man tag was affixed so readily to him because the
Leeds United team of the Don Revie era, in which he played, was justifiably viewed as a muscular and confrontational outfit, with Hunter and
Billy Bremner themselves also earning notoriety on account of their
physical approach. But this does not mean that Giles did not warrant the
moniker of 'hard man'.

The Leeds team of the time was not merely a collection of individual hardmen: they worked in combination as a team of nigglers and bruisers. Certainly, Kevin Keegan blames Giles for setting in motion the notorious punch-up between himself and Bremner in the 1974 Charity Shield,
which led to both being shown the red card: 'I allowed myself to be pro-
voked by the infamous Leeds tactics,' Keegan later reflected, 'first an off-

the-ball whack from Giles, followed soon afterwards by a crafty dig from Bremner that brought on the red mist of temper'.[21]

Giles and his team-mate Jack Charlton used to have fierce rows in the dressing room after games, with Charlton furious at what he perceived to be the Irishman's reckless behaviour, which, in his view, needlessly placed him and the team in jeopardy. 'John Giles used to do some awful things to players,' Charlton recalls. 'I once said to him, "What do you do it for, John?" And he said, "Well, I once got my leg broken, and I'm gonna make sure nobody ever does it again".'[22]

Charlton believed that Giles did not have to resort to the stereotype of the 'fighting Irishman': Giles possessed enough talent without having to descended to such levels. He was a creative and composed tactician, working in harmony with Bremner, the ball-winner in midfield. Giles's temper, which would snap if he was harassed by an opposing marker, was nonetheless an intrinsic component of his personality, and was the result not merely of the broken leg. Growing up on the streets of inner-city Dublin, and standing five feet six inches in height and weighing little more than ten stone, Giles had developed an inclination for sharp reprisal as a defence mechanism – a mechanism that became more pronounced with what the veteran Fleet Street football journalist Hugh McIlvanney believed to be the 'abuses he suffered as a young Irish immigrant'.[23]

Giles had grown up in Ormond Square, behind Merchants Quay, and started playing soccer on the streets and by the quays along the Liffey. He acquired his skills as a master of ball-control largely as a result of circumstances: he had only a bouncy, erratic rubber ball to play with, so out of necessity he soon acquired a sharp eye for judging its movements when collecting and passing it. By the age of eight, he was playing schoolboy football, and he soon developed a burning ambition to play for Manchester United one day, following in the footsteps of his childhood hero, fellow Dubliner John Carey.

By a stroke of good fortune, Manchester United's scout in Ireland, Billy Behan, was a friend of Giles's father, and helped to set up a trial for Giles junior when he was fourteen. This led to a trial, and in 1956, less than a year later, he moved to Manchester permanently. Behan signed Giles as an amateur, while also finding work for him as an apprentice electrician. He made his debut soon after the Munich air crash, which had decimated the team. As with Charlie Hurley, he had a baptism of fire, with United being walloped 5–1 at home by Spurs. Not long afterwards came what Giles remembers as the proudest day of his life, when he made his debut for the national team at Dalymount Park. Not only did Ireland claw their way back from a 2–0 deficit, but they did so with considerable help from the eighteen-year-old, who scored on his debut to help bring about a 3–2 victory.

Giles featured regularly in the United side in the next four years, helping to set up a goal that saw them beat Leicester 3–1 in the 1963 FA Cup final. Yet the reality of life at Old Trafford did not correspond to his childhood dreams. Initially, he found it tough leaving home at such a tender age. His mother was not keen on the idea of him moving to England, and while Giles exuded self-assurance on the pitch, he was otherwise a shy and self-conscious teenager who did not mix easily with the other lads. When it came to football, he was also an individualist, and a man of conviction: his tendency to question United's methods and tactics riled his superiors, particularly Matt Busby. Soon after the FA Cup win, Giles handed in a transfer request – a request that was duly accepted.

For a fee of £33,000, Giles was taken on by Don Revie's Leeds United, then in the Second Division, where he was converted from an outside-right to being a central midfielder. He didn't mind dropping down a tier: 'I'd rather join a Second Divison club trying to do something than a First Division club who weren't trying to do anything.'[24] Although Revie was never going to put out a team to entertain – he believed that a team's objective was not to score more goals than the opposition but to concede less than them – he was a deep thinker and a cute tactician who knew how to turn a team into a ruthless footballing machine. John Giles was literally placed at the centre of the Leeds United side, cajoling and marshalling those around him, his tactical wisdom (which belied his age) complementing Bremner's aggression, Eddy Gray's dribbling, and Peter Lorimer's pinpoint shooting. 'He could grab a match, tuck it into his back pocket and carry it around with him,' was Brian Clough's judgment of Johnny Giles. 'He didn't need to find space; it was as if space found him. It was always available to him – a tribute to his perception, [his] footballing brain and the wonderful natural instinct that separates great players from the rest.'[25]

With Giles at the helm, Leeds not only emerged as champions of the Second Division in 1963–64 but, in the following season, almost won the

First Division: they were denied at the last when they were pipped to the title by Manchester United on goal average. In fact, in 1964–65 they almost secured the League and FA Cup double: they lost to Liverpool 2–1 in extra time at Wembley.

The luckless Leeds were soon dubbed 'the nearly men', an epithet that seemed all the more appropriate as they finished runners-up again the following season. Nonetheless, they won both the FA Cup and the Inter Cities Fairs Cup (the precursor to the UEFA Cup) in 1968, against Arsenal and Ferencváros of Hungary respectively, and then made the First Division theirs in 1969 – and in riotous fashion. Their haul of sixty-seven points at the end beat the record set by Arsenal in 1931. Frugal at the rear and creatures of necessity in attack, they conceded only twenty-six goals and netted a relatively modest – but effective – sixty-six.

The beginning of the seventies, however, saw Leeds resume their role as also-rans – the victims, as in 1965, of ambition. Seeking an unprece-dented 'treble' in 1969–70, they were exhausted by the end of that cam-paign, knocked out by Celtic in the European Cup semi-finals, denied at the end by Everton for the title, and losing to Chelsea in the FA Cup final. Again, they were left with nothing. The 1970–71 and 1971–72 seasons saw the title slip from their grasp again, in the latter by a single point to Derby County, on the very last day of the season, while in the 1973 Cup Winners' Cup final, despite conspicuously outplaying AC Milan, they were let down by Norman Hunter's temper (he was sent off for retaliat-ing after receiving a crunching challenge) and by some poor decisions by the referee, who was consequently banned by UEFA from officiating at games.

There was some consolation. Leeds regained the Fairs Cup in 1971, and overcame Arsenal with a solitary goal to win the FA Cup in 1972 – but lost the final the following year to unfancied Sunderland of the Second Division, a result Giles to this day regards as a 'huge blow' and the biggest disappointment of his career.[26] They more than made amends the following season, beginning the 1973–74 campaign with a twenty-nine-match unbeaten run, and securing the title at the end when a victo-ry by Arsenal at Anfield meant that Liverpool could no longer catch them. It was ironic that Leeds had let the title slip from their hands when they were in charge of their own destiny, but had now won it while sit-ting on their backsides – and thanks to their old foes, Arsenal.

When Revie quit in 1974 to take up the job as chief England coach, Giles, now Leeds's most senior player – following the departure of Jack Charlton the year before – was a favourite to fill Revie's shoes. Indeed, Revie had recommended the thirty-four-year-old Giles, then player-manager of the Republic of Ireland, as his successor. But the board of directors at Elland Road dismissed Revie's advice and, unwisely, chose Brian Clough instead. The players had wanted Giles, and they hated Clough: he had previously been coruscating about several of them while he was Derby County manager, singling out individual Leeds players for criticism both in print and on television. He lasted only forty-four days at the club.

Although Johnny Giles did not replace Clough – the manager's job went to former Blackpool and England right-back Jimmy Armfield – he did remain at Leeds. He was no longer an automatic choice, but he excelled in Leeds's 1974–75 European Cup campaign, which they ended as runners-up to Bayern Munich. He then left the Yorkshire club, for which in twelve years he had made 521 appearances, scoring 114 goals, many of them from the penalty spot.

While maintaining his position as Ireland's player-manager, he accepted an offer from West Bromwich Albion to become their player-manager as well: in his first season in charge at West Brom, 1975–76, he led them into the First Division. After a period in charge of Shamrock Rovers, the Philadelphia Furies and the Vancouver Whitecaps, he returned to West Brom again, before retiring from domestic and international management altogether in 1980. His two periods with the English midlands club helped to set up the following sequence: between 1973 and 1988 West Bromwich Albion were managed, in succession, by Don, Johnny, Ronnie, Ron, Ronnie, Ron, Johnny, Ron and Ron. (Don Howe, John Giles, Ronnie Allen, Ron Atkinson, Ronnie Allen, Ron Wylie, John Giles, Ron Saunders and Ron Atkinson.) He eventually came to the conclusion that the role of manager was a thankless one, and decided to quit the game after Ireland's failure to reach the 1980 European Championships. But he had no regrets. 'I was very lucky,' he concludes. 'I had ambitions going into the game as a young player to play in England and win things in England, which I did. I feel very privileged and very lucky to have done that.'[27]

A genial character famed in his time for his handsome looks, rich brown hair and penchant for Bacardi and Coke, Giles moved into the media, graduating from writing columns for the *Daily Express* and *Daily Mail* to television punditry on RTÉ, having been encouraged to do so by Eamon Dunphy, whom he has known since he was fifteen and Eamo was ten. They had previously played together at the renowned Dublin youth team Stella Maris, at Shamrock Rovers, and on the Irish team, and they were contemporaries at Manchester United. Their recent differences have been well documented, with Dunphy touching on that long-time sore point of Giles's: that his style as a player was hooligan-esque. The pair fell out in 2002 when Dunphy alleged that Giles had deliberately broken John Fitzpatrick's leg during a match in 1965 while playing for Leeds against Manchester United, comparing it to Roy Keane's tackle on Alf Inge Haaland – a challenge that ended the Norwegian's career. 'That's life and you just have to get over it,' Giles said about his public disagreements with Dunphy. 'I wouldn't go so far as to say we are friends again, not at all in fact. But we have to work and sit beside each other every week, it's part of the job.'[28]

It's not so much that Giles resents being remembered as a hard-man but that he resents being called a dirty player. For him, there is a clear distinction. The bruisers of old were chivalrous, gladiatorial men of honour, and he freely admits that he deserves to have been sent off for punching Keegan in the 1974 Charity Shield.[29] 'In those days there was a code among players whereby you'd never try to get someone carded. You could get stuck into each other during the match but at the end you'd shake hands. There was violence, and I'm not saying it was right, but at least no one ever tried to influence the referee – there was no diving or any of that rubbish.' Today's notorious players do not achieve infamy through good-old-fashioned manly bellicosity, but through theatrical underhandedness. In his day, he says, there was no 'diving or rolling around or making silly gestures telling the referee to give cards. Some of the stuff that goes on today is shocking. Dreadful. Just dreadful.'[30]

In many respects, Giles's philosophy harks back to a very British Victorian ideal, which viewed soccer in a sacred, militaristic manner, as a game that both promoted and embodied honest muscularity. One E. A. C. Thomson would have subscribed to his appreciation of the game. Mr Thomson was the author of an article published in 1901 in the imperialist magazine *The Boys' Champion Story Paper,* in which he concluded: 'There is no more manly sport than football. It is so peculiarly and typically

British, demanding pluck, coolness and endurance, while the spice of danger appeal at once to a British youth who is not of the namby-pamby persuasion. He loves the game for the sport's sake and thrives upon it. A sound mind in a sound body is produced by healthful exercise, and effeminate habits are eschewed. He glories in the excitement of a hard-fought match, disdains to take notice of a little bruise, and delights to be in a vigorous charge, giving knock for knock.'[31] I would hazard a guess, however, that Mr Thomson would not have approved of Mr Giles's use of profanities, and he might have deemed any promises to break any 'f—king leg's very poor form indeed.

DON GIVENS

Irish soccer has been reawakened.

RTÉ COMMENTATOR JIMMY MAGEE, 30 OCTOBER 1974

Like his fellow Irish international Johnny Giles, Donal 'Don' Givens was a fanatical Manchester United supporter as a boy, realised his dream of playing at Old Trafford, but went on to make his name elsewhere. Just as Giles became a legend at Elland Road, Givens became a hero at Loftus Road, an elegant and prolific striker who was top scorer in Queen's Park Rangers' finest-ever season – when, in 1976, they almost became the champions of England.

This was quite a feat for the west London side, who as recently as 1967 had been a Third Division outfit. By the time Givens had joined them in 1972, they were a promising Second Division side. He got off to a good start at the club, scoring in his second game of the 1972–73 campaign, against Sheffield Wednesday. QPR were a team with ambition, signing not only Givens but also, in order to strengthen the front-three attacking line, Dave Thomas and Stan Bowles. This approach reaped rewards: in the ensuing months, QPR sparred with Burnley at the top, eventually ending up as runners-up to them.

QPR had been promoted to the First Division in 1968, but they were immediately relegated; were it not for the introduction as manager of Dave Sexton, a similar fate may have awaited them in 1973–74. However, Sexton, who took over from Gordon Jago, not only averted such a calamity but consolidated Rangers' First Division status. 'Gordon was a lovely man,' says Givens, 'but I thought Dave had a lot more football knowledge. Dave was ahead of his time. We'd play on a Saturday and he'd fly out to Holland and Germany and watch games there on a Sunday to see what he could learn and use to help us. . . . He was a great coach.'[32] Sexton was greatly influenced by Ajax, and at QPR sought to employ the Dutch style of 'total football'. And he did so successfully, as Rangers went on to become one of the most exciting and entertaining soccer outfits of the 1970s.

After some indifferent finishes in the early part of that decade,

1975–76 saw QPR almost snatch the title. Their ascent up the table was partly due to the introduction from Arsenal of the experienced Frank McLintock, who, like Sexton, possessed an experimental mind, and David Webb from Chelsea, who, contrary to expectations, arrived not to play out his autumn days but to enjoy an Indian summer. Givens, good with his head and his feet, and blessed with both power and accuracy, was at his peak.

The Hoops just got better and better as the season progressed. They took twenty-seven points from their last fifteen games and, with just one game to play, against Liverpool, stood at the top of the table. In fact, QPR finished their campaign ten days before the Reds were to finish theirs, away to Wolves: Liverpool needed to win to steal the title from the Londoners. It was an agonising wait. Givens was at Old Trafford that afternoon, watching United play, and at half-time the score came through: Wolves were 1–0 up. Givens was not celebrating, though. 'Deep down I always had the feeling that because they did it year in, year out, they would do it again that day,' he recalls. Liverpool duly scored three goals in the second half, with Wolves drawing a blank. 'I had a feeling inside that you couldn't rule them out, and unfortunately they proved me right.'[33] Givens would later move to Birmingham City, Sheffield United and Neuchatel Xamax of Switzerland, before becoming Ireland's under-twenty-one coach.

Like Johnny Giles, Don Givens was somewhat awestruck to find himself mixing it with such childhood heroes as Best, Charlton and Law when he came to Old Trafford. The young man had arrived from Dublin in 1966 but he would have to wait another three years before making his first-team debut in the League. (He even made his international debut before this.) United had been on a close-season tour of Ireland, and with some of the regulars missing, he was chosen to play in a few friendly games. This brought him to the attention of the FAI: he is probably best remembered for his performances at international level.

Givens made his international debut against Denmark in Copenhagen in May 1969 and was a constant in the Irish team throughout the 1970s, scoring four goals in his first seven matches. Prior to their European Championship qualifier meeting with the Soviet Union on 30 October 1974 – Giles's first competitive match in charge of the national team – Givens had hit a lean patch, failing to hit the target on eleven previous occasions. Earlier that morning, Muhammad Ali had beaten George Foreman in Zaire: no one expected Ireland to pull off a similar feat and beat the mighty Soviets – let alone for Givens to get all three of the Republic's goals without reply.

As much as he wanted to celebrate with the lads in what was hailed by many as the coming-of-age of soccer in Ireland (in what proved to be a decade of raised-and-then-dashed expectations), Givens needed to return to London quickly for QPR's next game. He left the ground early and, together with Eoin Hand – Givens with the match ball tucked under his arm – thumbed a lift to the team hotel. 'Eoin had his car parked at the hotel and when we got there we didn't even have time to shower,' Givens recalls. 'So we got to the airport and flew to Heathrow and I'm there in my tracksuit bottoms and my legs caked in mud. Word had obviously spread because when we got to Arrivals there were a few reporters and photographers there. And there I am still filthy and the match ball still under my arm.'[34] A year later Don went one better, scoring four goals against Turkey, who finished goalless.

Givens had made his Manchester United full-team debut in August 1969, brought on as a substitute for Tony Dunne against Crystal Palace in a 2–2 draw, but he struggled to secure a first-team place, invariably deputising when Denis Law was injured. The youngster was to make only eight more appearances, scoring once, in a 3–1 home victory over Sunderland. Eventually, Man United let him go, as there were simply better players at Matt Busby's disposal. Although heartbroken at the time, Givens was thankful for this development in retrospect: 'Manchester United did me a favour really rather than letting me hang around for another year or two.'[35] As with Giles before him, he dropped down a tier, signing for Luton Town in 1970 for a fee of £15,000.

Whereas Giles had arrived at a team with a mission, all Givens sensed at Luton was complacency and a team resigned to remain as a second-rate outfit. He remembers them making little concerted effort to push for promotion in his first season there: in the summer, when they sold their star striker Malcolm MacDonald to Newcastle United, it became clear that Luton were unlikely to go anywhere. He wanted to move and saw a Second Division club that had a sense of purpose: 'QPR meanwhile had just missed out on going up and looked like they were more willing to give it a go in the coming season, so I just thought QPR had more ambition at the time and that seemed to be a better move for me.'[36] Playing with

Givens as centre-forward in the 1975–76 season, and captained by twenty-three-year-old Gerry Francis, the Hoops went unbeaten at home all season: they defeated every team in the division except West Ham, and won thirteen of their last fifteen games, becoming the firm neutrals' favourites in the process.

QPR were subsequently to fall prey to complacency and bad management. The 1975–76 season proved to be an anomaly for them. Within eighteen months the team had broken up, and within three years the Hoops had returned to the Second Division. By now Givens had left for Birmingham City – who, as it turned out, were relegated along with QPR at the end of the 1978–79 season.

Givens was never to match the quality of football he had produced at Rangers, and after a spell at Bournemouth he ended his career at Sheffield United, and on a decidedly bum note. Managed by World Cup winner Martin Peters, Third Division United, who had initially led the table during the 1980–81 season, spent the remainder of the year sliding down the table, so that by the last day of the season they faced the prospect of slipping into the Fourth Division. They faced Walsall, needing only a draw to stay up, but conceded a penalty with two minutes to go. Walsall scored, but with one minute remaining the Blades were themselves awarded a spot kick. Don Givens's effort was poor. Peters remembers it as 'the most traumatic moment of my whole career' and promptly resigned. As for Givens, it was his last-ever kick in English league football.

He had been approached by some Dutch clubs but eventually moved to Swiss side Neuchatal Xamax, at the recommendation of Harry Haslam, the scout who had recommended him to Luton eleven years before. Givens became the Swiss team's captain, and took them to the first league title in the club's history – and eventually became their player-manager. He has since coached Arsenal's under-nineteen youth squad, been acting manager of the Irish national team in the interim period between Mick McCarthy and Steve Staunton, and is today the Republic's under-twenty-one manager. He retains fond memories of his days with QPR, and of his hat-trick against the Soviets – as do the many others who claim to have been there. 'An awful lot of people seem to have been at Dalymount that day. Everybody I have met since was at the game.'[37]

MARTIN O'NEILL

Of all the husbands living an Irishman's the best
No nation on the globe like him can stand the test
The English there are drones, as plainly you may see
But we're all brisk and airy, and lively as a bee.

CAPTAIN O'BLUNDER IN THE PLAY
THE BRAVE IRISHMAN, BY THOMAS SHERIDAN, 1745

There was something so enticing about them, that even John Smith –
plain, plodding, prosy Smith, cold, calculating, unimaginative John
Smith – could do no less than fall in love.

FROM AN 1848 TRAVEL GUIDE TO IRELAND,
WRITTEN BY AN ANONYMOUS ENGLISHMAN

The English have always regarded the Irish as a people given to extremes.
Indeed, this is why they viewed them with suspicion in the bad old days,
yet admired them at the same time. When an Englishman says that an
Irishman has 'the gift of the gab', he is both paying a compliment and
delivering an insult, intimating that the man to whom he refers is entertaining and possessed with an admirable way with words, but is also unre-
liable because his mischievous verbal dexterity may be employed to
deceive. While the English liked to pride themselves on being a calm,
dependable, phlegmatic and plain-spoken people (but now seem to dislike themselves for the same reasons) , they have always regarded the Irish
as unstable – a nation of both alcoholics and Pioneers, a people run by a
puritan Church yet given to sexual licentiousness, genial yet aggressive,
hot-headed and lazy, clever yet stupid.

This is probably why the English have warmed to Martin O'Neill –
why he is perpetually in demand on British television as a talking head.
They 'get' him. He can be meticulously well-mannered, yet also rude and
offhand, arrogant then meek, quick-witted yet sluggish, garrulous then
pensive, absent-minded and methodical. Known for his wide-eyed, mani-
acal performances on the touchline, prancing around in celebration or
disgust, his arms flapping, forever taking swigs from his bottle of water,
he is the complete reverse in post-match interviews: doleful, even dejected – even in victory.

If he represents the relationship between England and Ireland of old, he simultaneously embodies the better times we enjoy today. He represents a confident Ireland that no longer feels ashamed to play and excel at a foreign game: he not only played among the best in England but now commands some of the best English players. More striking still, the English have displayed no objection to this, perceiving no threat of resurrecting the kind of post-imperial gloom and embarrassment that the 1–0 win in Stuttgart generated eighteen years ago. Indeed, when Sven Goran-Eriksson announced his retirement from his post as England manager, O'Neill was not only tipped to succeed him in the post – many Englishmen actively desired him to do so. If you could rewind fifty years and ask an Englishmen whether he thought an Irish Catholic should manage the national football team, you would probably have got a rather different response.

Of course, O'Neill's achievements with Wycombe Wanderers, Leicester City, Celtic, and, provisionally, with Aston Villa, made him to football purists simply the obvious man for the job. The fact that he displays such a sheer, schoolboy-like passion for the game in an era dominated by managers who are either dour (Ferguson), arrogant (Mourinho), plain (McClaren), charmless (Sven) or robotic (Wenger) has endeared him to the English public even more.

O'Neill was one of nine children brought up in a fervent nationalist household in Kilrea, County Derry, in which the family were devout Catholics and Celtic supporters. His father Leo was a keen follower of Gaelic football and was one of the people who founded the Kilrea GAA. Young Martin was also a talented Gaelic footballer, winning the MacRory Cup in 1970 with St Malachy's College, Belfast. Like so many of his peers, he was also interested in soccer; unlike his siblings, who supported Celtic, he chose to follow Sunderland: 'Charlie Hurley was my favourite – my all-time hero'.[38] As with so many of his fellow youths, when placed in the position of choosing between Gaelic and football, he chose the latter, mainly due to the fact that he knew that one day he could potentially make a living from it.

He attended St Columb's College in Belfast before beginning a degree in law at Queen's University, Belfast, where he studied criminology. His interest in this area was aroused by the James Hanratty case of 1961 (Hanratty was a car thief hanged for murder), and he has since remained fascinated by the subject, attending the trial of the Yorkshire Ripper and the Black Panther. While at college, he had been turning out for Lisburn Distillery, where he was spotted by a scout for Nottingham Forest. He moved to England without finishing his degree.

He had stood head and shoulders above the rest of the team at Distillery, scoring twice in a 3–0 Irish Cup victory over Derry City. This, and his successful strike against Barcelona in the European Cup Winners' Cup in September 1971, aroused interest from Everton, Manchester United and Arsenal, and among scouts from many other teams. Nottingham Forest were the first to make a substantial offer.

His initial period at the City Ground club was unremarkable, but the arrival of Brian Clough saw his, and the team's, fortunes improve markedly. In 1976–77, he helped Forest achieve promotion; as with Giles's Leeds of 1963–64, the club did not rest on their laurels but aimed for the top. In 1977–78, they led from the outset, with the aid of a mean, industrious defence and a versatile attack, with O'Neill in midfield partnered by John Robertson, who acted as the provider. In thirty-eight appearances, O'Neill netted eight times on Forest's march to their first-ever First Division title – with four games remaining. The next year, Nottingham Forest built on their success in the European Cup; they went on to win the tournament with a dazzling performance in the final against Malmö of Sweden, with Trevor Francis netting the only goal of the game. Further success came in 1979, with Forest beating Southampton 3–2 in the League Cup final. In all this, O'Neill was an integral part of the team – except in the European triumph.

O'Neill had been trying to work off various minor injuries in weeks prior to the game, and insisted that he was fine, but Clough was not convinced, and Martin played no part in the European Cup final. Devastated at being told of his omission from the team by the manager, he said nothing and, according to Clough, 'it took him weeks to get over it. He avoided me at every opportunity'.[39] He hated being left out, and reacted to it either with sulky silence or by losing his temper.

Comparisons are often drawn between O'Neill and Clough. Like his mentor, O'Neill is passionate, intelligent, outspoken, demanding, and possessed with a righteous streak – which probably explains why the two had such a stormy relationship. 'He was bright, highly charged-up even on the field, hyper-active almost. If there was one player I clashed with more than any other during my time in management, it was Martin O'Neill,' remembered Clough. 'He definitely had an inflated value of his own playing ability and I was constantly having to put him straight about that.'[40]

These encounters usually arose when O'Neill was left out of the team. 'I was forever hearing him moan "I might as well pack my bags and go back to university." I heard it once too often and pulled him in front of all the other players.

"Martin," I said. "I've done you a big favour."

"What's that, Boss?" It was a growl or a sulk more than the civilised tone I was entitled to from an educated young man.

"I've arranged that flight for you back to Ireland and I've organised a place at university. Get on it."'

According to the manager: 'He never mentioned university again.'[41]

Perhaps it was a clash of like versus like, in that Clough saw too much of himself in the Ulsterman. He certainly admired his protégé, calling him 'a man of the world in a young man's clothes. He had an awareness of life beyond his years.'[42] Yet comparisons between the two can be simplistic and misleading. Martin O'Neill has an impish, self-deprecating side to him that was lacking in Clough, who said outrageous and conceited things to the media not in the spirit of half-jest, but with complete sincerity. For instance, when O'Neill was asked, upon his arrival at Celtic in 2000, what he would do if he failed to break Rangers' stranglehold on the Scottish Premier League (which they had won every season bar one since 1989), O'Neill replied simply: 'I will kill myself.'

By the time Forest reached their second European Cup final in a row, against Hamburg in Madrid, O'Neill was fit. Again, one goal would suffice, this time from John Robertson. The Forest keeper Peter Shilton gave a first-rate performance in keeping out the Germans, while O'Neill and the captain, John McGovern, shone, displaying courage and skill in frustrating a determined opposition who were looking for their first European Cup.

After 348 appearances for Forest, during which he scored sixty-two goals – including a hat-trick in a 6–0 win over Danny Blanchflower's Chelsea in March 1979 – O'Neill left the club in 1981. While his playing career was somewhat pianissimo during his days afterwards at Norwich City, Manchester City, Notts County, Chesterfield and Fulham, he did have a swansong by becoming the first Roman Catholic to captain

Northern Ireland in the World Cup finals: in 1982 he led them in Spain, famously beating the home nation in Valencia. He was capped sixty-seven times in all.

O'Neill was soon drawn back into the game after his retirement as a player. He began his managerial career right at the bottom, in 1987 at non-league Grantham Town. A brief spell at Shepshed Charterhouse followed, and he went to Wycombe Wanderers in 1990. He guided Wycombe into the Football League for the first time in its history three years later, and helped them win the FA Trophy in the same year. After a short spell at Norwich City, in 1995 he continued his managerial ascent by taking the helm at Leicester City: he took them into the Premiership in his first season in charge, then to three Cup finals and into Europe. He transformed the Foxes into a competitive Premiership outfit, and their victory in the 1997 League Cup, where they overcame Middlesbrough in the replayed final, ensured qualification for the UEFA Cup. Although Leicester were runners-up to Spurs in the same competition in 1999, the League Cup returned to Filbert Street in 2000.

He achieved all this with scant resources, and he has gained a reputation as an extremely successful manager. His conspicuous talents as a gaffer, and his background, made him an ideal candidate to take the top job at Celtic. He had previously turned down an offer to move to Leeds, out of respect and loyalty to Leicester, and after thousands of supporters had held up placards at games reading 'DON'T GO MARTIN!', but the offer of the Parkhead post was one he could not turn down. The advice of his late father must have been ringing in his head: 'If you ever get the chance to manage Celtic,' his da had once said, 'walk to Parkhead, son.' In his five seasons there, Celtic won three League titles, three Scottish Cups and a League Cup, and reached a UEFA Cup final. In the meantime, Leicester, who always finished in the top half of the Premiership during O'Neill's reign, have been relegated twice, and are currently languishing in the Championship.

When he retired from Celtic, and the game itself, in May 2005 to look after his seriously ill wife, it was widely assumed that this would be a brief hiatus. Consequently, whenever managerial positions become vacant, O'Neill is invariably tipped as a candidate. He has been linked to Derby County FC, Nottingham Forest, Newcastle United, Sunderland, Middlesbrough – and England, a position Martin O'Neill (who was awarded an OBE in 2004) said he would have no qualms assuming, 'because I'm kind of British.'[43] Eventually, with the departure of David O'Leary, Aston Villa secured O'Neill's services in August 2006. Unlike O'Leary, whose team's awful performances had led them to their worst-ever finish in the Premiership – and who was hounded out by the fans – Martin O'Neill is a motivator of men and has an uncanny knack of bonding with the fans. Already, the omens are looking good.

DAMIEN DUFF

Blueprint for the modern football star: eye-catching hair-do, designer suit and a swish pad in the trendiest part of town. Then there is Damien Duff.

SHOOT MAGAZINE, DECEMBER 2003

For a player who had a three-year association with the club that is regarded as the embodiment of everything that is diseased, debased and just plain wrong in English football today, and in an age in which most people recoil in horror at the wages commanded by players in the Premiership – players whose petulant theatrics on the field and often vulgar, ostentatious lifestyle off it, replete with even-less-endearing wives and girlfriends – Damien Duff is a refreshingly old-fashioned, homely kind of fellow.

Whereas many Premiership show-offs are happy to spend a hundred quid on a haircut and two grand on a designer outfit, Duff is a scruff – a man who often looks like he has just got out of bed and put on the first clothes that came to hand. And whereas his contemporaries have been exposed as being partial to spending their earnings on booze, cocaine and prostitutes, Duff does not spend, he *sends* – forwarding most of what he earns back to his ma in Ballyboden. So somehow it seems appropriate that he joined Newcastle United just as Alan Shearer, the man who celebrated winning the league in 1995 by creosoting his fence, had ended his career there. Duff thus now carries the flame at St James's Park for footballers who are untainted by much of the ghastliness of the modern game in England.

The Duffer is not one for bright lights and late nights. When the Dubliner was playing for Blackburn, he decamped to live in a nearby, sleepy Lancashire village. 'It's near lots of old people,' he boasted during his time with Rovers. 'Some of the other lads live near but they're all in love or whatever . . . mostly I just sleep.'[44] Duff, like Johnny Giles and Niall Quinn before him, is one of Ireland's legendary soccer soporifics: it is said of him that he could sleep for his country, and Brian Kerr believes he suffers from 'adhesive mattress syndrome'.[45]

When Damien moved to London in 2003 to join Chelsea, one of his first concerns was to move out of the capital as soon as possible. Despite being a city boy himself, he found it all a bit too noisy, too awake-inducing. 'I find it all a little mad and intense here. There are lots of beautiful restaurants and shows to go to in London,' he remarked in December 2003, 'but I am looking to move out to Surrey as I want to live back out in the sticks.' He is a man, in the opinion of one journalist, 'just about as earthy as Ireland's peat bogs.'[46]

In contrast – or perhaps because he saves so much energy in his rustic slumbers – Damien Duff is often a thrilling spectacle on the field of play. He plays as a support striker as well as a winger, is capable of bursts of acceleration, and has good balance and ever-improving versatility. His dribbling acumen torments opposing right-backs, while he is a master provider, swinging in cross after cross to his centre-forwards, while scoring more than a few himself.

He nearly might not have been a successful soccer player, as when he was a boy he attended De La Salle in Churchtown, a rugby college where, for two years, he played as full-back for the school team. His pace for the rugby team suggested that any sporting career in front of him might lay with egg-chasing. As an eight-year old, however, he had played for Leicester Celtic, and he returned to soccer for Lourdes Celtic and St Kevin's Boys. By the time he was fifteen, a Blackburn scout had spotted him, and soon the Rovers manager Kenny Dalglish convinced the Irishman to cross the water.

Duff made his debut for the club in the final game of the 1997–98 season, earning himself the accolade of Man of the Match that afternoon. In more than two hundred appearances for Blackburn, he netted thirty-five times, helping the club to make a return to the Premiership in 2001 and to take the League Cup the next season. While he had settled in as a player, though, emotionally he struggled against homesickness. 'It didn't get to me until the second year and that's when I wanted to go home,' he remembered. 'But the club and the youth-team manager Alan Irvine were brilliant. I went in on one occasion and saw Alan Irvine and I was just crying in front of him, a big cry-baby. Ray Harford, the manager, came in as well. They were brilliant with me. They thought the best thing for me to do was not to go home because that would make it worse. So they brought my family over and looked after me.'[47]

When Graeme Souness took over the reins at Ewood Park, the Scotsman came to recognise in Duff the same talents he had witnessed in Alan Kennedy, whom the moustachioed one had played with in the seventies. 'Ray Kennedy was arguably the best wide man I ever played with. He was guaranteed a dozen goals a season but he still got up and down the line, defending and building up attacks,' Souness said. 'Damien is learning that art. He does things that excite people and he can turn a game with a bit of brilliance.'[48] Souness encouraged Duff to model himself on Kennedy, while simultaneously concentrating his own efforts on fending off covetous outfits in the Premiership who were increasingly taking an interest in the Dubliner.

Duff's domestic performances, which helped Blackburn reach an impressive sixth place in 2002–03, and his appearances on the international field, particularly his outstanding performance in Ireland's defeat to Spain in the 2002 World Cup finals, saw him finally prized away from Lancashire. Manchester United, his father's team, had been tipped to get his signature, but it was a persistent Chelsea who, after a reputed three bids, eventually signed him for £17 million, a record for the club in the pre–Roman Abramovich days, and a fee Duff himself laughed at as 'ridiculous'.

The incumbent manager at Stamford Bridge, Claudio Ranieri, was famous – or possibly infamous – for his rotation policy at the time, which determined that only a select few of his players were guaranteed automatic selection for games. Duff was aware of Ranieri's tactics and was resolute in wanting to become one of the select few. 'I want to play every game and I think that there must be something wrong with any footballer who suggests otherwise,' he said after signing for the Blues. 'It is the competition for places that makes training tougher here. Everyone is going all out to impress the gaffer.'[49]

Unluckily for Duff, he wasn't to be a regular at Stamford Bridge. Initially, this was not on account of tactical considerations, but through the Irishman's chronic injury problems. His first season at Chelsea, 2003–04, was blighted by hamstring injuries, and when he was omitted from the team, it showed – particularly towards the end of the season, when he missed the Champions League semi-finals. (Similarly, his omission from the Blackburn team resulted in their fortunes declining.) Nothing could stop Arsenal from running away with the title that season; Chelsea ended as runners-up, their highest position for forty-nine years.

Duff scored six goals in that campaign, one of the most notable being the one he scored in Chelsea's 5–0 trouncing of Newcastle, when he blocked a throw from goalkeeper Shay Given, chipped the ball over a defender's leg, and volleyed the ball into the net past his hapless compatriot. Duff scored another spectacular solo effort away to Lazio, when he jinked his way past four Italian defenders before putting the ball in at the far post with his right foot.

When the new Chelsea manager Jose Mourinho signed Arjen Robben in the close season that summer, Duff's status as automatic first-team choice was placed in jeopardy, but this time it was Robben who was kept out of the side through injury. However, Mourinho initially preferred to play in a narrower, wingless formation, leaving Duff on the bench at the outset of the campaign. By the time Robben was match-fit, Mourinho had decided that a more expansive attacking formation would be most effective, and played both men, with the Dutchman on the left wing, and the Irishman being switched to play wide on the right. Scoring ten goals, he helped Chelsea to their first top-flight title for fifty years and, with the help of Duff, who had scored the winner against Manchester United in the semi-final second leg, to League Cup victory against Liverpool.

Although he would help Chelsea to a second consecutive League title the following season, he struggled to hold down a regular place, thanks partly to recurring injury, partly to competition from Robben and now Joe Cole, and partly also to Mourinho's failure to play him in the position for which he was best suited: as a left-wing attacker. In all, his performances did not do his talents justice, and he registered his lowest League tally of goals in five seasons – three. As the season neared its end, there was already talk of his desire to leave, and Chelsea's willingness to let him do so.

The fact that Duff was held in high esteem by the Chelsea fans during his time at the Bridge was an achievement in itself. In the late 1970s and 1980s, the London club's fans were notorious not only for displays of hooliganism, but for elements who attached themselves to the far right and indeed the Loyalist cause. When Chelsea's first black player, Paul Canoville, made his debut in April 1982, coming on as a substitute against Crystal Palace, he was met with a chorus of boos, hisses and racist chants – from his own fans. During those dark days, many of the team's supporters, by wearing 'No Surrender' scarves and hats, and chanting anti-Irish slogans, openly aligned themselves with Glasgow Rangers and Linfield, with some creating an organisation called the 'Blues Brothers', linking all three clubs.[50]

Songs such as 'No Surrender to the IRA', 'Hello, Hello, We Are the Billy Boys' and – neatly combining two prejudices for the price of one – 'I'd Rather Be a Darkie than a Tim' were sometimes heard. Unlike Liverpool, Arsenal or Millwall, who had a sizeable contingent of Irish and second-generation-Irish fans, and Irish players, Chelsea were regarded not merely as not an 'Irish team' but as a positively anti-Irish team. I remember standing in 'the Shed' at Stamford Bridge as a teenager in the late 1980s and having to listen to the man next to me spend the ninety minutes shouting abuse at Tony Cascarino, calling him a 'f—king Fenian bastard' whenever the Millwall player (who, incidentally, has no Irish blood in him and was later to play for Chelsea) touched the ball.

Until the 1980s, the club's only Irish-born Republic of Ireland internationals had been Dick Whittaker, who played once for Ireland in 1959, and Pat Mulligan, a defender who spent three years at Chelsea between 1969 and 1972. On the other hand, Chelsea had always employed the services of Irish northern Protestants, pre- and post-war, from Johnny Kirwan, who turned out for Ireland in 1906, to Sam Irving, the wing-half-back of the 1920s and 1930s, and a moustachioed Kevin Wilson in the 1980s. Their only Irish manager to date is Ulsterman Danny Blanchflower, who was briefly at the helm in 1978–79. While some lament the gentrification of soccer, particularly in Chelsea's case, the fact that the Duffer was welcomed at Stamford Bridge (where black people have not only been accepted onto the pitch, but can be seen in the stands too) shows that attitudes towards the Irish have mellowed considerably in England in recent years.

While Tottenham and Liverpool were said to have taken an interest in Duffer, Newcastle finally came in at the end of the 2005–6 season and, for the relatively cut-price fee of £5 million, shrewdly took him back up north, leaving Chelsea £12 million the un-wiser. 'Damien is still a little bit rusty and needs some more match practice,' said his compatriot and team-mate Shay Given – whom Duff had humbled three seasons previously – when welcoming him to the club. Given is, however, optimistic for the future: 'He will be a fantastic player for this club . . . Once he hits full fitness he is going be a great asset for us.'[51]

Damien Duff was marked out as a man of potential – a player with his best days perpetually ahead of him. In his early twenties, he was rated by Mick McCarthy as more skilful than Michael Owen, and by others as potentially superior to Ryan Giggs, Paul Gascogine and Juninho. When he was at Blackburn, a team-mate, Craig Hignett, remarked: 'I have played with some brilliant players during my career, but I've never seen a talent like Damien Duff.'[61] Now, at the age of twenty-seven, it is difficult to assess whether he has realised his potential, or indeed whether his potential has passed him by. Some might say that winning two League titles is pretty much any boy's dream, but in truth it was Chelsea who won the League: Lampard, Terry, Cole, Robben, Mourinho (and Abramovich's money) who essentially took the trophy to Stamford Bridge, with Duff being a peripheral presence. Now, after having signed a five-year contract with Newcastle, time will tell whether this in some ways very ordinary man capable of playing extraordinary football can finally play sublime football on a permanent and regular basis.

SHAY GIVEN

> Shay Given almost single-handedly won the match for Newcastle against Everton, although obviously he didn't score the goals.
>
> GEORGE HAMILTON[52]

Like Damien Duff, Shay Given is a quiet, relaxed and amiable family man who spends his spare time not on hedonistic pursuits but on raising awareness for the Macmillan Cancer Support. But while the Duffer has won the League at a club without ever really being *of* it, Shay Given has become intrinsic to a side without ever securing any silverware with it. An honorary Geordie by his own admission, Given has spent almost a decade at Newcastle United, a club that was to the turn of the millennium what John Giles's Leeds were to English football in the early 1960s: that era's team of 'nearly men', who, after so many promising finishes to so many seasons, ended up trophy-less.

Were it not for Given, Newcastle would not even have achieved that, for the Donegal goalkeeper has been responsible for sparing the Geordies' embarrassment on numerous occasions, both through his sheer shot-stopping ability – he once kept a clean sheet in 425 consecutive minutes of competitive football – and owing to his stamina. He is rarely injured, earning him the moniker 'Lazarus' from his team-mates (although his absence from Newcastle at the beginning of the 2006–7 season means that this nickname might have to be dropped) and he set a record for the number of consecutive games played in the Premiership, a record only recently superseded by Chelsea's Frank Lampard. Like his team-mate Alan Shearer, he has been a rock at Tyneside, one of the few constants in a club that always seems to be in transition, and in a team that is prone to inconsistency and has a tendency to self-destruct at precisely the wrong time.

Born in 1976 and named after his father, who was also a goalkeeper, Seamus Given comes from Lifford in County Donegal. He was playing with the big boys at an early age: by the time he was fourteen he was turning out for local adult side Lifford Celtic. The young, slight-of-build teenager's appearance for that team in the semi-final of the FAI Junior

Cup, in which they lost 1–0 at Dundalk, brought him to widespread attention, not least that of Frank Stapleton, now the manager of Bradford
City. Given was brought over to Yorkshire to play in a youth tournament,
where his performances aroused much interest from local clubs, but it
was Glasgow Celtic, managed by Liam Brady, who signed him after having seen the sixteen-year-old in a pre-season tour of Ireland.

Although Shay spent two seasons at Parkhead, he never played for the
first team, being shut out by his fellow Donegal keeper Packie Bonner.
The nearest he came to appearing in the Scottish Premier League was
when he was on the bench as a potential substitute for an Old Firm game
on New Year's Day 1994. He generally spent his time with the under-
eighteen team instead. His failure to break into the first team did not dis-
suade a former Celtic legend, Kenny Dalglish, now managing Blackburn
Rovers south of the border, who saw in the Irishman potential as a future
replacement for, and current understudy to, Blackburn's serving keeper,
Tim Flowers. Signed for £1.5 million to move south, Given again found
himself frustrated by the proficiency of the incumbent. Flowers was an
immovable object in the 1994–95 season, and while Blackburn went on
to win the Premiership that season, Given found himself loaned out to
Swindon Town and then Sunderland.

In performances that prefigured those he would go on to make later
in the north-east, he made seventeen appearances for the Black Cats,
keeping a clean sheet in sixteen and helping Sunderland to achieve promotion to the Premiership for the first time. The Sunderland manager
Peter Reid was so impressed that he sought to sign him, even promising
to make him their first-choice goalie. But Shay still believed he could
make it at Blackburn, and Dalglish didn't want to let him go.

While the Irishman failed to achieve first-team status in England, he
had suitably impressed Mick McCarthy, who gave him his international
debut at Lansdowne Road against Russia at the age of nineteen; Given
soon made Dean Kiely's Number 1 shirt his own. At Blackburn, though,
he made only two appearances in the space of three years. When Dalglish
went to Newcastle in 1997, he persuaded Given to come to the side that
had finished the previous two seasons as runners-up in the Premiership.

Finally Given became an established player, making thirty-four
appearances in the 1997–98 season. The Magpies shone in the
Champions League, with Given playing in their first-ever game in the

competition, a momentous 3–2 victory over Barcelona. The domestic campaign was gravely disappointing by comparison: Newcastle needed a replay to see off non-league Stevenage Borough in the FA Cup, before being beaten by Arsenal in the final, and they finished a comparatively dismal thirteenth in the League. When his mentor Dalglish was sacked, to be replaced by Ruud Gullit, Given retained his place as automatic Number 1, appearing in thirty-one of Newcastle's thirty-eight League games. Again, there was disappointment in the FA Cup, with the Magpies making it to Wembley, only to lose the game at the last by two goals to nil, this time to Manchester United. It was the culmination of a season that was made all the more disappointing for Given by the fact that he wasn't even chosen for the final, being replaced by Steve Harper.

Given saw Ruud Gullit come and go – the dreadlocked one unable to make the Magpies play 'sexy football' – as he has so many managers at a club that is impatient for success. Newcastle, now flirting with relegation, appointed Bobby Robson as the Dutchman's replacement in 1999, with the ageing former England manager pitting Given and Harper against each other to fight for the right to be first-choice keeper. He made only seventeen appearances in Robson's first year at the helm. Frustrated, and with memories of his wasted years at Celtic and Blackburn surely in his mind, he handed in a transfer request at the beginning of 2000–1. It was more of a gesture of discontent than a sincere plea to leave the club, and it was duly rejected by Robson, who, manifestly annoyed, scolded the Irishman, telling him to show some loyalty to the club, pull himself together and fight for his place. Given backed down, and after Harper was injured, he regained his place.

Given's decision to follow Robson's advice was a wise move, as he had a season to remember in 2001–2, with Newcastle finishing fourth, qualifying once more for the Champions League. He appeared in every single game in the Premiership, and was included in the PFA Premiership Team of the Season. He also made what is regarded as the save of the season, in the north-east derby at the Stadium of Light, when he tipped over with one hand a superb shot from the Sunderland striker Kevin Phillips. Newcastle built upon these achievements by finishing one position higher in 2002–3; during this season, Given became Newcastle United's most-capped player when he earned his forty-first international call-up, beating the record held by Ulsterman Alf McMichael. The season afterwards saw Newcastle finish a respectable fifth.

Keeping up the tradition of its revolving-door management policy, Newcastle sacked Bobby Robson just as 2004–5 had got under way, replacing him with Graeme Souness, whose tenure was calamitous. Having failed to qualify for the Champions League, the Magpies had to settle for the UEFA Cup, only to be beaten by Sporting Lisbon in the quarter-finals. They were defeated by Manchester United in the FA Cup semi-final and finished in a derisory fourteenth place in the League. Throughout Souness's forgettable time at St James's Park, Given's performances were one of the few that stand in the memory.

In the last five seasons, Given has missed only two League games and, after having been at the club for nine seasons, he was made captain of the side towards the end of 2005–6, a season during which he kept eighteen clean sheets. Such is his reliability at the back – he was voted goalkeeper of the season by his fellow professionals – that many have wondered why he has remained with Newcastle, a team which has not won anything since the Fairs Cup of 1969 and which, to those of a suspicious disposition, seems jinxed, destined not to win anything in the near future. Although there is no doubt that he could move to a club who are real champions contenders, Given is not the mercenary type.

Thus many people were surprised when, in 2006, he signed a new five-year deal with Newcastle, his previous contract having come close to expiring. 'I get the sense now that Newcastle is my home. I have committed to another five years and I cannot see myself playing anywhere else to be honest,' says the man who calls himself 'an adopted Geordie'.[53] 'This new contract keeps me going until I'm thirty-five, although I'll play a few more years after that . . . and, as I've said from day one, I want to win some trophies at Newcastle.'[54]

ROBBIE KEANE

'SILVIA says: Robbie is the World greatest and he is the best because he scored at germany. He is so sweet and i love him so like i love my familie. he is so great and amazing. our whole town in germany knows him because he is the best footballplayer in the world. ROBBIE I LOVE YOU I WILL SEE YOU 2006 IN GERMANY. I WILL TAKE YOU FROM THE AIRPORT. YOU HAVE TO WIN IN MY LAND: ROBBIE CHAMPION 2006 IN GERMANY: IM YOUR BIGGEST FAN KISSS FROM A LITTLE GIRL FROM GERMANY'

'Gemma says: Keano sad 2 c u go babe! Agh well we still hav u on r Ireland team babe! Luv u 2 bits baby!!!!! Go Keano! XXXXXXXXXXX'

MESSAGES POSTED ON LEEDSFANS.ORG.UK, JULY 2002[55]

['sic' throughout]

[Robbie Keane is] generally regarded as the future of Irish football

THE GUARDIAN, 12 NOVEMBER 1999

Turning on his heel, he motions away from the penalty area, runs to the side of the pitch, performs a clumsy cartwheel, and bends down on one knee to fire an imaginary longbow, or let loose volleys from two non-existent revolvers. It's the inimitable indication that Tottenham and Ireland's Robbie Keane has scored a goal. The ritual is as much his trademark as his shy, sunny demeanour off the field, that twinkle in his eye, the happy disposition that marks him out and sets him in such stark contrast to his near-namesake and predecessor as captain of Ireland, the one with the scowling, impatient expression and gorgon-like glare.

Robbie Keane may have matured as a tactician and all-round footballer in recent years, but he still has the aura of a boy who can't believe he's playing with men. But paradoxically, it has been his childlike passion for the game – a passion that belies his professionalism – that has transformed him into the accomplished leader of men that he is today.

In the true spirit of a gifted teenager, he was a fast learner, and with all the enthusiasm of a teenager who finds an early calling, he was obsessive in mastering his *métier*. He has always had a childlike quality to him, what with his wide, honest eyes and a grin that catches up on him unawares. By the time he signed for Inter Milan, Robbie still spent his spare time watching television – he never read the papers – and enjoyed sojourns back to his Dublin home, where he was still sharing a room with his younger brother.

He came to the English midlands as a sixteen-year-old, a stranger in a strange land, but nonetheless determined to make it with the big boys. When he was at Coventry, Keane relished training every day, and would stay behind for more. It was this kind of youthful resolve that has transformed the boy from Tallaght into the man who now captains club and country – the man in him leading from the front, the boy in him infecting his team-mates with his indefatigable positivity. 'He's natural company,' says his former Ireland team-mate Niall Quinn. Glenn Hoddle, his former manager at Spurs, is of a similar opinion: 'He's such a bubbly lad that anyone who meets him loves him. He is great for team spirit.'

Robbie Keane started his footballing with the under-ten team at Crumlin United, where he was paid fifty pence for every goal he scored. He earnt £24 in one season. (You do the math.) English scouts were on the prowl during his youth, and he was soon hunted down by Wolves. He had been offered a place by Liverpool, but he felt he had a better chance of breaking into the first team at a club outside the Premiership; he also felt that the presence of a couple of school friends who had also been signed by Wolves would alleviate any potential feelings of homesickness. His rise through the ranks of the second-tier club was rapid – after only a year playing in the youth and reserve teams, he made his full debut aged seventeen, away to Norwich City, and scored. In eighty-eight appearances in two seasons at Molineux he scored twenty-nine goals. Then, in 1999, he was lured, at the age of nineteen, to nearby Premiership outfit Coventry City for £6 million, a British record for a teenager.

Robbie made a dream debut for Coventry against Derby County in August 1999, scoring twice, slotting the first away from a tight angle. The Coventry fans, who had been despondent about their team's chances that season after the club had sold their favourite, Darren Huckerby, gave Keane a standing ovation as he left the pitch, substituted six minutes from time. The Irishman was to net ten more times that season, and after only two months at Highfield Road, commentators were making great play of Keane's cautious professionalism, allied to his ability to take the ball, run past defenders and score from distance, and were making comparisons to Alan Shearer and Michael Owen. According to Niall Quinn, however, Keane – by now his striking partner for the Republic – was already 'a better all-round player than Owen.'[56]

Robbie's worth in pounds more than doubled within a year, as he made the move to Italy, signed by Marcello Lippi of Inter Milan. Only twelve months after having had to play the likes of Barnsley and Bristol City, he had arrived in Serie A to play alongside Ronaldo and Christian Vieri. Players who have made the jump from English to Italian football have had mixed fortunes, and it was hoped that Keane's time there would be less akin to that of Ian Rush (who complained that living in Turin felt 'like being in a foreign country'[57] or Luther Blissett (whose time with AC Milan was also brief and even less successful) and more like that enjoyed by Liam Brady, twice Serie A winner with Juventus. Alas, when Lippi was sacked, his replacement, Marco Tardelli, decided that Keane was surplus to requirements.

Keane's failure to break into Inter's first team had seen him loaned back to England, to David O'Leary's Leeds United – an arrangement that was made permanent in 2001 for the price of £12 million. Once more, Keane had started brightly, netting nine in fourteen games, but he and the Yorkshire side's performances began to take a dip. In 2001–2, he registered only ten goals, and at the end of the following season's campaign he joined an exodus of players from a club that was in dire financial difficulties – and that, in 2004, was sent back down to England's second tier. Just as Roy Keane, the Tottenham Hotspur supporter, made his name at Manchester United, Robbie Keane, the Man United fan, was to prosper at Tottenham.

Since moving to Spurs, Robbie Keane has finally, albeit tentatively, come into his element. Tottenham's New Age manager Glenn Hoddle believed that Keane was so perfectly suited to the club that White Hart Lane could become his 'spiritual home', and in his first two seasons there he scored on twenty-nine occasions. But the 2004–5 season was unsatisfying for him, despite his haul of seventeen goals, as he found himself third choice behind the preferred strike force of Jermain Defoe and Mido, a trend that continued into the beginning of 2005–6. There were rumours that he was about to move to Everton, while talk of his departure increased after he stormed out of the dugout towards the end of an encounter against Birmingham City in April 2005 after not even being brought on as a substitute – a tantrum that earned him a £10,000 fine.

But as Tottenham progressed up the table in 2005–6, Defoe's form took a dive, and in November 2005 he was replaced by Keane, who took the opportunity with relish, playing some fine, commanding football, arguably his best to date. By March, he had overtaken Mido as the club's top goalscorer, and when Ledley King became injured, he was made Spurs' stand-in captain. He was becoming an inspiration to a team given to inconsistency, a saviour to a side that for so long has suffered from attacks of nerves. Keane's double strike against West Brom that month helped an otherwise jittery and stagnant Tottenham, who had been out-played and outmuscled by the Baggies, turn a 1–0 deficit into a 2–1 victory. This put the north Londoners into fourth spot and in contention for a place in the Champions League (something only denied to them on the last day of the season by Arsenal amid some talk of the team succumbing to food poisoning before their final game).

Robbie Keane ended the season with a flourish, signing a new four-year contract with the club, being appointed captain of Ireland by Steve Staunton, and being made permanent captain of Spurs after King was finally ruled out for the remainder of the season. Spring saw him net eight goals in nine games, including one against rivals Arsenal, and at the end of the 2005–6 season he was voted Player of the Year by the White Hart Lane faithful. Still in his mid-twenties, his international scoring record has passed Niall Quinn's haul of twenty-one and is nudging its way towards thirty. We can probably look forward to plenty more goals from Robbie Keane – and many more inelegant somersaults – in the years to come.

4

UNITED IRISHMEN

> Driven from their native shores by hunger, many thousands of Irish
> poor . . . have found their way to Manchester . . . in feeble health, to a
> cheerless lodging (if lodging many of them can be said to have), in the
> midst of strangers, out of the reach of sympathy, to sicken and to die
>
> THE *MANCHESTER AND SALFORD ADVERTISER,* 6 MARCH 1847[1]

If one club has come to be regarded as a quintessentially – or at least an
honorary – Irish side, it is Manchester United. This is due not only to
Ireland's traditional links with the Lancashire city, which since the 1840s
has had one of the greatest concentrations of Irish emigrants in England
– the first generation of which arrived to flee poverty, the most recent
generation to seek their fortune – but to the sheer number of Irish players who have turned out for the Red Devils. These players include Jackie
Carey, FA Cup and First Division title winner with United in 1948 and
1952, and Liam 'Billy' Whelan, one of the most promising players of the
1950s, whose life was cruelly cut short in the 1958 Munich air disaster.
Then there are the heroes of the 1960s and 1970s, such as Noel Cantwell
and Tony Dunne, the luckless Frank O'Farrell – the only Irishman ever
to have managed the club – the entertainers of United's Cup-winning
sides of the 1980s, such as Paul McGrath and Kevin Moran, and the manifest, multiple-trophy-winning talent witnessed at the turn of the millennium in the form of Denis Irwin, John O'Shea and, of course, Roy
Keane, who helped to make Manchester United one of the most successful football sides in English history. This is not to forget the likes of
Harry Gregg, George Best, Shay Brennan and Norman Whiteside –
Ulster Protestants or children of the diaspora whose feats will be
explored in Chapter 6.

JOHN CAREY

In soccer, you find two kinds of temperament at the 'genius' level. There is the explosive type like an Alex James, an Alex Jackson, a Billy Steel, or an Eddie Baily. Then there is the reserved, pensive type like a Matthews, a Ramsey or a [Wilf] Mannion. Similarly, there are two types of Dubliner. First, the volatile, talkative type who is apt to pull up a chair and talk for five hours on Michael Collins, 'the darlin' man'. Second, the canny thinker who holds his words too precious to squander. Into the latter category in each case must go Dublin's Johnny Carey, captain of Manchester United, and one of the really great players of the last decade.

THE *DAILY MIRROR*, 7 FEBRUARY 1957

Kick the ball up the field lad, it will take longer to come back.

JOHN CAREY

John Carey is regarded as one of the finest players to have appeared for Manchester United and Ireland. Were it not for the interruption of the Second World War, in which he served, he would be remembered today with even greater reverence by United and Irish football fans, both North and South, because Carey captained both the FAI's and the IFA's sides.

English Footballer of the Year in 1949 and captain of the Rest of Europe team that played Britain in 1947, Carey was known as 'Gentleman John' for his tranquil disposition, his abiding sense of fair play, his self-discipline and his unwillingness to rise to provocation. In his time, he captained Manchester United for longer than any other previous player in the club's history, and in 333 League games, during which he scored twenty goals, he played in nine different positions. A graceful, talented leader of men, Carey, under Matt Busby's guidance, was instrumental in Manchester United's ascendancy in the 1940s and 1950s, winning the FA Cup with the side in 1948 and then topping the First Division in 1952 – Manchester United's first League title since before the First World War.

Carey was one of many to have graduated as a schoolboy from the Home Farm club in Whitehall, Dublin, and, like many who would make their way to England to ply their wares as soccer players, he was a GAA player for the Dublin Minors football team – but was eventually banned from appearing at Croke Park after having been discovered playing this 'foreign sport'. Carey also shone at athletics at Guinness's Brewery team, St James's Gate, where he was spotted by Manchester United's former goalkeeper and then Dublin scout, Billy Behan.

Jackie Carey had played alongside Kevin O'Flanagan. Mr O'Flanagan – or Dr O'Flanagan, as he would become – was never particularly well known in England, but he deserves at least a footnote in a history of Irish soccer players in England. He was a champion sprinter, becoming the champion of Ireland in the 60 yards, 100 yards and long-jump national titles. And he was a man of protean talents, appearing for Ireland both in rugby and soccer internationals. Like Carey, O'Flanagan was also banned from the GAA for playing the foreign game.

O'Flanagan made his debut as a part-time amateur for Bohemians at the age of sixteen and in the 1938–39 season netted a record thirty-four goals in all competitions in Ireland, a feat that was only surpassed in 2001.[2] His talents had come to the attention of Liverpool, Manchester United and Aston Villa, who all tried to sign him, but his parents refused, insisting that he continue his studies.

At the age of 18, while studying medicine at UCD, O'Flanagan made his international debut for the Irish soccer team in a 3–3 draw against Norway at Dalymount Park – scoring in the process. In Budapest in 1939, he netted two goals against Hungary, with both efforts being the result of passes supplied by Carey, to give Ireland a 2–1 lead; only a late equaliser by the Magyars prevented an Irish victory. He also played alongside his brother Michael in Ireland's 1–0 home defeat to England in 1946.

O'Flanagan later went to work as a doctor in London, where he played on an amateur basis for Arsenal and then Brentford. He was also proficient at rugby, first playing for UCD's team, and then for the Ireland team. By 1946, he was playing for Arsenal and London Irish on alternate weekends: on one fortnight that year he played for Ireland at soccer against Scotland and for Ireland against France at rugby.

O'Flanagan's modest, Corinthian spirit was far removed from that of the Premiership today. He was so keen to continue to be eligible to play as an amateur rugby player that, when Arsenal's manager asked him to declare his expenses, he asked only for his bus fare. He later became a member of the International Olympic Committee and continued to practise as a doctor in Dublin's Upper Fitzwilliam Street. Dr O'Flanagan died in May 2006 at the age of eighty-six. In contrast, Jackie Carey's postwar career as a footballer in England proved more august.

John Carey had signed for Manchester United in 1936 for £250, and made his international debut against Norway soon afterwards – playing alongside Mr O'Flanagan. When the seventeen-year-old Carey arrived in Manchester, he spotted – to his delight, if not his expectation – a newspaper hoarding declaring 'UNITED SIGN STAR'. Alas, when he purchased the newspaper, he discovered that the headline referred to Ernie Thompson of Blackburn Rovers. Carey's acquisition merited only a two-line mention in the last paragraph of the report.[3] Whereas Thompson would play just three games for the Red Devils, before disappearing into obscurity, it was Carey who would become United's true star of the future.

John Carey began as an inside-forward and broke into the United side in the 1937–38 season, helping them to win promotion to the First Division, and he would go onto earn twenty-nine international caps. But with the outbreak of hostilities in 1939, Carey decided not to return to Ireland and opted to join the British army. 'A country that gives me my living is worth fighting for,' he declared. He served in North Africa and in Italy, where he continued to play football, making guest appearances for several teams. He was dubbed 'Cario', and on account of his performances he received offers from Italian clubs to remain in the country after 1945.

Fortunately for United, he politely turned down such offers, and at the end of the war returned to Old Trafford, where the former Manchester City and Liverpool half-back Matt Busby had assumed responsibility as manager. Busby recognised in Carey qualities of discipline, leadership and versatility. Carey was played in every position except outside-left, even being used as a goalkeeper. Busby warmed to Carey's temperament, too: Carey, like Busby, was a quietly spoken fellow who liked to smoke a pipe.

Busby had originally employed Carey as an inside-right, but at the beginning of the 1947–48 season he moved him to right-back, where Carey's steady nerves, control, intelligent passing and neat tackling were used to superior effect. While League triumph was tantalising elusive in the immediate postwar years, with United coming runners-up on four out of five seasons, in 1948 they made it to the FA Cup final.

Facing a Blackpool side containing the might of Stans Matthews and

Mortensen, United were 2–1 down with twenty minutes to go. The steady patience of their captain Carey, whose calming half-time talk averted panic in the ranks, saw the Mancunians score three goals in sixteen minutes. Their 4–2 win made Jackie Carey the first Irishman ever to captain an FA Cup–winning side.

'On the field a cool, elegant defender, off it calm, frank and unassuming' was the *Daily Dispatch*'s assessment of this reserved, contemplative Irish footballer,[3] and in 1949 Carey was named England's Footballer of the Year. He jubilantly declared this to be the greatest honour he had ever received – sentiments that endeared him to the *Sporting Chronicle,* a newspaper that took the occasion to indulge itself in characteristic, corny Hibernophilia: 'It was typical of the man. What he had achieved both on and off the field was not enough – his warm Irish spirit moved him to a further contribution. It was as though he had said in that rich brogue of his: "Bedad, I feel as though I haven't given half enough yet!" '[4]

In 1951–52, Carey helped United finally take the First Division title, making him, in the words of one English tabloid, the 'best-known and best-liked Éire international' in the country.[5] At the same time, he was beloved by the Old Trafford faithful, who saluted his exploits with the chant:

> Hello Johnny Carey, you can hear all the girls cry,
> Hello Johnny Carey, you're the apple of my eye,
> You're a decent boy from Ireland, there's no one can deny,
> You're a harum scareum, devil may care-um, decent Irish boy.[6]

This was generous praise, especially considering that Carey had helped the southern Ireland team beat England 2–0 at Goodison Park – the first time the English had lost to a foreign side on home soil (see Chapter 9). On account of his service in the British army, he was eligible to play for Northern Ireland – which he did, with distinction. He also captained the Rest of Europe versus Great Britain in 1947 – a distinction somewhat lessened by the fact that Great Britain won the fixture 6–1.

On his retirement in 1953, Carey was offered a coaching position at Manchester United, but he turned it down to join Second Division Blackburn Rovers, who, under his guidance in the ensuing years, regularly pushed for promotion, finally achieving it in the 1957–58 season. Like Busby, he favoured younger players and encouraged his sides to play an attractive, passing game. Upon promotion, however, he departed to take the reins of Everton, also of the First Division. The Toffees were at that time an unremarkable side, but Carey managed to improve matters by taking them to fifth place at the end of the 1960–61 season.

The Everton chairman, John Moores, was an impatient man. During a shared cab ride after a League Clubs Conference in London in April 1961, as the taxi was stuck in rush-hour traffic, Moores told Carey that he was sacked. 'You're fired as from now,' he explained.[7] 'I saw it that Mr Moores paid the fare,' Carey recalled.[8]

This was, obviously, a cruel way to terminate a contract, but the manner in which Everton eventually became champions in 1963 under Harry Catterick somewhat vindicates Moores's impetuous decision, and his ruthless ambition. But Jackie Carey proved again that he could lift dormant clubs to greater things, as at his next posting at Leyton Orient demonstrated. With few resources, he took the east London side to the First Division for the first time in their history. They failed to remain there, however – they were relegated in the 1962–63 season – and he and the O's parted company.

History was to repeat itself a third time when Carey became manager of Nottingham Forest. Employing an elegant, attacking style of football, Carey took Forest to their highest position in the First Division – runners-up to Manchester United in 1966–67 – and to the FA Cup semifinals. Again, despite these achievements Carey was hastily sacked, in December 1968, after Forest had begun that season appallingly, languishing in twenty-first place. Carey was bewildered, not only that he had been sacked when Forest still had more than half their games yet to play that season, but that the club's chairman, Tony Wood, ended his public statement relating to the sacking on a complimentary note: 'Personally I don't think there is a nicer fellow in football,' he said of Carey. 'He is one of nature's gentlemen. In my book he is one of the greatest administrators in the game.'[9] Admittedly, again the chairman's decision was vindicated, as Nottingham Forest survived relegation under their new manager, John Gillies.

Carey returned to Blackburn Rovers as manager before working for a textile company and then in the treasurer's office of Trafford Borough Council. He was, as one obituary of him noted in August 1995, 'one of the most accomplished full-backs the British game has produced.'[10]

LIAM WHELAN

If it happens, I'm ready to go.

LIAM WHELAN, 6 FEBRUARY 1958

While the world of music and acting is littered with talented men and women who were cut short in their prime, football has thankfully been mostly spared from this affliction. For this reason, when young, gifted footballers die before having had the chance to realise their dreams, it is all the more awful. The tragedy is all the more poignant in that, whereas the likes of James Dean, Marilyn Monroe, Jimmy Hendrix and Kurt Cobain were partly or wholly culpable for their own demise, young sportsman who meet an early end are generally innocents.

The fact that such rare occurrences tend to happen on a large scale lends a further layer of tragedy, as when the aircraft carrying the Torino team crashed into the side of a hill just outside Turin in May 1949, killing eighteen players, including the majority of the national side. Torino has never recovered from the event. Nine years later, a similar fate was visited upon Manchester United, who were robbed of one of the club's – and Ireland's – most promising footballers, Liam 'Billy' Whelan, a man often – and justly – described as British football's greatest lost talent.

On 6 February 1958, Manchester United's Busby Babes were struck down. They had touched down at Munich's Riem Airport to refuel, having returned from Yugoslavia, where they had secured a place in the semi-finals of the European Cup with a 3–3 draw against Red Star Belgrade. Snow was falling heavily as the BEA airliner prepared to make its third attempt to take off, after two aborted attempts. During the second attempt, the United goalkeeper, the Ulsterman Harry Gregg, began giggling, only to be reprimanded by Johnny Berry: 'I don't know what you're laughing at. We're all going to get f—king killed!' Whelan, a deeply religious man, touched Gregg's arm and reassured him: 'Well, if it happens I'm ready to go.'[11]

On the third attempt, the aircraft failed to achieve the required speed and over-shot the runway. It smashed through the perimeter fencing, hitting a house with its port wing, then veering right before crashing into

76

another building and bursting into flames. Fortunately, the fuselage did not explode, and as a result several of the crew and passengers were able to return to the wreckage to rescue the injured (Gregg himself was to rescue the pregnant Yugoslav ambassador's wife and her child). Berry, who had prophesied his own demise, survived; Whelan, who was prepared for his, did not.

Liam 'Billy' Whelan was one of eight United players who perished that afternoon. It was a cruel twist of fate, in that Whelan had initially asked permission from the club not to travel to Belgrade in the first place. He had recently lost his place to Bobby Charlton and asked Matt Busby if he could return to Dublin to rest, but the manager said 'it wouldn't look right' if he didn't travel with the squad.[12]

Just as Manchester and England mourned, so did Dublin. When Whelan's remains were brought home, Dublin's northside came to a standstill to bid farewell to their fallen son, with thousands lining the street as the cortège travelled from the airport to Cabra. One member of the schoolboy guard of honour that day was a seven-year-old called Bertie Ahern. As he has recalled: 'I think it was the disaster that started my interest in the club and I have followed them ever since.'[13]

Bobby Charlton, a survivor of the crash, had been in awe of Whelan at Old Trafford. 'As a youngster, I always wanted to be the best player in the world, but as long as Liam Whelan was around, I doubted if I could,' he remembers. 'He was able to do things with a football which were beyond the rest of us.'[14] Charlton is not a man to heap praise lightly or frequently, and his subsequent long and illustrious career only serves as a pitiful reminder of what might have been for Whelan.

By a cruel irony, just as Whelan should not have been on the doomed plane, he was only signed for United by accident to begin with. The United scout Bert Whalley had come over to watch Vinny Ryan of Home Farm with a view to signing him, but Ryan did not perform that day. His team-mate, Whelan, did, and Whalley returned to Manchester with the seventeen-year-old's signature. Unlike his brothers, Christy and John, who played for Drumcondra, Liam had never attracted interest from any League of Ireland clubs, and in his short career Home Farm and Manchester United were the only two teams he ever turned out for. One of the first pieces of advice Whelan received upon his arrival at Man United was not tactical but semantic. 'Liam, is it?' asked John Carey upon being introduced to his fellow Dubliner. 'Well hold on to that name for as long as you can. They're sure to try to take that away from you here.'[15]

Playing as an inside-forward, Whelan's initial assignment was to replace John Doherty in the 1953 FA Youth Cup final against Wolverhampton Wanderers: he excelled himself in the 7–1 first-leg victory. Soon Liam – or 'Billy', as his name had by now been anglicised by the Mancunians – was knocking on the door of the first team: in his ninety-six appearances he scored fifty-two times. In 1956–57, in fifty-three outings, he scored thirty-three goals and created countless more, helping United to their second successive First Division title win. This was quite a record considering the considerable pool of young talent Busby had assembled at Old Trafford – as well as the fact that he was often kept out of the side by Charlton, and indeed that Whelan was a midfielder.

Part of Whelan's weaponry was unwitting deceit. He looked disconcertingly laid-back, even awkward. But he was a complete player: a creative and composed passer and dribbler, nifty at playing dummies, lethal in a tight spot, and fond of embarrassing opponents with a 'nutmeg', which he did against Duncan Edwards in Ireland's 1–1 draw against England at Dalymount Park in May 1957. Yet he made only four international appearances, where he duly impressed. 'I watched Liam Whelan and Arthur Fitzsimons play together in my last game for Ireland in Holland in 1956,' remembers the great Con Martin. 'And they blended so well in a 4–1 win that I left Rotterdam that evening wishing it was my first Ireland game rather than my last.'[16]

Whelan mesmerised the opposition a year later in a quarter-final tie again Bilbao, when he picked up the ball deep within his own half, strode and shimmied his way half the length of the pitch, and past five defenders, to put the ball in the net. Two goals down in the tie, he helped to ensure that Manchester United overcame the Spanish champions.

Liam 'Billy' Whelan was a quiet, modest fellow, almost oblivious to his own talents. Everyone remembers the Munich air crash of 1958, and the Manchester United team of the 1960s, but it will forever remain a matter of conjecture as to what the team of that era might have achieved even more with Whelan, the lost talent of Irish football.

Noel Cantwell

Dear Noel, this is the most difficult letter I have ever written but you're sacked.

LETTER FROM COVENTRY CITY CHAIRMAN TO THE CLUB'S MANAGER, MARCH 1972[17]

It was an ignominious way to part company with one's chief coach. Noel Cantwell, a former player with Manchester United, had performed something of a minor miracle upon been given the post at First Division Coventry City, replacing Jimmy Hill, in 1967. With scant resources – but blessed with an impressive footballing intellect – Cantwell had saved the struggling Midlands side from relegation in two successive seasons by the narrowest of margins: under his management, City came third from bottom in 1967–68 and 1968–69 (at that time, only the bottom two were relegated), a single point above the second-last-placed team on both occasions. Within three years, he had guided them to sixth place in the top flight. But the club was impatient. As the chairman put it in his letter to Cantwell: 'We want jam today, not tomorrow.'[18]

The sacking was a particular shock for Cantwell, as it was his first real taste of failure, and he was widely regarded as a future manager of a top side. He had even been tipped by many to succeed Matt Busby in the future. As a left-back with United between 1960 and 1967, Cantwell, an FA Cup–winning Corkman, was a picture of composure. Tall, well-built and broad-shouldered, in his usual position of full-back Cantwell was a performer of touch, style and elegance. A precise passer of the ball, and useful with his head, he had both the footballing brain and paternal touch to qualify him as Sir Matt's successor.

Above all, Cantwell was an organiser. 'I remember Noel with particular fondness for his efforts to improve the financial prospects of young players,'[19] remembers Nobby Stiles. After United had qualified for the 1963 FA Cup final, Cantwell organised the players' pool and made the first steps towards establishing the Manchester United souvenir shop – an act of foresight if ever there was one – erecting a small hut outside Old Trafford, from where he directed commercial operations. He was perceptive in other ways too. In November 1957, while playing for West Ham, he suspected that there was something wrong with the Hammers' captain, Malcolm Allison, and urged him to consult a doctor. Allison followed his advice – to discover that he had tuberculosis – and consequently received surgery that saved his life.[20]

Noel Euchuria Cornelius Cantwell (as he was, understandably, *never* known on the terraces) was an all-rounder, and went on to represent his country at cricket as well as football, playing seven times for Ireland. His best cricketing performance came when he made forty-seven runs against New Zealand in Belfast in July 1958. Representatives from Essex Country Cricket Club had watched him at that game, and they asked him if he wanted to come to England to play the sport, but he turned down the offer, saying that he did not want to spend an entire year in England for personal reasons. [21]

Cantwell would later change his mind about that – and about which sport he would pursue. He began his football career at his local side, Western Rovers, before moving on to Cork Athletic. In 1953, he was signed by West Ham, then in the Second Division, who did bring him over to England, where he joined two other Corkmen, Tommy Moroney and Frank O'Farrell.

After struggling in the second tier, West Ham gained promotion to the first in 1958, with Cantwell shining, initially at left-back. He was ready, and usually willing, to push forward but was versatile enough to play at centre-forward, which he did for Ireland in the 1960–61 season. He appeared thirty-six times for Ireland over a fourteen-year period, setting a record for his country by scoring fourteen goals, including five from penalties.

At club level, Cantwell established a useful partnership at the rear with right-back John Bond. The Hammers consolidated their position in the First Division after being promoted, with Cantwell in particular making his presence known. Indeed, he coped with the game in the top flight with assurance, and his skills came to the attention of Matt Busby. In 1960, after 245 league appearances, and having scored sixteen goals for the side, he left West Ham for Old Trafford for a fee of £29,500, then a record for a full-back.

Busby was still in the process of rebuilding a team in the post-Munich era. Cantwell, who was both a gifted leader and relatively mature – he was twenty-eight when he transferred to United – would frequently captain the side. Roger Byrne's death at Munich had left Busby in need of a left-back, and for since 1958 this position was occupied by Ian Greaves, and then, for an even longer spell, by Dubliner Joe Carolan, but soon Cantwell was to make it his own. In this position, he helped the Red Devils to their first post-Munich trophy, when they overcame the favourites Leicester in the 1963 FA Cup final. He would play in United's 1966–67 title-winning season, but by this time he was well into his thirties and was being selected more infrequently, and he made only four appearances in that campaign.

To the surprise of many, who were perhaps reluctant to wait until Busby's reign had run its course, Cantwell left Old Trafford in 1967 to become manager at Coventry. 'The sack came as quite a shock,' he remarked of his inelegantly handled dismissal from the club five years later. 'I had no idea what to do for a living.'[22] Seven months later, however, he was invited by Peterborough United, then an indifferent side, doing nothing in the lower reaches of the Fourth Division, to rescue them from their sorry state. Cantwell began the process by giving twelve of the players a free transfer, and introducing ten other 'experienced performers who I knew would be suited to life in the Fourth Division. I was interested in skill, but a competitive streak was just as important to me. I settled on a squad of twenty, got them organised and sat back to enjoy watching them.'[23] In his first full season at the helm, he took Peterborough into the Third Division as champions, earning him the sobriquet 'the Messiah' from the Peterborough fans. Spectacularly, he was offered the job of manager of the esteemed Spanish side Atletico Bilbao; inexplicably, he turned the offer down.

By the time he left Peterborough in 1977, Cantwell was said to be the highest-paid manager in England outside the First Division. He went to the United States to manage the New England Tea Men and the Jacksonville Tea Men, before returning to manage Peterborough in 1986. Three years later, he retired to run a pub in the town. In recent years, he made a brief return to the game when Sven-Goran Eriksson asked him to become a scout for the England side.

A handsome and amusing man who enjoyed reunions at West Ham and Manchester United, Cantwell died in September 2005. 'I've had a very good life and a good, happy family life as well,' he said shortly before his death. 'So, all in all, I'm very happy about my little contribution to football.' He never begrudged being born at a time when footballers were not paid fortunes. 'I never look back and say to myself: "Oh, my God, why wasn't I born later? Why couldn't I be a Denis Irwin or a Roy Keane?"'[24]

It is apt that Cantwell should invoke the name of his fellow Corkman Keane. As one of Cantwell's obituarists noted, the older Corkman played briefly in the Irish league, moved to a small English club, was transferred for a record fee to Manchester United, became captain of the team, and led them to a notable Cup win.[25] Only time will tell whether Roy Keane will see history repeated on himself, and whether, if Niall Quinn does feel the need to pen 'the most difficult letter he has ever written', he will do so with the same brevity.

TONY DUNNE

At the end of that game I just said thank f—k for that . . . I was just so
glad this pursuit of European glory was finally concluded. Most people
celebrated that night, but it was a flat night for me.

TONY DUNNE, AFTER THE 1968 EUROPEAN CUP FINAL[26]

Tony Dunne was signed by Manchester United as an understudy, stand-
in and eventual replacement for Noel Cantwell, a process that took far
longer than the club had expected, and far longer than Dunne had hoped
it would – such was the manner in which the Corkman continued to dominate that position. But the quality of Dunne's performances when he
temporarily replaced an injured Cantwell meant that, when Cantwell
recovered, he found it impossible to displace his compatriot. Dunne had
become the third Irishman in succession to guard the rear left of the field
for Manchester United, and he is spoken of by some as United's pre-eminent left-back of all time.

Tony Dunne may have been short and wiry, but he compensated for
these apparent deficiencies with his tenacity and pace: 'he was as fast as a
whippet' remembers the Mancunian Nobby Stiles.[27] Dunne was a sensible and intelligent passer of the ball, quick in for the tackle and even
quicker to recover for a second; with Shay Brennan, the Manchester-born
Irish international, he formed an enduring partnership for both club and
country.

The Dubliner relished a confrontation. It was precisely on account of
Dunne's diminutive stature, and his failure to break into the first team,
that he became the player he did – one that would win the League twice
and go all the way in Europe in 1968. Faced with these two obstacles,
Dunne worked tirelessly to transform himself into one of the most athletic and hardy players in England. 'You're training too much,' Matt Busby
would constantly reproach him, but Dunne's ruthless fitness regimen
would make him such a nuisance to opposing wingers, whom he matched
them for pace, harassed, and forced into corners. It is said among United
supporters that Dunne was the first left-back since Munich to play in the
spirit of Roger Byrne. Whether he was as good as (or indeed better than)

Roger Byrne had been (or might have been) is a matter of opinion; what is less disputed is that Dunne was one of Busby's best bargain buys of the 1960s.

Although Anthony Dunne supported St Patrick's Athletic as a lad, he made his name in Ireland at Shelbourne via St Finbars, winning the FAI Cup with Shelbourne in their 2–0 victory over Cork Hibernians in 1960. On the way to that trophy, Shels met Shamrock Rovers – this time with Manchester United scout Billy Behan and Matt Busby himself in the crowd. The two men were instantly impressed. Later that evening, Dunne went to the cinema with his girlfriend, only for the following message to appear on the screen: 'Would Tony Dunne please go to the front entrance.'

'Frightened to death I was, I didn't know what was going on,' Dunne remembers.[28] When he made his way out, he found Gerry Doyle, the Shelbourne manager, waiting at the entrance to tell him some news.

'Manchester United want to sign you. I'm going to take you down to see your ma and dad.'

'Bloody hell.'

Dunne and his belle went to the Gresham Hotel – where they made a beeline for Busby and Behan.

'Listen, son,' said Busby, 'I've watched you play and I think I can make a footballer out of you, make you a professional if you're prepared to take the chance and do what I tell you. What do you think?'

'Well, yeah, sure, of course, if you can help me, yeah, that would be great,' Dunne said, pleased as Punch.

'Your club is having a Cup run and they would like to keep you till the end of the season. What we'll do is we'll sign a contract but we'll leave you here till you come out of the Cup.'

'Oh, that's marvellous.'[29]

With the deal done and the Cup won, Dunne moved to Manchester. The Corkman settled in with relative ease, becoming close friends with an Ulsterman called Willie Donaldson; Dunne's debut came on 15 October 1960. It was against the reigning champions Burnley, with Dunne facing John Connelly, the England left-winger and Dunne's future team-mate at Old Trafford. Connelly gave Dunne a game he would remember for a long time. 'The closest I got to him was when we came off the field and he shook my hand,' recalls Dunne. 'He ran me ragged and left me to face up to the reality that I could go one of two ways – raise my standards or accept failure at this level. We lost 5–3. I learned that if I was going to be a success I had to shut my corner off to give me another bite at the cherry.'[30]

Dunne's experience that day suggested to him that, if he was to defeat speeding wingers, he had to catch them first, and after training sessions he would put himself through sprinting exercises. Busby repeatedly admonished Dunne that he was pushing his body too hard, and even promised his new signing that he could take leave from occasional training sessions on account of the extra graft he was putting in. Tony, however, adamant that he needed the extra punishment, refused.

Dunne needed patience as well as punishment, though, as he failed to make it as a first-team regular in his first season at United. Nonetheless, when Cantwell was put out of the game in the 1961–62 season, Dunne was given the opportunity he needed; by the time he appeared in the FA Cup final – alongside Cantwell and Giles – in 1963 he had made the left-back position his own. Manchester United had yet to recover fully from Munich, and struggled in the League, even flirting with relegation in 1962–63, when they finished fourth from bottom.

During his time at United, Dunne made 530 appearances but, perhaps strangely for a man blessed with unusual pace, scored only two goals. His lack of goals was a result of his cautious, conscientious approach to the game: he preferred, having wrested the ball from the opposition, to deliver a simple, short pass to a midfielder or attacker, let them do the work, allowing him to return to his – remaining vigilant at the rear. When he did venture upfield, he provided the team with the benefit of his dead-ball skills: it was his free-kick which George Best headed into the goal, as United thrashed Benfica 5–1 in the own backyard in 1965.

Dunne made a relatively small number of appearances for Ireland, playing in just thirty-three games over a fourteen-year period. Again, he had been initially kept out of the team by Cantwell, but after being utilised as a striker for Man United, Dunne earned his first international cap, in a 3–2 defeat by Austria in 1962. Matt Busby resented losing his players to national sides – as well as losing their services, he was worried about them picking up an injury – and was alarmed that the Ireland team did not at the time have a physiotherapist. When Cantwell returned from a match in Spain with a limp, and with heavily bruised feet, Busby exploded. 'You play tomorrow because I need you, but you may never play for that f—king team again.'[31] In the end, Busby did not enforce his edict: in 1969, Dunne went on to captain the national side, and he continued to play for Ireland until 1976.

Having helped United on their way to the European Cup final in 1968, with a sterling performance against Gornik Zabrze of Poland (the second leg of which he played with a ruptured heel and in agony), Dunne ended the season relieved rather than elated. Dunne was one of three Irish players to appear for Manchester United in the European final at Wembley, alongside George Best and Shay Brennan. The Red Devils overcame Barcelona 4–1 after a gruelling encounter that went into extra-time. 'After the game I really tried to jump with joy but all I could think was: "Christ almighty, thank God that's over, thank God we've won",' Dunne said. 'I saw Bobby Charlton and I thought: "God, we've won, it's wonderful, it's absolutely wonderful." But inside of me there's something that's dragging me down and I'm thinking to myself: "Look at that silly twat jumping up there, he's happy." I was trying to jump and be part of it but it was really a low time for me.' Dunne just wanted to be on his own, with a well-deserved drink.[32]

By 1973, the old order at Manchester United was disintegrating rapidly. Busby had gone, Bobby Charlton had retired, Denis Law was moving on, George Best didn't know whether he was coming or going as a result of his drinking, and Dunne was being pushed out. The Corkman had continued to feature under the disastrous reign of Frank O'Farrell at the club; when the Irishman was dismissed as manager, Tommy Docherty came in, bringing in his own 'Tartan army', in the shape of George Graham and Alex Forsyth. Dunne did not feature in Docherty's future plans: the new manager played him only three times, the last being in the away match against Ipswich Town in February 1973.

'Docherty just wanted rid of me,' remembers Dunne. 'He just threw me out and it was a f—king nasty way he did it.' Dunne was due a testimonial, but just before it was to take place the club announced that they would hold one for Denis Law only weeks beforehand. 'Normally for testimonials they send out raffle tickets in the Development Association envelopes and in those days that usually raised about £3,000,' Dunne says. 'But when I approached them about doing it for my testimonial, they said they couldn't because they had just sent out tickets for Denis Law's.'[33] He describes the way he was treated as 'hurtful'; in the end a friend at Manchester City came to the rescue and organised a derby testimonial. A crowd of seventeen thousand turned up and Dunne received a cheque for £8,000 – of which Manchester United, in an appallingly charmless move, took a £1,500 slice for the cost of policing, and for the hire of the stadium.

Docherty's loss was Bolton Wanderers' gain, though: Dunne's six years at Burndon Park showed Docherty that the Irishman's playing days had been far from been behind him in 1973. His standards only declined right at the end: he was part of the 1977–78 side that gained promotion to the First Division. After a brief period across the Atlantic with Detroit Express, he returned to coach Bolton in 1981, before briefly taking the reins at the Norwegian side Steinjker between 1982 and 1983, where he replaced former Manchester United man Billy Foulkes. He now lives in Altrincham, Lancashire, and speaks with a Lancashire accent.

Frank O'Farrell

Frank O'Farrell was probably the nicest fella I ever met in my life, but the worst manager I ever played under.

Tony Dunne, 1999[34]

Have you any idea of how much there is to do? Do you ever think of that? Of course not, you're all too busy sticking your noses into every corner, poking around for things to complain about, aren't you? Well let me tell you something - this is exactly how Nazi Germany started. A lot of layabouts with nothing better to do than to cause trouble. I've had enough. I've had it.

Basil Fawlty

Like Tony Dunne, Frank O'Farrell eventually settled in England when his playing and managerial days had finished – in O'Farrell's case, in the English Riviera, in Torquay. Some, cruelly, might say that this was a fitting place for him, for under his guidance at Manchester United, the club was mismanaged in a manner befitting Fawlty Towers.

O'Farrell is remembered not as the only Irishman to have managed Manchester United but as one of Busby's brief and unsuccessful coaches: someone who oversaw the once-great club's freefall down the First Division in 1972 and was much criticised for his aloof and elusive manner. It is a harsh judgment. Admittedly, his managerial methods may have not been suited to the team. In particular, he employed zone marking, in which players were assigned areas rather than men to keep in check; this led to confusion and countless arguments between players, with one blaming another for failing to take up the man who had encroached into his zone, and the second man blaming the first for failing to chase him there. O'Farrell was not the most hands-on of managers: he was not a manic manager in the mould of Basil Fawlty but was painfully shy, and an almost-ghostlike figure at Old Trafford. 'We hardly ever saw him,' remembers Denis Law.[35] 'He came a stranger and left a stranger' has been the judgment of the many people who played for Manchester United during O'Farrell's time at the helm from June 1971 to December 1972 – a period during which he took Manchester United to victory in only ten victories in forty-two games.

This is perhaps an unkind and unfair judgment, for O'Farrell. Politeness and decorum is often mistaken for aloofness and superciliousness, and O'Farrell belonged to a previous era that placed great emphasis on 'respectability'. He was also hampered by George Best's increasingly erratic behaviour and frequent disappearing acts, and the baleful effect this was having on team spirit, especially when Best did actually turn up for a game: the Belfast superstar now seemed less interested in playing for the team and instead tended to hog the ball so that he could show off. O'Farrell also became manager at the wrong time. Busby had rested on his laurels since the European Cup win of 1968, and had failed build on a team that was collectively ageing. This meant that – in a process very much in evidence at Leeds United in the same era – when a mass exodus began in the early 1970s, there were no players of similar calibre to replace them; this led to a spectacular collapse in form that would leave United bereft of a League title until the 1990s.

Frank O'Farrell was another son of Cork, born in 1927, the son of an engine driver who followed his father's footsteps in becoming a railway hand at the age of sixteen. He also played for Cork United before English football lured him away from his native land: he moved to Second Division West Ham United in 1948. His introverted nature, and his unwillingness to be pushy, worked against him from the outset: he failed to break into the first team. Eventually, his feet did the talking for him, and his gritty approach to the game earned him a full debut against Notts County in November 1950.

O'Farrell remained with the Hammers for six seasons, winning nine caps for his country in the process, before moving up a tier to join First Division Preston North End shortly after the start of the 1957–58 season – a campaign in which they ended runners-up in the League. He went on to become player-manager of Weymouth in 1961, and then to manage Fourth Division Torquay United, where he took the team into the Third Division at the first attempt, and then almost up again, into the Second Division, as Torquay finished seventh and fourth in the Third Division in the following two seasons. In December 1968, he leapfrogged over the Second Division by taking charge of First Division Leicester City. Although he couldn't prevent Leicester's relegation the following year, he led them to the 1969 FA Cup final and brought them straight back to the top flight, at the first time of asking, in 1969–70.

In August 1970, Busby finally handed over the reins at Manchester United, appointing Wilf McGuinness as head-team coach, while remaining general manager himself. McGuinness did not command respect in the dressing room, however, and there was even talk of a revolt. The season started badly under him, with the Red Devils winning just five of their first twenty-two games before Christmas. The high expectations placed on him broke him in February 1971. Jock Stein initially agreed to step in to take his place, but withdrew at the last minute, and Dave Sexton also turned down the offer. Both Stein and Sexton evidently realised that it would be an impossible task to work after, and under, Busby – something that O'Farrell, the eventual successor after months of searching for a replacement, had not recognised.

United nonetheless began the 1971–72 season in spectacular fashion, and were top of the table on New Year's Day. Best was on scintillating form, with him and Law netting twenty-odd goals between them, prompting Busby to write an article for the *Daily Express* under the headline 'Frank is probably the best signing I ever made.'

The Red Devils' 3–0 defeat to West Ham on New Year's Day was prophetic, however – an indication of the lamentable season that they would endure thereafter. Having won all but two of their twenty League games in the first part of the season, United notched up a meagre five victories in the new year, and ended the season in eighth position. The 1972–73 season began even more disastrously: United failed to win in any of their opening ten matches, and their 5–0 mauling by Crystal Palace on 16 December was the last straw – United were left second-bottom of the table, and O'Farrell lost all remaining respect from the players or the boss. Busby even offered the job of manager to Tommy Docherty at half-time. Three days later, with three and half years remaining on his contract, O'Farrell was summoned by the board and dismissed.

His zone-marking approach clearly hadn't worked, and his hands-off approach and reluctance to appear at training displeased the team. Bobby Previously Charlton had been infuriated with O'Farrell at being dropped, and went straight to Matt Busby to express his displeasure. The upshot of this was that Busby, who had told O'Farrell's wife at a function that her husband was 'an independent sod', summoned the manager to his office to tell him that he should keep Charlton in the team. O'Farrell also failed to get George Best under control, and after the Ulsterman was put on the transfer list, he, too, did not speak to the head coach about the matter but instead went behind his back to consult Busby.

Throughout 1972, Best was regularly absent from training, initially returning to Belfast – concerned about his family's safety with the escalation of violence there – and later to Marbella. In May, he announced his retirement the day before his twenty-sixth birthday, but O'Farrell persuaded him to change his mind. Best later disappeared again, eloping with the actress Sinead Cusack. This prompted O'Farrell to drop him and Busby to put him on the transfer list.

'The press really hammered him,' remembers O'Farrell. 'It might have been time to say, "Bye bye George, thanks for everything" but the team wasn't good enough to say that.' O'Farrell had made tactical and personal errors, but the squad itself was reaching the end of its lifespan; he was essentially fielding a team of old men. O'Farrell believed that the healthy start made in 1970–71 season had been 'an illusion. People like [Paddy] Crerand, Law, Charlton, Tony Dunne, they had been great players, but that was in the past. When I looked at the team I realised their reputations were better than their performances. Except for Best.'[36] And after 1971, O'Farrell didn't even have him.

Then there was Busby, who should have either stayed and consolidated his team, or retired altogether, and stopped interfering with the coaching side of the game. The omens were not good from the beginning. On O'Farrell's very first day at Old Trafford, he was shown into the general manager's office – the same office he had had as coach for twenty-five years. 'It had the lettering "Sir Matt Busby" and a papal knighthood or something over it,'[36a] while O'Farrell was shown to his office, a poky room down the corridor. 'Alarm bells started ringing. I'm quite a polite person and I was somewhat in awe of him, but I said to him, "Matt, before I came here the press were speculating that whoever took over would always be in your shadow. It won't look right for you and it won't look right for me, not because I want a bigger office but everybody recognises this is where the manager is. You'll find him here." He said, "Okay, I'll move my stuff out." But I should never have had to ask. I got off to a bad start.'[37]

Busby's reluctance to be rid of the players who had been so loyal to

– and effective for – him in the 1960s was also responsible for United's dramatic fall from grace in 1972, and for the barren years that followed. No one coming up was of the same calibre as Best, Law and Charlton. Without O'Farrell, United finished eighth in the spring of 1973, and despite Docherty's efforts to buy his way out of trouble, they were relegated to the Second Division in 1974. 'He should have started rebuilding years earlier,' insists the Corkman; or, as one director put it to him: 'Matt sat on his arse for the last number of years.'[38]

Like Dunne, O'Farrell couldn't leave United without the club's now-customary display of parsimony – and an attempt to humiliate him. The club asked O'Farrell to return the club car, a Jaguar, even though he had offered to purchase it with his compensation money. The club upped the price tag and there ensued a squabble, with O'Farrell being advised by his lawyers to sign on the dole until the matter was resumed. This was the final humiliation for a proud man: 'At the time, to sign on the dole you were seen as the dregs. I used to see the poor men in Cork outside the labour exchange and I always felt sorry for them, that they couldn't work. I parked a mile away from the exchange in Salford and the manager was very good, he let me in the back. I was always afraid that the *Sun* or the *Daily Mirror* would be outside and that my kids would see the picture in the paper. So they put me through that, but eventually they settled just before it came to court.'[39] Although he is not the kind of man to seek revenge, he did exact some when the dispute ended with him accepting £50,000 – the largest pay-off made to a sacked manager.[40]

In 1973, O'Farrell moved to manage Cardiff City, but in April 1974 and in 1976 he returned to Torquay, where he was appointed manager (in 1976), general manager (1977), manager (1981) and general manager (1982).

Although he will not be remembered as the greatest-ever Manchester United manager, O'Farrell did become, for a time, a national hero in Iran. During the period between Cardiff and Torquay, he went to the Middle East to manage the Iranian national team, and in September 1976 became the toast of Tehran when he guided Iran to victory in what could be understatedly called a 'grudge match', beating Israel 1–0.

He still lives in Torquay.

KEVIN MORAN

Kevin Moran, oldest man on the pitch today, thirty-five years of age, of course the referee could possibly be older than that, and technically he is on the pitch too, but then again his linesman could be even older than him, but are they technically on the pitch?

GEORGE HAMILTON[41]

Although all-rounders used to be a common sight in top-level English sport, with many athletes customarily playing soccer in the winter and cricket in the summer, few have managed to excel in both football and another field of endeavour – to have been decorated on account of both their footballing prowess and their exploits elsewhere.

The hostile medium-fast swing bowler and destructive batsman Ian Botham may have beaten the Australians with England, but when it came to playing with a larger, bouncier ball, he never got beyond Scunthorpe United. Charles Burgess Fry, that legendary figure of the Edwardian age, may have played football for England, captained four cricket Test matches for his country, become India's representative at the League of Nations, earned a First in Classics at Oxford, held the world long-jump record and been invited to become the king of Albania, but when he appeared in an FA Cup final in 1902, his Southampton came out second best. Denis Compton fared better, appearing for England at both football and cricket, winning the FA Cup in 1950 with Arsenal and helping to wrest back the Ashes from the Aussies in 1953. Then there is goalkeeper Bert Trautmann, who guided Manchester City to glory in 1956. Trautmann, a former paratrooper and prisoner of war, is the only man to have won an FA Cup winners' medal and the Iron Cross – a record, as one writer has observed, 'he is likely to hang on to for some time.'[42]

Then there is Kevin Moran, the only man to win an FA Cup–winner's medal and the Sam Maguire trophy – twice, in each case – with Manchester United and Dublin. Moran is arguably the best-known Gaelic footballer in England, and certainly the most successful in mastering both codes of football. The 'Blood Donor', as he was known, owing to his reckless bravery on the pitch and the manner in which he threw himself

93

into tackles, also has a degree in business and commerce.

Although an unknown in England then, Moran's courage and determination on the field of play became familiar to Gaelic-football aficionados in the 1970s, particularly for the critical role he played in the 1977 All-Ireland semi-final encounter with Kerry. This game is still talked of today, and is regarded by some as one of the finest games of the 1970s, if not of all time. 'Twenty-nine minutes still remaining in this game, hallelujah,' as commentator Micheál O'Hehir famously remarked during that clash. With Dublin, Moran had beaten the Munster side in the final in 1976, and he then went on to secure another All-Ireland win against Armagh, after helping to beat Kerry in 1977.

Seven years after appearing at Croke Park, Kevin Moran walked out at Wembley for the FA Cup final against Second Division Brighton, where United were rather embarrassingly held to a 2–2 draw. In fact, were it not for the seasiders' Gordon 'He Must Score' Smith hesitating in front of goal at the last, in front of Gary Bailey, United could easily have succumbed to humiliating defeat. Order was restored in the replay five days later, when United punished Smith's vacillation with four goals, and with no reply from Brighton.

If the 1983 final was an occasion for red faces at United, the 1985 final was remembered for a red card. Playing against an Everton side that was chasing an unprecedented treble of League, FA Cup and European Cup Winners' Cup, Moran made history by becoming the first person to be sent off in an FA Cup final – for a foul on Peter Reid. It was also one of the harshest decisions in an FA Cup final – one cited as a reason why top-flight football needs video technology in games played for such high stakes.

The incident happened with twelve minutes of normal time remaining, and with the game still goalless. Reid had intercepted a pass from Paul McGrath and dashed forward; Andy Gray and Graeme Sharp following his lead, flanking Reid on each side, only for Moran to storm in and for Reid to hit the floor. It was a foul, but it was no worse than the comparably innocuous challenges committed by Kevin Ratcliffe and Frank Stapleton earlier on in the final – tackles which did not even solicit a caution. Moran had gone for the ball, not the man, and Reid's collapse to the turf was mainly the result of his own momentum.

To the surprise of the hundred thousand fans assembled at Wembley

– and to the Irishman's horror – the referee, Peter Willis, took a red card from his pocket and presented it to Moran's face. Moran's indignant reaction, and his refusal to leave the pitch, may have appalled those who believed Wembley to be a place of reverence, and the FA Cup final a solemn and very English competition that should embody national characteristics of sportsmanship and decorum, but it was understandable. 'I went through a whole range of emotions,' Moran recalled some years later. 'When I got sent off I honestly believe I was totally numb, I do not remember anything. I was just numb on the bench. I was watching the game all right but I was not taking it in. I was just devastated at being sent off.'[43]

Happily for Moran, United's Norman Whiteside stole the tie in extra-time, denying the Toffees their treble, and their place in posterity. Instead, the game will go down in history for Moran's undeserved dismissal. He is still bitter at that decision – for the ref ruining his big day – or perhaps he just is annoyed by the fact that his name is mostly uttered or written down these days on answer sheets in pub quizzes.

The Dubliner was born in April 1956 and harboured ambitions to be a professional footballer as a boy, preferably for Manchester United. He wanted to support United in his youth, but it was a rule in his household that no two members of the family were allowed to support the same team; with an older brother having already 'bagsied' Manchester United, young Kevin half-heartedly opted for Liverpool.[44] By the time he reached his teenage years, the GAA had removed its rule forbidding its members playing foreign games; like many of his generation who were educated by the Christian Brothers, he played Gaelic at school and football outside it. Did Gaelic take priority? 'Yes Gaelic did, like it did for every kid, or schoolboy. But once eighteen, no, not really,' he recalls.[45] Unusually for a footballer, he went to university: he studied commerce at UCD and spent a year as an accountant, while continuing to play both sports with equal vigour.

Moran was another discovery of United's ever-vigilant eye on Ireland, Billy Behan, who was among the 150 spectators in attendance at an FAI Cup first-round tie between Pegasus and Dundalk. Behan successfully convinced his boss, Dave Sexton, that this multifaceted sportsman could have a future playing soccer in England. Moran did not need much persuading to take the plunge, and in February 1978 he moved to England.

The transition to a different country proved difficult at first for Moran, who had just made it to the top in Gaelic, and he would not make his United debut for another fourteen months. In the meantime, the club allowed him to return to Ireland to appear in the 1978 All-Ireland football final; this time, the Dubs, now hailed by their devotees as the 'team of the century', came out second-best – to Kerry.

Moran's English soccer debut came on 30 April 1979, the day after his twenty-third birthday, away to Southampton; in his next 286 appearances for Manchester United he was occasionally employed as a midfielder, before settling in at the rear. (By coincidence, the following year another Dubliner, Anto Whelan, made his debut for the side, coming on as a substitute for the injured Moran in a home game against Southampton. Whelan never played for the team again, thus securing his own place in history – as the Irishman with the shortest playing career at Manchester United. Whelan, who had been signed from Bohemians, soon returned to Dublin to play for Shamrock Rovers. For those who really want to know, the player with the briefest-ever first-team record as a Manchester United player was York-born Nick Culkin, who enjoyed an eighty-second-long stint with them in the Premiership, coming on for the first and last time in their 2–1 victory at Arsenal in 1999.)[46]

Moran's timing was not always perfect, as the scars on his face attest, but he came to master his game as a central defender with United, learning the art of distribution; despite his relatively short stature, he was always useful in the air. His first appearance at Wembley came in the 1983 League Cup final, where Norman Whiteside put the team 1–0 up against their traditional foes, Liverpool, after twelve minutes. Liverpool were in truth a superior outfit and thereafter took control of the game, with Moran and Gordon McQueen at the back shutting out Scouse incursions – until, that is, the sixty-ninth minute, when the Irishman fell to the ground with a twisted ankle. Moran was to play no more part in the game, and McQueen was crippled by cramp, and his hamstrings were flaring up again. United nonetheless struggled valiantly, with Frank Stapleton moving back to marshal the rear. But only six minutes after Moran's departure, Alan Kennedy's long-range, swerving twenty-five-yard effort eluded Bailey, to level matters. United might have stolen the game at the last when, in the final minute, Liverpool goalkeeper Bruce Grobbelaar blatantly body-checked the hobbling McQueen, but appeals for a penalty were dismissed. Decimated and exhausted, United capitulated to the Liverpool machine in extra time. Ronnie Whelan's ninety-ninth-minute goal, and his team's subsequent outrageous time-wasting, won Liverpool the Cup but also lost them many friends.

Manchester United secured England's pre-eminent Cup competition some weeks later, and again in 1985, but Moran's dismissal in that final cast a shadow on that occasion. As Moran had set a precedent, he was not even sure if he could walk the steps to collect his medal, but the manager, Ron Atkinson, told him to make the ascent anyway. He did so, but did not put out his hand to pick up his decoration. It was later posted to him.

'Big Ron' Atkinson's departure from Old Trafford, and Alex Ferguson's arrival in 1986, marked the beginning of the end for Moran, and many others at the club. Atkinson had tolerated the drinking culture at the club – it even mirrored his own public persona as a gauche playboy – and Moran, alongside Whiteside, McQueen, Paul McGrath and Bryan Robson, were in the inner circle: the 'booze brothers', as they were known. But Ferguson took a dim view of Bacchanalian bonding sessions, and all of these players, bar Robson, were to become victims of Ferguson's intolerance of other people drinking alcohol to excess. The Presbyterian Scotsman had also introduced Steve Bruce from Norwich City, making competition for a place in defence even fiercer.

In August 1988, Moran was released from his contract, and he moved to the Spanish side Sporting Gijón, before returning to England to spend five useful seasons at an ever-improving Blackburn side. He retired the year before the side won the Premiership, an achievement in which his time there played a significant part. Fergie has since admitted that by, letting Moran go, he had possibly made 'a mistake'.[47]

Kevin earned seventy-one caps for Ireland, later playing in midfield alongside Mark Lawrenson. According to the FAI, Moran 'epitomised everything that was good about the game in the Eoin Hand and Jack Charlton eras'.[48] He appeared in all five World Cup qualifying games when the Republic so nearly made it to Spain 82. Moran has since formed, with Paul Stretford and Jesper Olsen, the football agency Proactive Sports Management, which has handled John O'Shea, Steve Finnan, Andy Cole and Wayne Rooney, the last of whom is no stranger to seeing red – and being shown the red.

Despite the fact that he is a two-time FA Cup winner, Moran wishes he had won the League with United or Blackburn. Overall, though, he says: 'I've no regrets about anything. I've played with some great players and for some great teams.' His proudest achievement was winning the Sam Maguire trophy. That, he says, was 'a bit more special'.

PAUL MCGRATH

I played against Paul McGrath a few times at United. His skill and athleticism were a nightmare for me. He'd just nip in and pinch the ball off my toes. Against Kevin, I'd feel like I'd been beaten up; against Paul, it was more like having my pocket picked.

NIALL QUINN, 2002[49]

Ooh, Aah, Paul McGrath!

TERRACE CHANT

Beer makes you feel as you ought to feel without beer.

THE AUSTRALIAN POET HENRY LAWSON, 1867–1922

Although he was a winner that day, Paul McGrath felt responsible for the role he played in Kevin Moran's sending off in the 1985 Cup final. 'I still feel guilty about that red card,' he said in 1994. 'It was my poor back pass to Kevin that let Peter Reid in to pick up the ball and sweep towards goal. I had given Kevin no choice but to go for Reidy after that hospital pass.' As regards Moran's medal: 'Had they refused to give it to him point-blank then I would have given him my medal – after all, I was responsible for his dismissal.'[50]

It is a somewhat harsh self-indictment on McGrath's part – Peter Willis was the true guilty party that day – but characteristic of the defender's modest and self-effacing nature. Few recall that 'hospital pass' today; instead, the softly spoken 'Black Pearl of Inchicore', with his whimsical grin, is remembered as one of the bravest players to appear for Manchester United, Aston Villa and the Republic of Ireland.

While Moran is the most famous Gaelic-football player in England, Paul McGrath is one of England's best-known Irishmen of African or Afro-Caribbean descent, along with Phil Lynott, Samantha Mumba – and André Shoukri, the leader of Egyptian descent of the north Belfast wing of the UDA. Despite a catalogue of injuries as long as the number of column inches he has generated in the press, and eight operations – his damaged knees made him unable to train for matches – Paul McGrath continued playing well into his thirties. After Moran's dismissal in May 1985, he almost single-handedly shut Everton out in that game.

One of the best central defenders in England in his prime, Paul McGrath was strong, speedy and versatile, and was comfortable playing as a midfielder too. But he was also rather accident-prone. Considering that he did not, because he *could* not, prepare for matches, he enjoyed a career of surprising longevity, being, in the opinion of his former Villa team-mate Derek Mountifield, 'the best centre-half with dodgy knees in the business.'[51] From the outset, football was his first love – and, sadly, his only real love: when he became too old to play it, he seemed to have no idea what to do with his life.

Paul McGrath was born in Ealing, west London, to an unmarried mother from Dublin and a Nigerian doctor – a father he has never met. His distraught mother was not in a position to raise him, this being an era where unmarried Irishwomen with brown babies were not treated with approval in England, let alone in Ireland. She journeyed with her six-year-old son and arrived at Dun Laoghaire docks, tearfully placing him in the hands of a foster agency.

McGrath's older foster brother, Denis, introduced him to football: Paul's first memory was, as a three-year-old, standing up and kicking the ball with Denis against some gates.[52] His brother also chased away the kids who teased him about his colour before Paul was old enough to fight his own battles – something which he subsequently did on numerous occasions. He immersed himself in football as a means of escape. He grew up in Whitehall in Dublin's northside, supporting Chelsea, and though he was raised a Protestant, he came to regard himself as a Roman Catholic. In Italia 90 he even met Pope John Paul II – an event he still regards as one of the greatest of his life.[53]

McGrath began playing soccer with Pearse Rovers, moving to Dalkey United as a seventeen-year-old before graduating to St Patrick's Athletic. Perhaps inevitably, he had already come to the attention of Manchester United scout Billy Behan during his Dalkey days, and he was offered a month's trial at the club. This unnerved McGrath. He had been continually uprooted throughout his life – foster care was followed by spells in three orphanages – and he didn't want to move again. A summer tour of Germany in 1978 with Dalkey – when he left Ireland for the first time, flew on a plane for the first time, and had his first taste of alcohol – had already unhinged him badly: two months after returning home, he suffered a mental breakdown. Depression was diagnosed, and his mental state deteriorated further, landing him for a period in rehab. But such was his state of mind – he was practically mute – that he later had to be readmitted, to St Brendan's Hospital in Grangegorman.[54] Although he recalls this as a 'horrendous' place, McGrath liked the security it offered. With the help of some pills, therapy, long walks, and the encouragement of his friends, he was to recover, and six months later he had returned to playing with the Dalkey team.

He also plucked up the courage to take up Manchester United's invitation. He warmed to Ron Atkinson, despite the fact that, when meeting him for the first time, the big man immediately (and, one might say, a tad hypocritically, given his own penchant for the stuff) ordered McGrath to remove his jewellery: 'If we're going to buy you, the one thing we don't want is centre-halves with earrings.'[55] After his month's trial had elapsed, Big Ron decided that he wanted to keep McGrath, and he was duly signed in April 1982 for a mere £30,000.

McGrath's confidence on the field made an immediate impression. Much to his relief, leaving Ireland for a second time had not had the catastrophic effect on him that it had had the first time. He fitted in well, and rapidly, partly because of the presence of his countrymen at the club. 'The big thing for me was that Frank Stapleton was there. Kevin Moran was there. Ashley Grimes was there. There was a great splattering of Irish there, which helped enormously,' he says.[56]

McGrath made his League debut for Manchester United as a substitute for Kevin Moran against Tottenham in November 1982, but the presence of Moran and Gordon McQueen as regular centre-halves meant that he made just fourteen appearances in 1982–83, scoring three goals in the process. The next season, he appeared only nine times. By Christmas 1984, however, McGrath had cracked it: not only was he making himself a fixture on the team, but in February 1985 he also made the first of his eighty-three international appearances, against Italy at Dalymount Park. After Jack Charlton took over as manager of the Ireland team, McGrath would become a regular presence for his country, playing in one European Championship finals and two World Cup finals

McGrath made twenty-three League appearances in the season United returned to Wembley, 1984–85, and forty in 1985–86, when

United came closest to taking back the title for the first time in almost twenty years. The Red Devils won all ten of their opening games but dropped too many points in the second half of the season, slumping to fourth, and surrendering a ten-point advantage to the eventual champions, Liverpool. United's appalling start at the beginning of the 1986–87 campaign, in which they won only three of thirteen matches, cost Atkinson his place at United, and would eventually cost Paul McGrath's his too. When, in 1990, asked by the journalist Paul Kimmage if he would ever consider go into managing, McGrath replied, only half-joking: 'Me! Manage a team! I can't even manage myself!'[57]

Unlike Norman Whiteside, Bryan Robson and Kevin Moran, McGrath was not just occasionally getting drunk; he was *becoming* a drunk. 'By 1987, I was drinking for fun,' he recalled. 'We weren't supposed to drink two days before a game but if I went out on the Wednesday, I would wake up feeling that bad that I would have to have a drink just to get through Thursday. And suddenly it would be Friday, the day before the game, and I'd think, "You've just got to leave it alone", but inevitably I'd push it right to the limit. And then I'd run out and face top-quality people who've been on pasta diets all week. Some people say there's an excitement to living on the edge but it wasn't very exciting for me. It was horrendous.'[58]

That year, after a night out with Whiteside and Robson, McGrath crashed his car through not one but three gardens on his way home, the vehicle coming to a halt in a garden pond. He was found spread across the bonnet, covered in blood. A paramedic, taking him to be dead, attempted to put a blanket over him, before McGrath spoke out. 'I've got to get back,' he cried. 'I've got training tomorrow.'[59] His drinking caused him to start missing training sessions, and later, even international games.

In the first week of January 1989, McGrath and Whiteside spent much of Monday and Tuesday bar-hopping in south Manchester and Cheshire; their disappearing act prompted many concerned supporters to phone the club. Ferguson was eager to find his errant players, McGrath and Whiteside, but the absconding pair thought it was all a bit of a laugh. McGrath envisaged his manager 'sitting at his desk with a map of the Greater Manchester area plotting our drinking routing [*sic*], putting down pins wherever we'd been spotted. I'm glad he was keeping note of where we were. Usually by the end of the night we wouldn't have a clue if we were in Hale or Altrincham – and we'd care even less.'[60] They were behaving like naughty schoolboys bunking off from school, hoping that teacher wouldn't find them, and when they were punished they acted according-ly. 'Norman used to be in Alex's office and Alex would be giving him a dressing down,' McGrath recalls. 'Norman would be on the way out and I'd be on the way in. I'd be saying to him "How much did you get fined this time?" and he'd be saying "Oh, it's a big one this time." It was all a bit of a giggle for us. We were that daft at the time that we used to think that it was a bit of craic. We thought he was just going to slap us with a fine and it would all be forgotten.'

Fergie is not, however, the kind of headmaster who makes idle threats, and by the end of the 1988–89 season he had had enough. In his autobiography, Ferguson said that he persistently tried to impress on McGrath how much damage alcohol was doing to his life: 'He would sit there and just nod in agreement, then walk out the door and carry on as before, seemingly indifferent to the threat his behaviour posed to a career already jeopardised by chronic knee problems. The methods that had served me so well over the years in dealing with the serious personal dif-ficulties of players achieved nothing with him. But I went on trying, for my sake as well as his.'

McGrath was at a barbecue at Bryan Robson's house when the phone rang. 'It's for you,' his host said. It was Ferguson on the line. He said: 'Graham Taylor has been on for you and I've said he can speak to you', and then simply hung up.[61] McGrath duly spoke to the Aston Villa man-ager and a deal was swiftly done: he was bought by Villa for a fee of £400,000, a price that proved, once again, to be a bargain for his new club.

Despite being battered (in more senses than one) and now in his thir-tieth year, McGrath would go on to play seven seasons for Villa, in what some (especially Villa fans) believe to have been the best days of his play-ing career. His Indian summer prompted Eamon Dunphy to appear on *The Late Late Show* to declare him, alongside John Giles and Roy Keane, one of the three greatest Ireland footballers.

Having signed for the midlands club in the summer, McGrath made an immediate impact with his commitment, strength and versatility, play-ing in midfield as well as in central defence. His resilience impressed his new team-mates. 'Paul McGrath's ability to go out week after week with-out training through the days between matches was exceptional,' said Villa goalkeeper Nigel Spink. 'He read the game brilliantly. His positioning, passing and heading ability was immense. He was international class.'[62] Towards the end of his career, McGrath's weekly training regime consisted of spending one hour on a cycling machine.

McGrath helped Villa to win the League Cup twice and took them to the runners-up spot in the League in 1990 and 1993, the year he became the second Irishman to be voted by his fellow footballers as PFA Player of the Year.

Villa thoroughly deserved both League Cup victories. McGrath's partnership with Andy Townsend in midfield made the difference in the 3–0 win over Leeds in 1996, but the victory two years beforehand was even more special. 'Imagine if we beat them,' he said to his team-mates before heading out to face a Manchester United team looking to secure a first-ever League, FA Cup and League Cup treble. 'What a result that would be! What a kick up Fergie's arse!' Aston Villa's manager at the time, Ron Atkinson, must have also derived a degree of satisfaction from the 3–1 result.[63]

Voted FAI Player of the Year in 1990 and 1991, McGrath was also Aston Villa's Player of the Year on four consecutive occasions, and he remains the club's most-capped player, making fifty-one of his eighty-three appearances for Ireland while with Villa. He had brief stints at Derby County (with whom, for good measure, he helped knock Aston Villa out of the FA Cup in 1997) and Sheffield United, before announcing his retirement from club and international football at the age of thirty-eight.

'I will miss what goes with being in the Irish squad,' he said in April 1998, 'but I still hope to see all those lads again. I was an Ireland supporter long before I was an Ireland player. Now I will just go back to being an Ireland supporter. And that suits me fine.' But it didn't. Instead, he just drank more. Like Best or Greaves before him, or Gascoigne or Paul Merson after him, McGrath took to the bottle perhaps because, having devoted his career to becoming a successful soccer player, he was left with a void in his life upon retirement. Upon announcing that he was retiring, he added: 'I don't know what I will do after football, and I have to admit I'm a little bit frightened.'[64] That was an understatement: he was actually dreading retirement, and this was part of the reason why he spent so long in the game. In effect, he had had wrenched away from him the only safe, stable thing he had ever had in his life.

McGrath's alcohol consumption had increased steadily throughout the years, particularly after Italia 90, when he missed each European Championship qualifying game against Turkey after a massive drinking session, and he went missing again for a World Cup qualifier against Albania in 1994. Luckily, Jack Charlton was a more forgiving manager than Alex Ferguson. Although Charlton could be even more foul-tempered than Ferguson and give McGrath what the player called the occasional 'bollocking'[65], he was constructive, too, sitting down to talk with Paul to try to sort things out.

By the time McGrath's playing days had finished, he was positively in self-destruct mode. He turned up so drunk for the opening ceremony of the Special Olympics that he couldn't march with the athletes and was unable to meet one of his heroes, Nelson Mandela. He was sacked from the BBC's team covering the World Cup in 2002 on account of his drinking, and after returning from Japan, the situation got even worse. 'I became an animal over a period of that time,'[66] he says. He was also ashamed about the kind of person he had turned into. 'I didn't want anyone to see me. What I was doing was shutting myself away. From my kids even. . . . I was going hiding in some hotel room – anywhere. I didn't mind where, so long as there were no friends around.'[67]

Then he was arrested in November 2003, charged with causing a breach of the peace after begging his first wife Claire Maguire for somewhere to stay following another binge. McGrath, who once owned a £2 million mansion, had recently split with his second wife, and been ordered to leave the house. Giving his address as 'no fixed abode' when he appeared at Manchester Magistrates' Court, McGrath was effectively homeless. Only hours before his arrest, he had been discharged from hospital, having been treated for a cut to his forehead.[68]

McGrath has had a couple of stays in Dublin's Rutland Centre in an effort to dry out, but each led to only a temporary cessation in his drinking. 'I know some people think you enjoy drinking,' he said. 'But people who know realise it's one of the loneliest places you can be.'[69] The cruel paradox is that, were it not for the demons that turned him to drink, he could have been a superlative centre-half rather than a fine central defender, but also that, were it not for his demons, he may not have sought a place of refuge in football in the first place.

DENIS IRWIN

Denis was quiet, intelligent, composed, sensible. . . . We got on well.

ROY KEANE, ON SHARING A ROOM WITH DENIS IRWIN, 2002[70]

A boring old shite

JACK CHARLTON, PAYING TRIBUTE TO DENIS IRWIN
AT HIS TESTIMONIAL DINNER, 2000[71]

While McGrath shone at Old Trafford but won himself only a solitary winners' medal, Denis Irwin quietly – even almost invisibly – won twenty-six medals at the club. Irwin was a consistent and dependable presence at the back, and his lengthy, multiple-trophy-winning association with the club spanned two generations of Manchester United teams: the maturing side of the early 1990s, of Paul Parker, Gary Pallister, Brian McClair, Bryan Robson and Mark Hughes, which won the team the title for the first time since 1967, and the youthful twenty-first-century team of David Beckham, Paul Scholes, Roy Keane and brothers Phil and Gary Neville, which took the treble in 1999.

Irwin is often compared to Tony Dunne. Like his United predecessor, the Corkman was similarly reliable, exuded confidence when in possession, and was quick to get in a second tackle after having been felled. He could also play as either a right-back or a left-back. Irwin was a rock in defence, Fergie's 'little diamond', a man who didn't steal the limelight, in the fashion of a Ryan Giggs or an Eric Cantona, but instead, with deceptive repose, put a stop to any enemy raids. His relative lack of height also disguised his usefulness in the air. Unassuming yet plain-spoken, in a twelve-year association with the club Denis Irwin saw other full-backs come and go, earning seven Premiership winners' medal in the process. Like McGrath, he was one of Fergie's best bargain-basement buys. Like Dunne, he won the European Cup with Manchester United.

Born in October 1965, Denis Irwin played Gaelic football as a youth but, unusually, he was proficient both at football and hurling, and harboured no ambitions to become a professional soccer player. 'I just wanted to play Gaelic,' he remembers – and he did so at Croke Park.[72] He did, however, drift towards association football, going on to play for his local club, Everton AFC, and in the Cork Schoolboys' League, and he would tune in regularly to BBC television's *Match of the Day* on Saturday evenings.

Irwin made his first steps in English football when he signed as an apprentice for Leeds United in 1982, turning professional for the Second Division side the following year. But he struggled with the Yorkshiremen. In four seasons at the club, he made only seventy-two appearances, and in 1986 Leeds let him go on a free transfer. Joe Royle, manager of Oldham Athletic, also of the Second Division, had made a note of Irwin, and signed him in May 1986. Denis Irwin remains to this day most grateful to Royle. 'Joe Royle got my career up and running again and I owe him an awful lot,' he said in August 2001. 'I got released and Oldham picked me up. I had four years there and they were the stepping stone for me to the success I've had at United. I had four great years there.'[73]

In those four years, 'the Wizard', as Irwin came to be known at his club and beyond, played 167 league games for the Latics, helping unfancied Oldham to the FA Cup semi-final in May 1990, in a tie in which Manchester United needed a replay to see off the second-tier side. Irwin's impressive presence there finally convinced Alex Ferguson, who had seen Irwin play on more than twenty occasions, that he wanted him for his own team. He made known his intention, and Irwin was overwhelmed: 'When I heard United were interested in me I didn't even want to talk to anyone else.' Manchester United signed him two months later, for a fee of just £650,000. Along with the £550,000 he paid to Brondby to secure Peter Schmeichel, it is considered one of Ferguson's shrewdest and most inexpensive purchases.

Irwin adjusted to the move swiftly and easily, playing initially as a right-back. He won the first of many trophies when, in the European Cup Winners' Cup final in Rotterdam, he helped the Red Devils overcome Barcelona 2–1 – a result that was infused with both significance and irony. It was the first season in which English clubs had been allowed to compete in European competitions, having been banned after Liverpool fans had caused the death of thirty-nine people at Brussels' Heysel Stadium in 1985; the fact that an English club had reached the final at the first time of asking had restored some dignity to the country. On the pitch, Mark Hughes, who had been deemed a failure at Barcelona, scored both goals against his old club, while Alex Ferguson matched Barcelona manger Johan Cruyff's record of winning the competition with two different clubs – the other being Aberdeen.

Paul Parker's arrival in 1991, however, saw Ferguson switch Irwin to the left, a decision that would have brought tears and tantrums from others not gifted with Irwin's ambidexterity and calm professionalism. He was a constant in that position as United lifted the Premier League in 1993. He also helped the team to the double the following season and continued to thrive into the next millennium, becoming, alongside Giggs, one of the most decorated players of the Ferguson era.

Irwin was a critical component of United's treble win of 1999 but, like Roy Keane, he did not pick up all three medals: the booking he received at a game at Anfield ruled him out of the FA Cup final with Newcastle United. Four days later, on 26 May, he compensated for his absence in the Champions League final in Barcelona when he prevented Bayern Munich adding to their solitary goal – a goal that was overturned with two injury-time strikes to win United the trophy for the first time in thirty-one years. United had otherwise played poorly that evening and were lucky to have the solidity at the back of Irwin, who confounded Bayern's Mario Basler after he had scored in the fifth minute. Irwin and United had relied on their resilience to contain the opposition, and the team, as one pundit put it, 'had been out-thought by the Germans but never out-fought' by them.[74]

A dead-ball expert at Old Trafford before Beckham came up through the ranks, Irwin scored thirty goals from free-kicks and penalties in almost five hundred club appearances. By the time United had won the title for the third time in a row in 2000–1, Irwin's first-team appearances were becoming more sporadic, owing to the ascendancy of Mikael Silvestre and the Neville brothers, but he continued to sign one-year contracts: being the intelligent and canny man that he is, he conducted the negotiations himself, without the use of an agent.

Although Irwin had been tempted to leave Man United after winning the League in 2001, Ferguson persuaded him to stay on for another season. Irwin remembered the words of his former team-mates: 'Steve Bruce and Gary Pallister told me they probably left the club too early and I don't want to turn around and feel that way.'[75] Irwin also cut short his international career, having made fifty-six appearances for Ireland, to concentrate on club duties. In August 2001, with characteristic under-statement, he told a *Manchester Evening News* reporter that he was going to retire at the end of the season.

Irwin moved to Wolverhampton Wanderers afterwards – the team that, alongside Cork Hibernian, he had supported as a boy – and became a favourite at the club. He was conscientious to the end: after Irwin made his last appearance in May 2004, Wolves manager Dave Jones praised him as a model of professionalism who would be greatly missed by the club. 'The biggest honour I can give Denis is that he has trained this week as if it was his first,' he added. 'I was quite emotional when I came off at the end because I knew that was it, but I will have a few drinks and get over it,' said Irwin, leaving his adopted game. 'I think it will begin to really hit home when the new season starts in August, but I have got no regrets.'[76]

He has also been sad to see the sanitisation and gentrification of soc-cer in England in recent years, something which has been particularly in evidence at Old Trafford. His most cherished memory 'was the 1992–93 season, when we won the League. The atmosphere down there was real-ly unbelievable. But it has gone all-seater since then, and it hasn't been any help because there's now a lot of business people and the commercial people coming to games, to the boxes and all that, so it takes a bit away from it.'[77] Instead, he has returned to the amateur discipline of his child-hood, working with the GAA to promote Gaelic games in Manchester, launching the 'Gaelic Football Scheme' at Burnage High School, the pupils of which are now given coaching by Manchester's St Lawrence's GAA club.[78]

In the opinion of Joe Royle, the man that helped him on his way, Denis Irwin was the 'best British full-back of the past decade. Tell me someone who has been better or won more? I doubt there's anyone to touch him.'[79]

ROY KEANE

I welcome all signs that a more virile, warlike age is about to begin, which will restore honour to courage above all. For this age shall prepare the way for one yet higher, and it shall gather the strength that this higher age will require some day. . . . For believe me: the secret for harvesting from existence the greatest fruitfulness and the greatest enjoyment is − *to live dangerously!* Build your cities on the slopes of Vesuvius! Send your ships into uncharted seas! Live at war with your peers and yourselves! Be robbers and conquerors as long as you cannot be rulers and possessors.

FRIEDRICH NIETZSCHE, 1882[80]

If his 'ruler and possessor', Niall Quinn, is regarded as a saint at Sunderland, Roy Keane is often beheld as an honorary deity, frequently called a god − at least by his most fervent admirers and the more excitable pundits. But if Roy Keane is a god, which one is he?

A contender might be the God of the Old Testament, who believes in truth, justice and righteousness but as a consequence is greatly angered by, and unforgiving towards, those who cross or malign him. This God shows neither mercy nor pity. By temperament, Keane could also be Thor, the hammer-wielding god of thunder, or the Scandinavian deity's equally vigorous Hindu near-equivalent, Shiva, the violent ascetic who rejects society's norms and destroys worlds. In appearance, Keane could certainly be the Gorgon Medusa, whose icy stare turns people to stone.

Perhaps the strongest contender is a fellow creature from Greek mythology, Dionysus − and his Roman equivalent Bacchus − the god of frenzy, excess and chaos, whose attributed deeds once inspired ecstatic displays of worship. Dionysus honours those who honour him, but on those who cross him he inflicts madness and destruction. Just as Dionysus destroyed King Pentheus of Thebes for mocking his rites, Keane broke Alf Inge Haaland's leg for wronging him (cursing him, too, by admonishing him as a 'c—t'). Just as Dionysus inspired violent orgies of alcohol consumption, so Keano has had his own moments of Bacchanalian distemper − as Leanne Carey, an Australian tourist to Ireland, recalled in 1999: 'He was very, very drunk and as aggressive as

110

you can imagine. He had evil in his eyes and he gave me a good kick. I still have the bruise.'[81]

Were Keane to be a mere mortal, he would be the nineteenth-century philosopher Friedrich Nietzsche. For like the mad German philosopher, Keane is a quiet, intelligent, eloquent and exceptionally serious character, a thinker who, consumed by his own will to power, does not make friends easily. He eternally questions and scorns contemporary mores, upsetting and infuriating people in the process, especially figures of authority (whether they be referee or manager). He is given to delivering maxims and aphorisms: 'Fail to prepare, prepare to fail'; 'Happiness is not being afraid'. He shows contempt for weakness and mediocrity, and is single-minded in his desire to become superman. Brian Clough likened him to Dracula, and his team-mates at Manchester United nicknamed him 'Damian' on account of his crazed, wide eyes. More prosaically, Alan Hansen believes that Roy Keane is simply the best footballer ever to have played in the English Premier League.

In his playing days, Keane's vicious tackles – which led to him being sent off eleven times – lent to comparisons with Johnny Giles, but whereas the veteran Leeds man's conduct on the field was reactive, in that it was prompted by taunts about his size, Keane's manner was proactive. His forceful nature was and is driven by the desire to create in himself a being of excellence, who does not realise his potential but, impossibly, exceeds it. It was this compulsion to be the best that made him one of the best.

Keane is one of the most decorated players in English football, an agitator midfielder whose distribution skills and bold tackles, and his capacity to persecute, contain and break the opposition, and to fire up his own men, helped make the Manchester United side of the 1990s the team of the century, and win himself multiple medals in the process. In his own words, he has 'very little time for people taking things for granted and who go through the motions.' When he came to England in 1990, he told himself: 'I'm coming over here and I'm going to have a very good career.'[82]

Born in 1971 and growing up in Cork, Roy Keane cultivated from an early age an image as a person not to be messed with, and he initially channelled his anger by taking up boxing. Mike Tyson was his hero; having joined the Brian Dillon boxing club, he made four fights, winning them all. Still, soccer was the first love of the young Tottenham supporter, who idolised Spurs midfielder Glenn Hoddle for his pace and aggression, and Keane made it his ambition to make it as a professional, despite discouragement from those who said he was too small. He did concede, however, that he lacked the build to realise his ambition of being a centre-forward, and he moved back into midfield.

Like Robbie Keane, Roy Keane was an ambitious and industrious footballer in his youth: on successive weekends he played for the Rockmount under-10 team on Saturday morning, for the under-11s later in the afternoon, and then for the under-11s on the Sunday. By 1987, word of Keane was spreading around County Cork, and that year he joined League of Ireland outfit Cobh Ramblers, a step up – or rather a stepping stone – for the sixteen-year-old, who had his sights set on what he called realising 'the English dream'.[83]

Like so many Irishmen and Irish footballers in the days before the coming of the Celtic Tiger, England was not only a place where he could achieve his ambition: it also provided an escape from poverty. Keane had left school with no qualifications, and his prospects in the mid-1980s were bleak: by the time he had signed for Cobh, 17 percent of the workforce was unemployed in Ireland. 'Jobs were scarce,' Keane remembers. 'It makes this fairy-tale thing even more complete, if you like. Because if I hadn't got a contract with Forest and wasn't playing football for my living now, I know I would be on the dole back in Cork.'[84]

Keane had written to all of the First Division clubs in England asking for a trial – all the clubs, that is, except Manchester United, as he feared he was not good enough for them. The letters led to nothing, but in 1990 he was told by his team-mates at Cobh that a Nottingham Forest scout was in the vicinity. Sceptical, Keane remembers: 'People were always saying, "There's somebody looking at you today so if you could do well you might get a trial," so I thought no more of it.'[85]

Brian Clough was suitably impressed, and after bringing him over, he signed the teenager in May 1990 for a fee of £10,000. Like Johnny Giles before him, this bone-crunching footballing hardman was, after the ninety minutes had finished, initially introverted and withdrawn. 'You had to ask him a direct question if you ever wanted to hear him speak. He really missed his family at first and one night I remember, after he'd had a drink, he became quite misty-eyed about Cork and everything he had left behind,' remembers one of the staff at Forest, who also recognised that

Keane was a man who was prepared to see things through. 'He was never going to run off home because he was too desperate to make it as a footballer.'[86]

This paid dividends sooner than he had hoped, with Clough, a man not given to lavish praise, selecting him for the first team. 'He was shy off the field but a revelation once his feet touched the grass,' Clough recalled. 'I never remember him giving an ounce less than his utmost, his absolute maximum, in a Forest shirt' – even if the gaffer found it hard to understand the Corkman at first: 'His Irish brogue was so pronounced that we considered employing an interpreter in the early days.'[87]

At the outset of the 1990–91 season, Keane made his breakthrough. The day after playing against Rotherham reserves at a deserted City Ground, he was told he was to walk out at Anfield, in front of thousands, for Forest's away League tie against First Division champions Liverpool. Although the Scousers took the game with two goals, without reply, it was a serendipitous occasion for another club. Sitting high up in the stands was Manchester United scout Les Kershaw, who returned to Old Trafford to tell Alex Ferguson about one of Nottingham Forest's new talents. When Forest visited Old Trafford in September 1990, Ferguson saw the Corkman with is own eyes and became convinced that Manchester United had to sign him.[88]

Anfield hadn't been the easiest of baptisms, with Keane facing the kind of footballers he had regarded with awe and not as real-life, flesh-and-blood opponents on the field. If he had passed the test in his first away game for Nottingham Forest, he positively distinguished himself in his City Ground debut. Playing against Southampton, his omnipresence and control in midfield helped the team reverse a 1–0 deficit: Keane slotted the ball through to Franz Carr, who crossed for Terry Wilson to equalise. Forest scored twice, and Keane came close to getting one of his own, when his courageous header was cleared off the line. Such was his performance that when he came off with eight minutes to go, Brian Clough gave him a kiss.

By the time the 1990–91 season was reaching its conclusion, Keane had displaced former England international Steve Hodge in midfield, and netted three times in Forest's march to Wembley. In May 1990, he had been playing for Cobh Ramblers; in May 1991, he was appearing in the FA Cup final. Pitted against Spurs, it initially looked as though Forest were in with a chance of taking the trophy for the first time since 1959. Tottenham may have showed better skill, but Forest at the beginning displayed superior stamina. After Tottenham's danger man – or, as the *Daily Telegraph* put it, 'superman' – Paul Gascoigne was stretchered off in the fifteenth minute following an appalling challenge on Gary Charles, Stuart Pearce put Forest into the lead from a free-kick outside the penalty area that sailed over the Spurs wall. Gary Lineker had a goal disallowed, and then missed a penalty. But after Paul Stewart equalised for the Londoners, Forest withered, and lost 2–1 in extra-time. Keane returned to Wembley the next season, this time for the League Cup final against Manchester United, and again came away with a runners-up medal.

The process that led to Roy Keane signing for Manchester United was the result of both 'push' and 'pull' factors. First of all, there was Nottingham Forest's performance during the 1992–93 season. Despite attempting to play attractive football, and despite Keane's efforts, they began atrociously, losing six of their seven opening games. They never recovered and were relegated from the first tier of English football at the end. A man of Keane's calibre and ambition was simply not going to play in anything but the top flight. Then there was Old Big 'ead's announcement in April 1993 that he was to retire after eighteen years at Forest. Clough may have lost his grip, owing partially to his own Bacchanalian tendencies, but he had been a father figure to Keane. Indeed, Clough was not only the reason why Keane had come to the club, but the principal reason why he had stayed there. 'He was the one who gave me the chance in the first place and I was banking on him being with us for quite a bit longer,' said Keane. 'I was planning on him helping me out. I was with the Ireland team when I heard the news of his retirement, so obviously it was a major shock. I was absolutely shattered.'[89] Thirdly, there was Alex Ferguson, who had coveted Keane for three years, and who would persuade him to make what would turn out to be a life-changing move.

Keane initially spoke to Blackburn Rovers, and he had agreed contract terms before returning home to Cork to mull over finalising the move. On the Sunday, he was pleasantly surprised to receive a telephone call from Ferguson, inviting him to fly over to Manchester the next day – which he did. They met at the manager's home, and over lunch and a game of snooker Ferguson spelt out how eager he was to sign Keane, and what a potentially bright future lay ahead for him at Old Trafford.

Ferguson was impressed by Keane, seeing in him a maturity uncommon in players his age.[90] His £3.75 million transfer fee was regarded as substantial at the time, but in retrospect, it was one of Ferguson's shrewdest purchases.

Having arrived at the club, Keane was not initially welcomed by his new team-mates, who, after all, had been former foes. He had clashed with nearly all of them, even the placid Lee Sharpe, but his performances on the pitch soon eased matters. In his debut, away to Norwich, his cross led to United's first goal of the season, from Ryan Giggs, and on his home debut, against Sheffield United, he was given a rousing reception by the 42,000-strong crowd. He scored twice in the encounter, first slamming a header from Giggs into the back of the net and, in the second half, accepting a pass from Mark Hughes to score from close range – much to Keane's evident elation.

Having proved that he could play alongside the Premiership's finest, his transformation into an Old Trafford hero commenced when United visited Maine Road for the derby against Manchester City on November 1993. United had just been knocked out of the European Cup by Galatasaray of Turkey, and conceded two Niall Quinn goals in the first half without reply. The City fans gleefully taunted the United players by hurling bars of Turkish Delight onto the pitch as they went in at the interval. When play resumed, Eric Cantona added two of his own, and as the game neared the end it looked as though United had snatched an impressive draw. But with three minutes remaining on the clock, Denis Irwin made a galloping break down the left wing before launching a deep, high cross in to the box. The ball sailed over the City defenders to meet a sprinting Keane at the far post, who extended his leg to force the ball into the bottom right-hand corner of the net. Keane's momentum took him up to the corner flag, where he threw himself down in a sliding dive in front of the shell-shocked home supporters and was mobbed by his jubilant team-mates.

Despite his joy at having stolen victory for the red half of Manchester, Keane claims to be non-plussed about the match in retrospect: 'We've played a lot more important games since then but supporters actually keep bringing it up. I wouldn't mind if it was the European Cup final or something, but it was just a League match if you look at it that way. But yeah, 2–0 down and to win 3–2 was great, to be fair.'[91]

Keane is not given to sentiment: his only concern is winning. When a journalist for the *Daily Telegraph* asked Keane how he felt about winning his fiftieth cap for Ireland, Keane replied: 'Absolutely nothing.'[92] In Keane's first season with his new club, the Red Devils confounded Alan Hansen's disparaging assertion about the young United outfit – 'You canna win anything with kids' – by doing precisely that, and winning the Premiership title.

By the beginning of the 1994–95 season, Keane was a millionaire – and the youngest millionaire in English soccer, to boot. He had previously partnered United's anchorman Paul Ince in central midfield, but in his second season at the club Keane was beginning to overshadow Ince. Ferguson thus decided to sell 'The Guv'nor' and make Keane the midfield supremo. By 1997, he was to replace Eric Cantona as team captain, something his commanding display in the 1996 FA Cup final helped him to secure.

Although, for neutrals, that encounter was possibly the most boring final in living memory (its closest rival being that between Chelsea and Villa four years later), it was for Keane a day to remember. Ferguson – on Cantona's advice – deployed Keane as a deep-lying midfielder, positioned just in front of the four defenders and in support of three midfielders, a tactic designed to thwart Stan Collymore and deny Liverpool the space to create chances. From the outset, this approach proved effective, with Keane nullifying Steve McManaman and Jamie Redknapp in the opposition's midfield, shutting out Collymore and forcing John Barnes so far back as to render him impotent. Policing the middle of the Wembley turf, he hacked away at the Scousers, his bruising tackles knocking the wind out of the opposition. He was central to United's attritional approach, which paid off with five minutes to go when, with the match still goalless, David James feebly punched out an inswinging corner, only for the ball to be met by Cantona, who slammed it through a crowded penalty area and into the net. On the final whistle, the Frenchman sprinted towards Keano to deliver a clenched-fist salute, before embracing the Irishman. Deservedly, Keane was named Man of the Match.

Upon assuming the captain's armband on Cantona's retirement, Keane would be a consistent presence in the ensuing seasons, and he and United won every title from 1996 to 2001, with the exception of 1997–98, a campaign that he missed, mainly owing to a badly timed challenge on Leeds United's Alf Inge Haaland. As Keano lay on the ground in agony, his cruciate ligament ruptured, his Dutch opponent stood above him, accusing the Irishman of feigning injury – an act that would come back to haunt him. Without Keane, the team that had led the League by thirteen points at one stage – leading one Manchester bookie to pay out on United winning the title – faltered in all competitions, and was helpless in the face of Arsenal's bullishness and impervious defence.

Keane's temper and muscular approach to the game would also deny him a place in the European Champions League final the following season, when United secured an unprecedented League, Cup and European treble. It was largely thanks to Keane that they realised this in the first place: his stimulating, workhorse performance helping United (again) recover from a two-goal deficit, in the semi-final second leg against Juventus, even after he had received a yellow card that would rule him out of the final. Keane had got the first goal himself.

Teddy Sheringham and Ole Gunnar Solskjaer may have been the heroes at the final Barcelona, each man scoring in stoppage time at the death to steal the trophy from Bayern Munich, but the United faithful were keen to pay their dues to the man who had made it possible. Soon after the final whistle, the crowd started chanting 'Keano! Keano! Keano!' Keane emerged from the tunnel and made his way to the halfway line before gingerly making his way on to the pitch, beckoning to Paul Scholes (who had also missed the game) to come with him. Together, they joined the celebrations, with the cries of 'Keano!' become ever louder, and some of his team-mates joining in. The other United players formed a guard of honour, applauding him and Scholes, who together held aloft the trophy – to the cheers of the travelling supporters.[93]

Keane had been superlative throughout the treble-winning season, the engine at the heart of Fergie's Manchester United machine. Unbeaten in their last twenty league games, and breathing down the neck of the reigning champions, Arsenal, they won back the Premiership title on the last day of the season with a 2–1 victory over Tottenham. At full-time, Ferguson's first reaction was to embrace Keane – only the third Irishman to have captained a team to the English title. Also, United dumped the Gunners out of the FA Cup in a thrilling semi-final replay (which saw Keane sent off again, for fouls on Marc Overmars and Dennis Bergkamp). Keano's efforts were recognised when he was awarded the

PFA Player of the Year Award for 2000; he became only the fourth Irishman to be given that honour, after Pat Jennings, in 1976, Liam Brady (1979) and Paul McGrath (1993).

After signing a new contract in 2000 that increased his weekly wage to £52,000, Keane would go on to enjoy more success with United in the new century, winning the title again in the 1999–2000, 2000–1 and 2002–3 seasons, but his later years were tainted by increasing irascibility and the growing number of arguments he was picking against colleagues and superiors. He decided to stop drinking in 1999, recognising that it only got him into trouble, and ever since he has been obsessively single-minded in his pursuit of excellence on the football field. In 2001, he was openly critical of his team-mates, accusing them of not wanting to emulate the successes of 1999 and, in 2005, damning the decision to make a pre-season tour to Portugal as unprofessional. Also, in 2005, after a 4–1 defeat to Middlesbrough, he condemned by name several of his players in an interview for the club's television station, MUTV – an interview that was never broadcast.

It was not only his sobriety that had concentrated Keane's attention: he knew that time was not on his side. He had reached the age of thirty, Ferguson's reign was looking as though it was soon to come to a close, and United's stranglehold on the Premiership was looking shaky. Arsène Wenger had assembled a fine squad, which wrested the title back from United in 2002 and 2004, while Chelsea had been making steady progress up the final League standings since the mid-1990s – United's 5–0 defeat at the hands of the west London side in 1999 signalling the shape of things to come.

Keane's propensity to snap on the field of play had always been there – his dismissal from the FA Cup semi-final in 1995 for stamping on Crystal Palace's Gareth Southgate being a vivid example of this – but he was now getting into trouble on a more regular basis. He quarrelled with international team-mates, such as Jason McAteer, whom Keane had once remonstrated with for having called him 'mate': 'I play with you, but I'm not your mate' is the family-friendly version of Keane's retort on that occasion.[94] In 2002, he was sent off at Sunderland for fighting with the genial Scouser: this earned him a three-match suspended ban, and aroused suspicion in the British press in the process, as Keane booked himself in for a hip operation that would have seen him miss the next three matches anyway. The fact that the injury was more serious than he had thought, putting him out of the game for four months, cannot have improved Keano's temperament: he was now seemingly always in a foul mood.

His most notorious act of brutality came when in 2001, when he faced Haaland for the first time since their clash in 1998. Keane was ready to serve vengeance on Haaland, who had mocked him and implied that he was a theatrical cheat, and thus questioned his integrity and authenticity. 'I'd waited almost 180 minutes for Alfie, three years if you looked at it another way,' he later revealed. 'Now he had the ball on the far touchline. Alfie was taking the piss. I'd waited long enough. I f—king hit him hard. The ball was there (I think). Take that, you c—t. And don't ever stand over me again sneering about fake injuries.'[95] Although the intentional nature of the assault was not made known until three years later, he was nonetheless fined £150,000 and banned for five matches, while Haaland never played football professionally again.

Keane had been appointed Republic of Ireland captain by Mick McCarthy in September 1998, but the two never really got on, to put it mildly, and Keane's ill-feeling towards the Yorkshireman, which spilt out in Japan in 2002 in a volley of invective and spleen, reflected not merely Keane's doubts over McCarthy's talent or whether the Barnsley-born McCarthy – whom one British pundit has recently described as 'the most northern-sounding bloke on the planet'[96] – had the right to call himself Irish, but also Keane's philosophy of never settling for second-best. Keane's fury at the poor facilities that the parsimonious FAI had provided for the national team was itself an attack of the 'sure it'll do' attitude of that organisation, and indeed of the Ireland of old. Keane embodied the new Ireland. As Fintan O'Toole has written: 'It is tempting to regard Keane as the embodiment of the Celtic Tiger: ambitious, tired of being patted on the head, not wanting to settle for "heroic failure".'[97] Keane was to play no more part in the competition, much to the disgust of one half of Ireland (including Eamon Dunphy, who discovered his African roots and wore a Cameroon shirt on RTÉ TV), and to the delight of the other – and Brian Clough. As Clough put it: 'Mick McCarthy was right to dispatch Keane from his World Cup camp. In his position I'd have done the same, but I'd probably have strangled or shot him first.'[98]

In 2002, Keane made philatelic history when he became the first, and to date only, soccer player to feature on an Irish postage stamp; two years later he made his stamp in a different way, becoming the first southern Irishman to be inducted into the English Football Hall of Fame. In 2004, he created a modern-era record by playing in six FA Cup finals. (The holder of the all-time record is Lord Arthur Kinnaird, who played in nine finals for the Wanderers and Old Etonians between 1873 and 1883. Lord Kinnaird, like Keane, put the fear of god into his opponents. His mother once voiced her fear that her son might one day come home with a broken leg, only to be reassured by Captain Marindin of the Royal Engineers football team: 'Don't worry, ma'am, it won't be his own.'[99]) Keane played in a seventh FA Cup final (on the losing side against Arsenal), in 1995, the year he was selected by Pelé to appear in the FIFA 100, a list of the greatest living footballers in the world.

Keano's recurring displays of petulance were increasingly testing Ferguson's patience, and Fergie, who is said to have wanted the Corkman to succeed him as Man United manager eventually, decidedly cooled to the idea after the 4–1 defeat by Middlesbrough in 2005. After a further injury – he broke his foot after challenging Liverpool's Luis García in September 2005 – had kept him out of the game, Keane left the club suddenly that November. He departed as the most successful captain in Manchester United's history, having won nine major honours with the club.

Keane's putative replacement in midfield at United has been John O'Shea, who, though having joined United after a loan spell at Bournemouth as far back as 1998, has come to show signs of fulfilling his substantial potential only earlier this year. Keane was very supportive towards the Waterford man, but simultaneously prevented him from gaining a first-team place with United. As a defender, he had enjoyed a distinguished season in 2002–3, prompting the *Guardian*'s Dan Rookwood to remark of his game against Real Madrid in April: 'John O'Shea, unfussy and unfazed, yet again impressed in a defence which was up against the world's most irresistible attack'[100], with the same newspaper's Kevin McCarra prophesying the 'major role' awaiting the player at the club.[101]

But O'Shea's *métier* is in midfield, and despite having won the League, FA Cup and League Cup at Old Trafford, he still appears somewhat unsettled, his transition from defence to midfield looking incomplete. The key role he played during United's eleven-game unbeaten run towards the end of the 2005–6 season may be an indication of greater

120

things to come. The club certainly appears to have faith in him becoming a future constant at Old Trafford: they agreed a new four-year contract with him in October 2005.

In December 2005, Keane moved north of the border for a brief sojourn at Celtic, helping them to the Scottish Premier League title and the Scottish League Cup in the 2005–6 season, but in June 2006, following medical advice, he announced his retirement. While he had left Manchester United on not the best of terms, his fans – the ordinary, loyal United supporters whom Keane had defended against the arriviste 'prawn-sandwich brigade' – were forgiving, and saluted his accomplishments by turning up in force for his testimonial, against Celtic, at Old Trafford in March 2006. Keano played for his new club in the first half and for his old one in the second, watched by a sell-out crowd of 68,000, the highest-ever attendance for a testimonial match played in England.

Contemporaries and pundits have lavished praise on Roy Keane the footballer. 'There's no better midfielder than him,' Bryan Robson, his predecessor in the Manchester United midfield, and a man with a similar approach to the game, once said. 'He is absolutely top-class. He has tremendous stamina, he's quick, he is a great tackler, he never gives the ball away, and he's good in the air.' Frank Lampard has labelled him 'the best midfielder in Europe', while the former England head coach Graham Taylor, in a lament made about many Irish footballers, has sighed: 'I just wish Roy Keane was English.'[102]

While his public persona as the solemn firebrand has entered the public consciousness to the degree that he has become the inspiration for a play, Colin Teevan's *The Roy Keaneiad,* in which he takes on the role not of Dionysus but Achilles, and a musical comedy, Peter Sheridan's *I, Keano,* a take on the 'Saipan Affair' set in ancient Rome, featuring General Macartacus (McCarthy) Fergi the Hair Dryer, and a tap-dancing nymph, Dunphia, there are those who feel that this is a misrepresentation. When the current-affairs journalist and Man United supporter Chris Moore met Keane in February 1999, he was happily surprised to encounter 'a charming, warm, friendly' character who was 'nothing like the terrier who defends the good name of United with such vigour and passion on the field of play'.[103]

While Alex Ferguson was typically exaggerating when he once called Keane 'the most victimised player in football', Keane has indeed been the subject as well as the instigator of violence. In a 2–1 win over Arsenal in

February 1997, during a confrontation that resulted from Ian Wright jumping on Peter Schmeichel, Ferguson was astonished to hear an Arsenal player call Keano an 'Irish bastard'.[104] While Keane has always said that he wanted to get into management, he thought he would do so by starting at the bottom, and make his way gradually to the top, even to Old Trafford. So it came as a surprise to many when the Sunderland chairman Niall Quinn, having sacked himself as manager, unveiled Keane as his replacement as head coach in August 2006. This move was surprising, even alarming, in that many believed that Sunderland, then in a parlous state, bottom of the second tier, were going to sign a mature manager – a safe pair of hands to guide them to security, not a rookie. It was also a shock in that Keane had publicly insulted Quinn before, calling him a 'coward' and a 'muppet' following Saipan, and mocking his virtuous public persona. Keane's reaction to Quinn donating the proceeds of his testimonial to charity had been: 'Mother-f—king-Teresa.'[105] The two men are, by temperament, completely contrasting figures – something the laid-back and genial Quinn knew all too well. In 2002, he wrote: 'Roy will have me down as too soft, too nice, too much of a goody-goody, too damn happy with my lot. For him, I'm football's version of the Singing Nun.'[106]

Keane has since apologised to Quinn, made peace with Ferguson, and admitted that his failure to control his temper 'cost me my World Cup place, and you could say my Manchester United career.' He has, he says, quarrelled 'with literally thousands of people but I'm humble enough to apologise if I've done something wrong'. He has yet to make his peace with General Macartacus, though. 'What happened at the World Cup, I would do again tomorrow,' he said.[107]

The future of 'Sundireland', as its fans now call it, lies in the hands of the gods, between Quinn as Apollo, the god of order and stability who made men aware of their own guilt and purified them, and Keane as Dionysus, the Greek god who would take on the form of the beast. Or, to put it more prosaically, for the Sunderland players the Stadium of Light may have become the Stadium of Fright.

5

THE GUNNERS AND THE REDS

They were great days for the Irish in London or thereabouts. I remember a Saturday when Arsenal fielded seven players from this small island. Of course you can name them – Pat Jennings, Pat Rice, John Devine, Sammy Nelson, David O'Leary, Liam Brady and Frank Stapleton.

CON HOULIHAN[1]

There's every race and colour of face and every kind of name,
But the pigeons on the Pierhead, they treat youse all the same,
And if you walk up Upper Parliament Street, there's people black and brown,
And I've also seen them Orange and Green in dear ould Liverpool Town.

'I WISH I WAS BACK IN LIVERPOOL'

Since Irish emigration to England began in earnest in the 1840s – a trend that only finally tailed off in the 1990s – the Irish have made their presence known in many English cities, notably Birmingham, Manchester and Leeds. But two cities remain indelibly linked to the Irish diaspora on English shores: London and Liverpool. It is thus fitting that many Irish footballers have made their mark at Liverpool FC and at the English capital's most successful team, Arsenal; as a result, these two clubs, alongside Manchester United and Celtic, have commanded a great deal of affection among the Irish.

This is the story of some of the players from Ireland who, in two different cities, have caused both Irishman and Englishman alike to utter the famous cry: 'Come on you Reds!'

RONNIE WHELAN

He's put on weight and I've lost it, and vice versa.

OBSERVATION BY RONNIE WHELAN[2]

If Manchester United were *the* team of the 1990s, Liverpool were the team of the 1980s: Roy Keane and his team-mates won nearly everything there was to win in the '90s, as did Ronnie Whelan and his team-mates in the previous decade. In more than four hundred appearances with the Reds, Whelan won six First Division winner's medals, two FA Cups, three League Cups and a European Cup.

Mockingly nicknamed 'Dusty' by the lads at Anfield, on account of the way he pronounced 'just', the Dublin-born midfielder was a precocious talent whose authority on the field and ferocity in going for the ball was all the more notable for the fact that he had a slim build and he had a slim build and an authoritative presence on the pitch from an early age. Whelan had a sharp eye and was intelligent when running off the ball. He possessed control and perpetually urged his team-mates to push forward – also often taking the opportunity to do so himself, with his sharp-shooting humbling opposition goal keepers on seventy-three occasions (and his own goalie on one occasion, to boot).

While eager to charge forward as a youth, by the end of the 1990s he was an unspectacular figure of stability for Liverpool, a club that had lorded it over English football for two decades but was then in the process of abdicating its proverbial crown. (The crown passed in 1991, when Arsenal denied Liverpool the title; Liverpool have yet to regain it.) Many of his fans feel that he never received the credit he deserved at Anfield, possibly because he did not have the flair, bravado or relentless goal-scoring skills of his team-mates Kenny Dalglish, Graeme Souness and Ian Rush, but principally because, like Denis Irwin, he just got on with the job. The irony of it all is that Ronnie Whelan was a Manchester United supporter!

Born in 1961, he was named after his father, who had also played for the Republic in the 1960s. Young Ronnie also took to soccer, playing for Home Farm. He came to the attention of his beloved Manchester United, with whom he trained, but he turned down the offer to sign for the club, opting instead to finish his education. When he had done so, he was ready to make the move across the Irish Sea: Liverpool scouts had seen him play at Home Farm, and Whelan took up Bob Paisley's invitation to come to Anfield.

Paisley regarded the eighteen-year-old as 'one for the future': although Whelan was signed on October 1979, it took him eighteen months to make his first full team appearance. In the meantime, the mid-fielder became a constant in Roy Evans's reserve side. Injury to Ray Kennedy gave him the opportunity to break into the senior side, and in a Friday-night game against Stoke City in April 1981 he made his mark immediately.

In front of the Kop, and with his mum and dad watching, the left-sided midfielder made a forty-yard dart to receive Sammy Lee's pass and slot it underneath the Stoke goalkeeper. This goal, on debut, would help ensure that he would become Ray Kennedy's permanent successor. Whelan was only one of the many youngsters who were then breaking into the team: there was concern that the young bloods could never hope to emulate the success of the now-departing stars of the 1970s – the Liverpool team that had won four League titles, two European cups, two UEFA cups and an FA Cup.

But Whelan's first full season, 1981–82, was to suggest that there was no reason for the fans to be downhearted. In fact, Whelan made the League Cup final that season his own. He approached the encounter, against Tottenham, with much trepidation, suffering a sleepless night beforehand, and when he saw the twin towers of Wembley approach in the morning from the team bus, suffered an acute attack of butterflies. Yet he had a memorable day in a memorable match, in a time when Spurs were a force to be reckoned with and the League Cup was treated more seriously than it is now. Steve Archibald had put Tottenham up in the eleventh minute, and they looked to increase this lead in the closing stages as they pounded away against a heroic Bruce Grobbelaar in goal. But with 180 seconds of play remaining, and after Archibald narrowly missed another chance, Whelan scored a dramatic equaliser. He struck again in extra-time, deflecting a cross from Dalglish into the net from the six-yard box; a final goal from Rush settled the matter.

Whelan would also exact 'capital' punishment on the Londoners in the League. While the new-look Liverpool struggled initially, standing in twelfth position in the table on New Year's Day 1982, they found their form by rising to sixth in March, and did not lose any of their final sixteen games. Their ascent up the table is largely attributed to Whelan replacing Kennedy as a permanent presence in midfield, coupled with Rush becoming established as Dalglish's partner up front. Whelan became a fixture in that side and was on the scoresheet when the Reds beat Spurs 3–1 at Anfield on May 15 to clinch the title.

Whelan would receive most of the plaudits for Liverpools's success in the League Cup final the following year, when the Scousers faced a Man United side who had taken the lead through a Norman Whiteside effort after twelve minutes. Liverpool started to dominate the game, then equalised, and although they won the trophy in a somewhat undignified manner, with time-wasting in extra-time, no one could find fault with Whelan, whose magnificent dipping shot gave Liverpool a 2–1 lead, a lead they did not surrender.

The Dubliner was justifiably gaining for himself the reputation of a goalscorer who rose to the big occasion. In the 1984 European Cup quarter-final, Liverpool took a 1–0 lead to Benfica and seemed determined to shut up shop in the away leg. Whelan did not follow the script, however, and after three minutes he gave Liverpool an invaluable away goal; another strike, on this occasion three minutes from time, sealed the match for the Reds, 4–1. They went on to win the trophy, against AS Roma, in Rome, on penalties.

Fifty-five of Whelan's goals for Liverpool came in his first five full seasons; by the last of these seasons, 1985–86, he began his transition from attacking midfield goalscorer to midfield marshal and goal provider. By this stage, he was no longer used for his pace, nor to release crosses from the byline, but instead to provide crosses from the inside-left. He demonstrated these newly developed skills in the 1986 FA Cup final against Everton, when, with six minutes remaining, he floated the ball across the penalty area to Ian Rush, who, unguarded, made the score 3–1, ensuring that Liverpool secured the double. When Graeme Souness left the Reds in 1987, his role as distributor came to the fore: he took over from the Scotsman as the foremost playmaker in central midfield, with John Barnes moving to the left side.

The fact that Whelan secured no more than fifty-three international caps between 1981 and 1995 owed much to injuries and club commitments. He had made his international debut soon after his club debut, coming on as a substitute for Gerry Daly in a 3–1 victory over Czechoslovakia on 29 April 1981. He was again used as a sub when Eoin Hand brought him on against Holland later that year. He would appear intermittently from then on, becoming a central part of the international team after Jack Charlton's appointment as head coach in March 1986.

His maturity and lengthy association with Liverpool made him the chief candidate to take over the role of captain upon Alan Hansen's departure in 1989, and although he consolidated his role as central-midfield guardian, age was beginnging to take its toll: increasingly frequent injuries saw his efficacy decrease. He eventually left to manage Southend United, and this was followed by periods at Panionios of Greece and Olympiakos Nicosia of Cyprus, before he became a media pundit.

Ronnie Whelan will forever, however, be associated with Liverpool, where his roll of honour reads: First Division winner, 1981–82, 1982–83, 1983–84, 1985–86, 1987–88 and 1989–90; FA Cup winner, 1986 and 1989; League Cup winner, 1982, 1983 and 1984; European Cup winner, 1984. Another of his memorable feats was scoring one of English football's most beautiful own goals, when, at Old Trafford in 1990, he sent a chip from twenty-five yards soaring, then dipping over Grobbelaar, who, startled, could only look on as the ball went under the crossbar.

STEVE STAUNTON

Because you have made a different life for yourself in another country, that doesn't make you any less Irish.

STEVE STAUNTON, 2001[3]

Like Ronnie Whelan, Steve Staunton was a strong presence for the Reds: Staunton's maturity on the park and leadership qualities prompted many to mistake him for a much older man. Yet the Drogheda-born defender has similarly been somewhat overlooked by posterity for the contribution he made as one of Liverpool's stars, just as the club was surrendering its grip on British football. Staunton, who also won the League with Liverpool in the spring of 1990 – the last time the club has done so – would go on to travel with the Republic's squad in its first World Cup finals adventure later that year.

Unlike Whelan, however, who preferred to snatch the ball when it was in motion, Staunton was a mean dead-ball merchant. Although he did not take many goals from open play, defences often knew what was coming when the Liverpool side of that era secured a free-kick well outside the area. The ball would invariably be unleashed by Staunton's potent left foot and, too often for his opponents' liking, would whistle through or fly over the wall and into the net. He had longevity, like McGrath, and like McGrath would enjoy an unlikely Indian summer at Aston Villa – a move that everyone assumed that he, like the Inchicore pearl, had made merely to play out his final days quietly.

The Drogheda boy, born in 1969, began his soccer career at Dundalk and was signed by Bob Paisley's replacement as Liverpool manager, Kenny Dalglish, as a seventeen-year-old in 1986. It took him two years to break into the first team – perhaps unsurprisingly, given that this was the side that had won the double – but he did make an impression in the reserves, under the guidance of Phil Thompson. After a loan spell with Bradford City, Staunton, like Ronnie Whelan before him, made an instant impression when he finally broke into the Liverpool first eleven. His debut, in a 1–1 draw at home to Tottenham in September 1988, and his no-nonsense tackling and lethal left foot ensured that he swiftly became

Northern Ireland goalkeeper Pat Jennings, March 1983

(Ray McManus/SPORTSFILE)

John Aldridge in action against Ronald Koeman of Holland in the 1988 European
Championships   (Ray McManus/SPORTSFILE)

Noel Cantwell (centre), seen here appearing for the Republic of Ireland, played for
Manchester United between 1960 and 1967, and was 'a performer of touch, style
and elegance'.   (Connolly collection/SPORTSFILE)

Charlie Byrne, Jack Charlton and Mick McCarthy

Paul McGrath in action against Roberto Baggio of Italy at the 1990 World Cup quarter-final in Rome   (Ray McManus/SPORTSFILE)

Tony Cascarino moving clear of Ivan Neilsen of Denmark in a World Cup qualifier in Lansdowne Road, November 1985   (Ray McManus/SPORTSFILE)

ark Lawrenson playing against Holland in a World Cup qualifier played at Lansdowne
oad in September 1980   (Ray McManus/SPORTSFILE)

iam Brady in action against Holland in the same match

(Ray McManus/SPORTSFILE)

Frank Stapleton celebrates with team-mates Michael Robinson (11) and Ronnie Whelan after scoring his second goal against France in a World Cup qualifier at Lansdowne Road October 1981   (Ray McManus/SPORTSFILE)

Northern Ireland's Norman Whiteside, March 1985

(Ray McManus/SPORTSFILE)

The Republic of Ireland team that played France at Lansdowne Road in October 1981. Back row, from left: Kevin Moran, Seamus McDonagh, Mark Lawrenson, Ronnie Whelan and Dave O'Leary. Front row: Dave Langan, Liam Brady, Frank Stapleton, Chris Hughton, Michael Robinson and Mick Martin. (Ray McManus/SPORTSFILE)

Damien Duff in action against Chile, May 2006

Roy Keane at Republic of Ireland squad training at Malahide FC, Dublin, September 200
(David Maher/SPORTSFILE)

a regular in the 1988–89 campaign. It was a triumph for the young man, considering that his new-team mates had won the League with ease the previous season. But injury had provided the opening he needed, too, with Alan Hansen's absence forcing Gary Ablett into the centre of defence and allowing Staunton to move in as left-back. Staunton was given a fairly free hand here and could easily move into central defence or midfield.

The 1988–89 season would end with Liverpool fans subject to three games that elicited contrasting emotions: success, disappointment and tragedy. The tragedy was of course the Hillsborough disaster of April 1989, when ninety-six Liverpool fans were crushed to death at the stadium in Sheffield as the Reds played Nottingham Forest in an FA Cup semi-final. The disaster was the result of the South Yorkshire Police failing to close the gates to Liverpool fans who were trying to get into the terraced part of the Leppings Lane end of the stadium; the ensuing surge meant that those in front were crushed against the railings and the perimeter fence.

After the disaster, Staunton went to comfort the bereaved families; at the risk of sounding flippant, he also heartened Liverpool supporters when the game was rescheduled, being vital in the Reds' 3–1 win. Just as Manchester United were determined to win the Cup in 1958, as a tribute to their fallen, Liverpool also resolved to lift the trophy, to honour their dead. Liverpool achieved their aim, beating Everton 3–2 in the final in extra-time, although Staunton was substituted off towards the end. Then came disappointment, in the final minutes of the very last game of the season, when Arsenal came to visit in what came to be a head-to-head battle for the title. The Londoners needed a 2–0 win at Anfield – something they achieved with the last kick of the game, with a goal by Michael Thomas. The Arsenal victory denied Staunton his first double, and Liverpool their second.

Staunton, who was already appearing for the national side, played another season and eventually secured a First Division winner's medal, but Dalglish's replacement as manager, Graeme Souness, decided he didn't want – or perhaps couldn't have – Staunton in his team. Souness was eager to prune the squad, particularly of foreign nationals, as this came at a time when clubs were permitted to field no more than three foreign nationals – which included the Republic of Ireland–born Staunton.

Souness later admitted that this was the biggest mistake he made as manager of Liverpool – some accolade for Staunton, considering the competition he faced for his place in the Liverpool team at that time.

For a fee of £1.1 million, he joined Aston Villa, the nearly-men of
the early 1990s. He settled in comfortably here, taking Villa to the runners-up spot in 1992–93 and winning the League Cup in 1994 and again
in 1996. He returned to Liverpool on a free transfer in 1998, but his second spell at the club was less successful: he struggled for two years to
command a first-team place, even in a team that was making hard work
of the 1990s. He was released on a free transfer and, following a spell at
Crystal Palace, made a second return to a former club, joining Aston Villa
for free in December 2000.

It seems strange that a player who would go on to distinguish himself
at international level in the World Cup finals of the 2002, taking over the
Ireland captaincy after Roy Keane had returned home from Japan, was
released for free on three occasions in the 1990s. Part of the reason for
this was that, unlike Mick McCarthy, league managers did not see
Staunton as a player of maturity: they erroneously perceived him to be a
footballer who was past his best. 'People have a misconception of me
age-wise because I started at a high-profile club at a young age,' said
Staunton in 2001. 'I just laugh about it. When I was twenty-five I was
described as thirty-two in one paper. It was after the '94 World Cup and
one paper had the nerve to say that "all Villa's Irish thirty-year-olds", Paul
McGrath, Ray Houghton, Andy Townsend and myself, were "well past
it".'[4]

Staunton's new manager at Villa, John Gregory, was one of the few
English managers not to confuse Staunton's advanced approach to the
game with him being over-the-hill. Gregory also warmed to Staunton's
determination to prove that he wasn't past it by getting into the first team,
and even his constant criticism of his fellow players. 'It's like having
another coach,' remarked Gregory.[5] 'He probably had that hammered
into him at Liverpool. He trains as if it is his last ever training session.
He's so fit; he always looks after himself so well. He is always banging on
the door, saying: "Why wasn't I on the bench? Why wasn't I in the team?
I can't believe you've left me out." That's music to my ears because it
shows he cares. . . . 'I can hear him down the corridor moaning. If we are
due to leave on the coach at ten, he will be moaning: "We should be leav-

ing at 9.30." Players who have played for Liverpool are the world's biggest moaners. Stan has always got that hunger. He's not financially driven. He just loves football.'[6]

Staunton was given another free transfer, this time to Midlands neighbours Coventry city in 2003, with whom he played until his contract expired; he went on to join Walsall, as assistant coach, in August 2005. He had always been keen to remain in football after his playing days were over. Asked in 2001 what his future was, he remarked: 'When my legs are past it, I will get my coaching badges done. Football is all I know.'[7] At the beginning of 2006, he did get a full-time coaching post, to the surprise of himself and others, when he was appointed Republic of Ireland manager. (His managerial career began promisingly, with the Republic beating Sweden on 1 March 2006, although defeat at the hands of Chile in May and a calamitous capitulation to Holland planted doubts in the minds of many about his suitability for the post.)

Like Whelan or Irwin, Staunton quietly got on with his work, and thus did not get the recognition he deserved. Like Terry Neill, former manager of Tottenham and Arsenal, he was a professional who did not care whether he was liked or not, and at the end of the day recognised that football was *not*, despite the famous saying to the contrary, a matter of life or death, and that, in the end, all that matters is family.

'I have never sought the limelight,' he said in 2001. 'I have a happy life. I don't need that limelight; that's for other people, for the strikers. Press comments are more hurtful for my family than me. I feel sorry for my family at times because they see what I put into my game, see how well I am doing. But a football match is not about me, it's about whether we win. As long as we are winning, everything else is irrelevant. Football is as much a passion as a profession for me'.[8]

STEVE FINNAN

There's always an unsung hero in great teams, and at Liverpool it used to be Jamie Carragher, but now Steve Finnan's the man. Since last year he has been the most consistent player still waiting to hear the Kop chanting his name, and he has been terrific this season.

STEVEN GERRARD[9]

Finnan is like one of those mid-range Japanese saloon cars. Very little about him is flashy or eye-catching, but he is unfailingly reliable.

ROY CURTIS, THE *SUNDAY WORLD*[10]

Anfield seems to be a magnet for victorious Irish players – and indeed Irish defenders – whose deeds go relatively unappreciated, and Steve Finnan is no exception. At first glance, it seems strange that it is the feats of British-born Irish internationals, rather than native Irish footballers, that are readily more remembered by Liverpool fans and those from other clubs – the likes of Mark Lawrenson, Jason McAteer, John Aldridge, Ray Houghton, and even Phil Babb. On closer inspection, however, this makes sense: Liverpool is a diaspora city, a place where for a century and a half Irish emigrants have settled and attempted to make a life for themselves.

Or perhaps this phenomenon is due to the fact that, while Finnan – like Blackburn's Steven Reid or Richard Dunne of Tottenham – may have proved himself only recently, he hasn't achieved quite enough to transform him into a great in Irish soccer history. Time will tell if Steve Finnan, Steven Reid or Richard Dunne will to future generations be held in the same affection as the likes of Carey, Brady and O'Leary. One suspects that Finnan, who has passed his thirtieth birthday, will be remembered in Merseyside, on account of his undemonstrative and efficient demeanour, as the 'Quiet Man' of English football.

Limerick-born Steven Finnan, born in April 1976, began his career in the English non-league with Welling United and moved up to Birmingham City in 1995. He found it impossible to break into the Blues' first team, and consequently moved to Notts County, where he went on to make almost a hundred first-team appearances. This brought him to the attention of third-tier side Fulham; the London side's manager, Kevin Keegan, paid £600,000 to bring the twenty-two-year-old to Craven Cottage, in November 1998. With the Irishman's assistance, the club romped home to win the old Second Division, notching up 101 points at the end of 1998–99 season (a record for the third tier), with Finnan, both a regular and a favourite at Fulham, named the club's player of the season. In 2001, Fulham made another jump, this time from the old First Division to the Premier League, again racking up 101 points.

Steve Finnan surpassed the expectations that he carried during Fulham's first foray in the Premier League the following season, helping the side qualify for the UEFA Intertoto Cup. At the end of that campaign, 2001–02, he was included in the team of the season in the PFA awards. Unsurprisingly, the Premiership's were beginning to take note, but it was Liverpool, beating off rival interest from Manchester United, who eventually secured his services, signing him in the summer of 2003 for £3.5 million

Finnan's first campaign at Anfield, 2003–04, was a let-down. He succumbed to a series of injuries, and these, allied with competition from Spanish player Josemi, kept him out of the side, despite his ability to play as a right-sided defender or winger. There was talk of his departure but, after Finnan shook off his injuries and secured his place in the team, the Reds secure the fourth spot in the Premier League, thus qualifying for the Champions League.

At international level, Finnan graduated from the under-21 squad to the full team proper in the Republic's game against Greece in 2000, and he helped secure his place in the 2002 World Cup after setting up Jason McAteer to score the only goal against Holland in September 2001, helping Mick McCarthy's boys to the finals. Again, he was hampered by injury for Ireland's campaign to reach the 2004 Euro Championships in Portugal, his absences being one of the reasons why the campaign endd in failure.

Finnan was to enjoy success on foreign fields the next year, when, with Liverpool in the Champions League and Finnan a first-team regular, he appeared in every one of the Reds' Champions League games in the approach to the final against AC Milan in Istanbul. He started on that occasion too, and earned the top prize in European football as Liverpool came from three down to beat the Italians on penalties.

Rafa Benitez's appointment and subsequent tenure at Liverpool seems to have finally brought out the best in Finnan, who as a right-back in 2005–06 was both consistent and dependable, helping Liverpool to the FA Cup final and to third place in the Premier League. According to one august watcher of the game, Finnan is reaching, or has reached, his apotheosis. 'Steve is the best right-back in the Premiership,' says Alan Hansen. 'The way he's been playing all season has been outstanding. I always thought Finnan was good on the ball but he's dramatically improved defensively since he's been at Liverpool.' Certainly, the nature of the new regime at Anfield has delighted the Limerick man, who remarked this year: 'It's been a brilliant move for me and after nearly 140 games here I could not be happier.'[11] This begs the question: can he get even better, and thus even happier?

PAT JENNINGS

I'm sorry, I don't quite agree.

PAT JENNINGS LOSES HIS TEMPER

Depending on your point of view, political persuasion or ethnicity (or, if you are a journalist, the audience you are writing for), Pat Jennings is either one of the greatest Irish goalkeepers of the postwar era or one of the greatest British goalkeepers of the same period. Like George Best, by hailing from that part of these islands that is both British and Irish — and neither at the same time — he is claimed by both. He is also claimed by rival camps among north Londoners, being regarded as both the best keeper in Spurs' recent history and the finest shot-stopper for Arsenal in living memory.

The 1970s were halcyon days for goalkeepers in English football — with Gordon Banks, Peter Bonetti, Ray Clemence, Peter Shilton, et al — and, were it not for such stiff competition, Jennings would be remembered as the finest keeper of that decade. He was without doubt Ireland's finest of that decade — and perhaps ever; he also had exceptional stamina and longevity, notching up a record 1,097 first-class appearances. More importantly for Arsenal and Tottenham, he was instrumental in bringing silverware, both domestic and European, to Highbury and White Hart Lane.

He helped effect this with the aid of his huge, floppy hands, which are of almost comic proportions. A calm, quietly spoken and avuncular character, he was widely admired in his playing days, by fans, players and even those not interested in football. 'It's almost impossible not to warm to this gentle Irish goalkeeper with the sweet smile,' wrote the *Dail Mail*'s Lynda Lee-Potter in 1985.[12] 'Jennings is one of the game's most loved and respected figures,' was the opinion of the London *Times* in September 1983.[13] (Jennings, unlike Danny Blanchflower, *did* take up Eamonn Andrews's offer to be the subject of *This Is Your Life* later that year.)

A gentleman in every respect, Jennings was keen to promote the values of discipline and sportsmanship. During his career, he only ever

135

received one booking and had a reputation for having lost his temper only once. 'I'm sorry, I don't quite agree' were the words he is reported to have uttered on that occasion.[14]

A native of Newry, Jennings grew up only a few hundred yards away from Peter McParland's house. He, like McParland, was faced with the decision at an early age to choose to play either the indigenous or the imported ball game. Initially, as a youth, there was no choice at all: he was passionate about the latter, spending every morning before school playing soccer with his brothers in the backyard. Later in the day, as soon as they had finished their supper, the boys would continue playing – even after it got dark. Their father would give them a new football each Christmas, but by the spring it was invariably warn out, and the brothers to spend the remainder of the year playing with a tennis ball.

At the age of eleven, however, devastated after being dropped for a local Cup final, he became disaffected and turned to Gaelic football; he also followed his father into the timber trade. Both moves, in the long term, were to stand him in good stead: Gaelic football honed his ball-handling skills, while chopping down trees in the Mourne Mountains improved his agility.

Pat's brother Brian eventually lured him back to association football at the age of sixteen, where his talents soon manifested themselves. He signed for Newry Town, and in 1963 Third Division Watford brought him over to England for a fee of £6,500. His parents were sad to see him go – Jennings was the first to fly the nest – but the money was useful: at the timber yard he had been making £4 a week, whereas at Watford he was making £15, much of which he sent home.

After fifty-two games at Watford, he made the leap to the First Division, signing for Tottenham in June 1964. He would enjoy thirteen distinguished years with the club, making 472 League appearances. His first piece of silverware came in the 1967 FA Cup final, in which Spurs overcame Chelsea 2–1: the scoreline flattered the west Londoners and Jennings had a quiet afternoon. He made his mark in the Charity Shield against Manchester United that summer, however. Holding the ball at the edge of his area, he launched a massive punt which, aided by erratic winds, landed in the opposition's goalmouth and bounced over Alex Stepney – the replacement for the Ulsterman Harry Gregg. Realising that the ball was going to clear his head, he started back-pedalling; Spurs' striker Alan Gilzean ran with him, but neither caught the ball as it bounced into the net. Jennings was unsure as to whether it would count, and he remembers seeing the look of bewilderment on his team-mates' face as they looked around, wondering whether the goal would stand and, if so, who they should congratulate. But the goal was perfectly legitimate, and it briefly made Jennings Tottenham's top scorer that season!

Although the Tottenham side of the late 1960s never enjoyed the League success achieved by the side in the early part of that decade, during Jennings's time they became masters in the Cup. In March 1973, he distinguished himself in a spectacular performance against Liverpool, when he saved two penalties to secure Tottenham a rare draw at Anfield.

In 1972, in a two-legged affair against Wolverhampton Wanderers, Spurs became the first English club to win two different European trophies (they had secured the Cup Winners' Cup in 1963). Spurs took a 2–1 lead from the first leg, at Molineux, to White Hart Lane, where Alan Mullery put the Londoners 1–0 up with a flying header. Wolves replied just before half-time and spent the remainder of the encounter launching repeated assaults at Tottenham's goalmouth. But Jennings was not to be beaten.

Jennings's career at White Hart Lane soured thereafter. Although he was awarded PFA Player of the Year in 1976, Spurs were on the wane. They lost the 1974 UEFA Cup final to Feyenoord, 4–2 on aggregate; the second leg, which Spurs lost 2–0, is largely remembered for a howler by Jennings in the forty-first minute and for the shameful behaviour of rioting Spurs supporters. Tottenham finished rock bottom of the table in the 1976–77 campaign, and they and Jennings parted company. Word was put around by sections of the press that he left because he felt too grand for the Second Division, or that he was greedy and feared a drop in his wages. But this was not the case. He had been paid pitifully little throughout his time at the side – as late as 1974 he was still earning £4,000 a year. Moreover, rather than jumping, he was pushed. The board felt that, at the age of thirty-two, his career was in its autumnal phase, and he was transferred to Arsenal for a paltry £40,000.

'While I was in the car park the directors all trooped out to join the coach and they walked past me without a single word of greeting,' he recalls. 'If somebody had stuck a knife in me at that moment, it couldn't have hurt me more. . . . I got elbowed out because they thought I was too old. I can't deny that I was shocked to the core by what they did and the way they did it. . . . I was loyal to Spurs for thirteen or fourteen years, they had the best years of my life, and at the end I didn't even get a phone call or letter of thanks.'[15] It was a decision that the board would come to regret.

Jennings had lost none of his reactions or nerves, however, and he would remain the first-choice keeper at Arsenal until the mid-1980s – a commanding, towering presence, still calmly collecting crosses in a manner befitting a GAA footballer, and intelligently employing his feet and legs as extra barriers too.

Owing to his popularity, Jennings was rarely the subject of anti-Irish insults, but in the heady days of hooliganism in England in the 1970s and 1980s, he faced more tangible indignities. 'I've had everything thrown at me, from door handles to snooker balls to beer bottles,' he recalls. 'They even used coins with the edges sanded down like razor blades.' In a game against Everton, a member of the crowd launched a Coca-Cola bottle at him, striking him on the head. In another encounter, against Nottingham Forest, his arm was pierced by a dart thrown by a fan. 'When I went in at half-time I said to the trainer: "Have a look at my arm, I've had a dart stuck in it." ' Jennings remembers his team-mates having a laugh about this, but Arsenal manager Don Howe was not amused and went to Brian Clough to complain about players being attacked with darts. The culprit was eventually found in the crowd and was jailed for the offence.[16]

Jennings made three consecutive FA Cup final appearances with Arsenal. Although he made the save of the match from a George Burley header in the 1978 final against Ipswich Town, the Gunners were otherwise comprehensively outplayed in a 1–0 defeat. Two years later, Arsenal were again runners-up, this time to West Ham United, but in the interim Jennings had gained another winner's medal, after Arsenal overcame Manchester United in the classic Wembley clash of 1979.

The early 1980s proved to be a barren period for the Gunners, and age was finally catching up with Jennings. By 1982 he was frequently being dropped from the first-team side, and by 1985 he was a regular in the Arsenal second eleven. Such was the affection in which he was held that when his testimonial, against Tottenham, was held in May that year, twenty-five thousands fans turned up at Highbury – five thousand more than had appeared at Arsenal's previous home game. Twenty-five thousand also turned up the following year for his international testimonial, where a 'Pat Jennings Select' team versus an 'International Select' team ended 3–3. Among those who appeared at the game for the home side was Liam Brady, who had travelled from Italy especially to take part in the game. 'He helped me a lot in my early days and it's an honour to be on the same team as him again,' Brady commented. Likewise, Kevin Keegan, another player in attendance that night, felt moved to honour him: 'There aren't many people I'd travel to play for, but I'd go anywhere for Pat Jennings.'[17]

Jennings's decision to remain in the reserves rather than retire while he was at the top was motivated by a desire to keep his skills in shape in order to help Northern Ireland qualify for the 1986 World Cup finals in Mexico. In the event, they did, and Jennings made his final international appearance on his forty-first birthday against Brazil.

The keeper had made his international debut against Wales in 1964, and although the Northern Irish remained minnows on the international scene, they had their moments. In November 1983, in Hamburg, Jennings made three superb saves from West Germany to help his team gain a surprise 1–0 victory. Likewise, his series of blocks against England's Kerry Dixon at Wembley in November 1985 ensured that the Irish made it to Mexico.

The greatest moment of Jennings's international career came in the 1982 World Cup in Spain, when a low, long-range shot from Gerry Armstrong gave Northern Ireland a shock 1–0 victory against the hosts. Jennings was on superlative form, performing one of his famous hanging-arm catches with one hand. He later remembered: 'Nothing in soccer has given me greater satisfaction than victory in Valencia. I didn't want to leave the pitch when it was all over. I think I was the last player to do so.'

Like Martin O'Neill, Pat Jennings is one the greatest Catholic players from Northern Ireland to have shone in English football; like O'Neill, longs for a time when Ireland might play on the international scene as one team. And like O'Neill, whom many Englishmen wanted to see become their national manager in the summer of 2006, Jennings has helped bring the two peoples on this island together through sport. In the end, it doesn't really matter whether Jennings is British or Irish: what matters is that he has given joy to followers of football in all these islands.

LIAM BRADY

HAS THERE EVER BEEN A FINAL LIKE THIS?
Socks tumbling around his ankles, the sweat of effort darkening his
shirt, Liam Brady stood in the centre of Wembley's vast stage and took
his share of the applause of a Cup final that will be written into history because of its sensational climax.

SUNDAY EXPRESS, 13 MAY 1979

He has a left foot delicate enough to pick a speck of dust from a baby's
eye, a nearly infallible sense of orientation in the midfield, along with
the variety of passes to exploit it, and the confidence frequently to
attempt and almost as frequently achieve the outrageous. On the field
he appears as a slight, rather slouching figure but he stands a shade over
five-eight and weighs eleven stones, and, since his heart is not readily
discouraged, he can compete where the fray is hottest.'

HUGH MCILVANNEY ON LIAM BRADY, THE *OBSERVER,* 22 JANUARY 1978

FA Cup finals are seldom named in honour of players. One thinks, if
prodded, of the 'Matthews Final' of 1953 – although this has always
seemed a very unfair misnomer, as it was Stan Mortensen who scored all
three of Blackpool's goals in their 3–2 defeat of Bolton. Mortensen died
in May 1991, and as he approached the end, cynics began to wag: 'I sup-
pose they'll call it the Matthews funeral.'[18] Other classic FA Cup finals
with their own monikers seem curiously named, with the 1923 final
becoming known as the 'White Horse Final', on account of a prominent
filly that appeared to control the crowd that had spilled on to the pitch.
In 1930, when a German airship arrival at the final between Arsenal and
Huddersfield, the game became known as the 'Graff Zeppelin Final'.

Only two FA Cup finals have come to be known in honour of the
men who were the true architects of their team's wins that day: Bert
Trautman, who helped win Manchester City the Cup in 1956 with a broken neck, and the hero of the 'Brady Final' of 1979.

Dubliner Liam Brady was one of the shining lights at Arsenal in the
late 1970s – and certainly Ireland's most naturally gifted player in the
post-Best era – blessed with a great first touch, superlative dribbling skills

and a left foot far neater than that of his successor for the Republic of Ireland, Steve Staunton. At club level, he was a jewel in an otherwise unremarkable side: the club had wasted the decade since winning the double in 1971. Arsenal had made it back to Wembley the year before, in 1978, but had been humiliated by minnows Ipswich Town in the Cup final: the game's 1–0 scoreline flattered Arsenal and masked the Tractormen's overwhelming dominance that day.

Twelve months later, on a stiflingly hot afternoon, and just twelve minutes into the match, Arsenal took the lead thanks to Brady, the Irishman beginning a move and Brian Talbot finishing it, to give the Londoners the lead. Two minutes from the interval, Brady was there again, bursting past United's Arthur Albiston and Martin Buchan to cross an inch-perfect pass to Frank Stapleton for the Irishman to head down emphatically and into the goal.

Arsenal were effective in containing the Mancuniuns in the second half, in what was becoming a pedestrian encounter – until Terry Neill made the unwise decision to take off David Price with five minutes to go and replace him with the rookie Steve Walford. As Arsenal fans jubilantly chanted: 'Ee-ay-addio, we've won the Cup', back in the ITV studio Jack Charlton informed the nation that this was the 'wrong' move and that, for Arsenal, 'the whole balance is upset'. Presciently, he added: 'Arsenal might even be in trouble now.'[19] The decision did indeed flummox the Arsenal players: their defensive line was thrown out of kilter, and they were given the impression that the game had been all but secured.

Many United supporters that day thought likewise, and with minutes remaining thousands of them began streaming out of the ground. Arsenal duly dropped their guard, and in the eighty-sixth minute Gordon McQueen duly took advantage, to net what looked like a consolation goal. But two minutes later, Sammy McIlroy, receiving a pass from Steve Coppell, mazed his way past David O'Leary and Walford to shoot, the bobbled past Jennings into the goal.

History – and a rudimentary knowledge of sports psychology – would have suggested that United would have taken that game, with Arsenal hopelessly shell-shocked. 'Unbelievable,' remembers McIlroy at his feelings at that stage. 'To get the equaliser was an amazing feeling. I could have played for another ninety minutes, the way I felt then. I just looked around and thought, "We can do it now."' Arsenal's Graham Rix remembers thinking along similar lines: 'We were beaten, no doubt about that,' he remembers thinking after McIlroy's strike. 'If it had gone into extra-time we would have lost, because we had lost the impetus and they had the upper hand.' For his part, Terry Neill did not want to contemplate such a defeat, after the embarrassment of the year before: 'There were a myriad of things going through my mind, including "You are going to be labelled losers now." '[20]

It would be tempting to succumb to romanticism and suggest that 'in the meantime, Liam Brady had different ideas', but the truth is that, with a minute to go, Brady began his run with the aim of getting the ball as far away from the Arsenal goal-line as possible. He galloped towards the heart of the United defence – a defence that was unsettled and alarmed at this unexpected counter-attack. The United defenders backed off, hoping to contain Brady rather than commit to the tackle. The Arsenal player then used his left foot to pass to Rix, who was now clear on the left wing, and Rix swung in a cross that found Arsenal's Alan Sunderland, who had made a covert run into the box and duly connected at the far post and knocked the ball in. Sunderland wheeled away in jubilation, yelping with delight, his head shaking in disbelief. Arsenal had finally got back their lead, and when the referee blew for full-time moments later, they had won, 3–2.

It was ironic that few had seen the spectacular nature of Sunderland's finish. While many United fans had left the ground, many others were still too busy celebrating, and many Arsenal fans were still in shock. 'A lot of Arsenal fans missed the goal,' recalls Rix. 'So many have told me over the years that they had their head in their hands thinking, "What have we done?" ' Graham Rix also recalls the unexpected display of catharsis from his Irish manager, Neill. 'There's a great clip of Terry Neill jumping like a nutcase when we scored the third goal. . . . And all of a sudden he realises he's Arsenal manager and straightens his tie and acts cool.' Meanwhile, Pat Jennings sought to console his fellow Ulsterman McIlroy, who had sunk to the Wembley turf. 'But no words could comfort me,' remembers McIlroy. 'It was like I thought I had won the pools and then realised I hadn't put the coupon in.'[21] Others chose different, more imaginative, similes, with Lawrie McMenemy declaring from the BBC studio: 'It was like being sentenced to death, being reprieved at the last minute – then walking from the courtroom and being run over by a bus.'[22] Liam Brady, like Matthews in '53, may not have got himself on the scoresheet that day, but the match is rightly known as 'Brady's Final'

The Dubliner, the youngest of six children and the son of a docker, was, like many boys from a similar background, a keen soccer player as a boy. He came from a soccer family: his uncle Frank played for Ireland, while his brother Frank played for Shamrock Rovers and two of his other brothers, Ray and Paddy, had spells in England, for Millwall and QPR respectively. Young Liam joined the local boys club when he was nine, to learn the sport outside school hours. He had mixed feelings about Gaelic sports. 'I wasn't too bad at Gaelic football. . . . But I wanted nothing to do with hurling. I didn't fancy all the sticks clattering around my skull.' He also remembers 'plenty of boys who shared my inclinations – David O'Leary and Frank Stapleton come from the same part of the city.'[23]

Liam was playing for St Kevin's Boys Club when he was discovered by an Arsenal scout at the age of thirteen, and the London club asked him and his family to come over for a trial in the holidays. Arsenal scout Gordon Clark took him and his parents out for a meal, but all Liam wanted was chips, and while his nickname 'Chippy' is said by some to have been meant as a compliment, on account of his golfing proficiency, his penchant for fried potatoes is believed to be the source for the epithet[24].

In 1971, at the age of fifteen, he was offered a two-year apprenticeship by the Gunners, and his parents took him out to Collinstown and placed him on a plane bound for Heathrow.[25] His £6 weekly wage, which excluded his free board and lodgings, did little to comfort a boy for whom emotional stability was far more important than financial security. 'I felt so terribly homesick,' he remembers. 'If my brothers hadn't been living in London too, I would have packed it in and gone home. I also felt the whole thing was a bit of a gamble because there was no guarantee that Arsenal would offer me a place in the team.'[26]

His brothers' support, and his own burgeoning maturity, saw that he did not pack his bags, and by seventeen he had turned professional with a weekly wage of £25. He made his debut against Birmingham City in October 1973, by which time he had perhaps become too certain of himself. 'I was so over-confident and I played so badly that the next week I was dropped,' he remembers.[27] By the next year he had settled and had become an Arsenal regular, employing his passing adroitness to act as provider for Malcolm Macdonald and Frank Stapleton and to attack himself. Stapleton's presence at Arsenal was no accident. Arsenal came to realise, long after Manchester United and Billy Behan had done, that Dublin was a fertile recruiting ground for future footballers. Arsenal, having secured Stapleton, went on to sign David O'Leary, John Murphy, John Devine and, later, Niall Quinn. Of the connection between the Dublin-born players who went over to play at Arsenal, Brady recalls: 'We were never particularly close. We never hung round together. But we were almost like brothers in that we looked out for one another. If one of us had a problem we'd try to help and get it sorted out. It was a bit like a family. Brothers don't necessarily pal around together but they look after one another. That's the way it was at Highbury at that time.'[28]

From the outset, Brady grabbed the attention of the Highbury faithful, with his, imagination and vision, not to mention his clinical left-footed passes. He was, like Staunton, Whelan and Whiteside, another Irish player whose performances belied his age. By 1978, he was, as one British tabloid put it, 'regarded by many astute observers as the most accomplished player in the country', with Johnny Giles observing at the time: 'You watch the way Brady gets a grip on a game and it's hard to believe he is still only twenty-two.'[29] His artistry also came to the attention of a young, intelligent, articulate Arsenal fan and future best-selling writer, who warmed to the Irishman because he perceived in him a kindred spirit: 'Liam Brady was one of the best two or three passers of the last twenty years, and this in itself was why he was revered by every single Arsenal fan, but for me there was more to it than that. I worshipped him because he was great, and I worshipped him because, in the parlance, if you cut him he would bleed Arsenal,' wrote Nick Hornby in *Fever Pitch*.[30]

Brady was spared the embarrassment of the 1978 Cup final, having been unwell and replaced by Rix in that game, but the result still weighed heavily on him. It was all the more important for him that the defeat against Ipswich would not be repeated. 'I can now live with the memory of the FA Cup final against Ipswich, when I had a nightmare,' he said later. 'But I'm not sure how I would have reacted had we not scored that last-minute winner against United. I doubt whether there will ever be a finish to match it.'[31]

Brady was involved in a memorable finish as a consequence of that win, which made Arsenal eligible for that season's European Cup Winners' Cup: they eventually met Valencia in the final in Brussels. Both teams applied defensive, attritional methods, although Brady had made some threatening runs, and after 120 goal-less minutes, the game went to penalties – the first time a European final was settled in such a way. Argentina's Mario Kempes missed Valencia's first spot-kick, and then Brady stepped up and missed too. The shoot-out thereafter see-sawed, before the tie reached 'sudden death'. Rix's final miss, with Valencia leading 5–4, lost the game for the Gunners, but many commentators blamed Brady, who had previously been both reliable and heroic, for the defeat.

The midfielder scored fifty-nine goals in 307 first-class games for Arsenal between 1973 and 1980, but he was soon to leave – as was his compatriot and team-mate Frank Stapleton, to Old Trafford. Both players found Terry Neill's attitude towards his players – the Ulsterman described his underlings as 'morons' – intolerable, with Brady and many others losing respect for him as a result. Brady left for Italy to join Juventus, with whom he won two Italian champions medals, but when Michel Platini joined the Turin side, the Irishman lost his place and moved on to Sampdoria, Inter Milan and then, finally, Ascoli. He returned to London in 1987 to play for West Ham for three seasons. Owing to suspension and injury, he did not appear for Ireland in Euro 88. He made seventy-two appearances for his country and scored nine goals. His managerial spells – first at Celtic, between 1991 and 1993, and then with Brighton and Hove Albion, from 1993 to 1995 – were less successful.

Brady, now a television pundit, is well-known for his laid-back disposition. Inded, he was not known for his powers of concentration during his playing days: 'I lose interest very easily if we are winning two- or three-nil', he once said of his playing days at Arsenal, where his daily regimen would consist of having a cup of tea at 8.30 AM, a visit to Arsenal's training ground in Hertfordshire at 10 AM, a maximum of two hours' training, and then a round of golf and a nap.[32]

FRANK STAPLETON

Stapleton was a tremendous leader of the forward line. A man who had an uncanny instinct for being able to somehow tell where his playing colleagues could be found on the pitch – even though they were behind him or extremely wide and therefore out of his line of vision. But when he scored, he scored important goals. Who can forget his winners against Liverpool?

CHRIS MOORE[33]

When Frank woke up each morning, he'd race to the bathroom and smile, just to get it over with.

TONY CASCARINO[34]

Frank Stapleton seems perpetually to wear the stern, poker-faced visage that one invariably sees in landlords in old-fashioned pubs in rural Ireland – places where proprietors and employees retain an old-fashioned devotion to respectability. Stapleton likewise bears the look of serious man who wants to be taken seriously because he takes his job seriously.

Steely by disposition, steely in his performances, Stapleton made up for what he lacked as a striker by what he had by way of determination – and particularly his heading ability. Stapleton looked hard because he trained hard: he was always seeking to improve his game, and his icy self-discipline ensured that he never lost his temper on the pitch. He was a players' player, always selflessly passing the ball when the occasion required it, and frightening his opponents, irrespective of whether he was in possession of the ball or not. 'There was an aura of danger surrounding striker Frank Stapleton,' writes Colm Keane. 'He had a towering presence in the penalty box. His strength and aggression were fearsome. His power with headers was respected far and wide. His sense of position was exceptional.'[34] Or as Tony Cascarino puts it: 'Anyone who has ever played with Frank and is honest will tell you he has never been the easiest bloke in the world to get on with. He's an extremely dour man who takes himself awfully seriously.'[35]

But perhaps Stapleton has reasons to be serious. Frank 'Stapo'

Stapleton was reared in a similar environment to Liam Brady, and supported Manchester United as a boy, but saw his favourite team play for the first time when he was on trial with them as a fifteen-year-old in 1972: 'United were at home to Liverpool, and they were stuffed by three goals to nil. George Best was playing, and Bobby Charlton and Denis Law, so it was a United team four years past its glorious peak of victory over Benfica in the European Cup final. The atmosphere was fantastic, as usual, but the United team was well beaten on the day.'[36]

Like so many Man U–supporting Dubs, Stapleton was not to make his mark with his favourite team. He played for the Dublin school team St Martins, and for Bolton Athletic from 1969 to 1972, and followed the great Dublin exodus to Arsenal at the beginning of that decade as the Gunners were in the process of building a team that could emulate that which had brought them to League and Cup triumph in 1971. He joined Brady, O'Leary and Johnny Murphy in the English capital, where they made their mark on English soccer – with the exception, that is, of Murphy, who would return to Ireland to become an outstanding rugby full-back with Greystones.

Stapleton, who had made his debut as an eighteen-year-old at Highbury in a game against Stoke in March 1975, was, like many Irishman, and Irish soccer players, affected by the Troubles. But Stapleton witnessed the effect of the Troubles on both sides of the Irish Sea. He had returned to Dublin in May 1974, the month the UVF took the 'war' to the south (with, it is believed, the connivance of elements within the British security forces), with the loss of twenty-two innocent lives. Stapleton recalls: 'I was at home and actually heard one of the bombs go off about five or six miles away in the city centre. What we heard was not a big bang, it was more like a motorbike backfiring and all of a sudden – well, it was just unbelievable.' He remembers his colleague Liam Brady being on the receiving end of the backlash after the Provisional IRA's bombings of Guildford and Birmingham later that year: 'Liam Brady got attacked on a Tube train,' remembers Stapleton. 'He was seventeen at the time and was with his girlfriend when he was beaten up by a group of lads because of his accent.'[37]

Stapleton played his own part in Arsenal's 1979 FA Cup win with a goal that Terry Neill's poor tactical sense that day almost cancelled out, but it was his displeasure, like Brady's, at Neill's approach to his staff that saw him leave, too. Stapleton also recognised that he was not going to win any medals with Arsenal, and when Manchester United offered £800,000 to take him to Old Trafford in 1981, he decided to make the move.

Although 'Stapo' did seek success at club level, he also wanted to succeed for his country: before the transfer to United was completed, he insisted upon a clause being inserted into his contract saying that he would be released for Irish international games, either friendly or competitive. His determination to play for Ireland almost took the team to the 1982 World Cup: even his goals against Cyprus, Holland and France could not avert the team being pipped to the finals by France on goal difference.

Although silverware would come to Stapleton with Manchester United, that long-waited title win would not come in Frank's time. He recalls: 'We should have won it twice and we were close on other occasions. I think under Big Ron we used to get a little too relaxed.'[38] Then there was the League Cup final of 1983, when the ball had ricocheted off Stapleton's shin in extra-time to fall to the feet of Whelan, who netted the Liverpool winner. Stapleton nonetheless helped United to their FA Cup victory, netting in the first encounter, in the final against Brighton in 1983. While the 2–2 result against Manchester United was inglorious, Stapleton made history by becoming the first man to score in an FA Cup final for two different teams (excluding own goals). His appearance in the 1985 final with United was Stapleton's fifth FA Cup final appearance (he had appeared for Arsenal in 1978, 1979 and 1980), equalling the record held by Johnny Giles.

Towards the end of his career – a career during which he scored 108 goals for Arsenal and 78 for United – Stapleton was playing centre-back with Mike Duxbury. He spent the final part of his career at Ajax, Derby County, Le Havre and Blackburn Rovers. He remains a pale and serious media pundit, who is nonetheless not averse to providing viewers with pearls of insight on the game, as Eoghan Corry has related:

'He's got a knock on his shin there, just above the knee.'

'You're not sure if the ball is going to bounce up or down.'

'One-one is probably a fair reflection of the score at half-time.'

'West Ham have to weather the storm, although it was really only a tempest.'[39]

DAVID O'LEARY

Now Dave, hoof the ball out of defence rather than fannying about on the ball the way you do at Arsenal.

JACK CHARLTON, GIVING ADVICE TO DAVID O'LEARY

When David O'Leary arrived at Arsenal as part of the Dublin contingent in the 1970s, few would have envisaged that this lanky, slight Irishman – nicknamed 'Spider' at the London club – would come to enjoy such a long and distinguished association with the Gunners. None would have predicted that he would transform himself into a rock at the rear at Highbury, his solid presence in defence and excellent reading of the game helping Arsenal finally reclaim the League-winning form seen by a previous generation of Gooners supporters.

O'Leary's later adventures in management, at Leeds United and Aston Villa, have been less kind to him, and his unwillingness to take responsibility for his errors of judgment have sometimes grated, but he nonetheless remains to the British public – apart from fans of the two above-mentioned clubs – inescapably a likeable character. He looks and sounds and acts as though he should have been Niall Quinn's less-good-looking, more serious older brother: a man blessed not with his former Arsenal team-mate's childish enthusiasm but nonetheless a genial man who carries heavily the responsibility always placed upon older siblings: forever wanting to please, and determined never to be regarded as the failure of the family.

Whatever O'Leary's managerial career holds in store for him (and he is still only in his forties), he will remain a star at Highbury, where his long, lumbering steps masked his ability to make ground on his opponents and then cleanly take away the ball with a swiping tackle. Having done this, the ambidextrous defender would release the ball with precision to his methodical midfield colleagues, his job done. Arsenal have until very recently had a reputation for possessing a mean, parsimonious defence: O'Leary, like Tony Adams after him, was part of the reason why Arsenal earned the accolade.

David O'Leary was not born too far from Highbury, in Stoke Newington, north London, in May 1958. The son of Irish parents, he moved with his family to Dublin in 1961 and became captain of the Ireland schoolboy team, which brought him to the attention of the by now apparently Hiberno-maniac Arsenal scouts. He had had a two-week trial as an apprentice with Manchester United in 1973 but chose instead to joined his 'local' team.

He signed with the Gunners as a fifteen-year-old, having played for Dublin junior side Reds United. On his debut (a 3–3 draw with Burnley in August 1975), he looked too delicate and brittle to complete the game, never mind a forty-two-game league season. Nonetheless, he went on to make more than six hundred first-team appearances for the club and sixty-seven international appearances for the Republic of Ireland – overcoming his previous differences with Jack Charlton to be chosen for the squad that went to Italy in 1990. It was a good time for Big Jack to overcome his differences with the Dubliner – who, as any fool knows, scored the winner in the penalty shoot-out against Romania to send the Republic into the quarter-finals in that competition.

O'Leary won every major honour in the English game with Arsenal, the first being the FA Cup in 1979. Like Brady, he found the Irish presence at the club comforting: 'It was nice to have lads from Dublin there to help you. . . . You had Sammy Nelson and Pat Rice there, who were great. They were very influential people. Pat Jennings came on the back of that. So Arsenal, through no intention of their own, was starting to build up a right Irish mafia.'[40]

O'Leary's dependability resulted in an approach from Manchester United in 1981, but he turned it down and signed a four-year contract at Highbury instead. The year after collecting £100,000 for his testimonial match against Celtic in 1986, he won the League Cup in a win against Liverpool, going on to collect his first league winner's medal in 1989, with Arsenal overcoming Liverpool again to win the First Division title on the last day of the 1988–89 season. In that season, he broke the club record for number of appearances, turning out for the Gunners for the 550th time before winning the First Division title with them again in 1991.

The Dubliner was always held in high regard for his sense of fair play, and was never sent off – until 1992, when he was dismissed for the first time in his career, in a reserve game away at QPR. In 1993, having secured another League Cup winner's medal, against Sheffield Wednesday, he came on as an extra-time substitute in the replay against the same Yorkshire side to gain an FA Cup winner's medal. His appearance in the

2–1 victory was his 721st competitive game for Arsenal.

Later that year, O'Leary moved to Leeds on a free transfer, but chronic Achilles-tendon problems meant that he played only twelve times for them, and he retired in 1995. The following year, however, he returned to Elland Road as assistant coach to manager George Graham; O'Leary took temporary charge in 1998 when Graham moved south to Tottenham. After Martin O'Neill declined chairman Peter Ridsdale's invitation to take up where Graham had left off, in October 1988 O'Leary signed a two-and-a-half-year contract to become manager on a full-time basis.

O'Leary's initial tenure as full-time manager seemed to suggest that his lengthy experience as a player had been a useful apprenticeship: he took Leeds to fourth place in the Premiership in 1998–99 and third in 1999–2000 – bringing Rio Ferdinand and, in turn, Champions League football to Elland Road. Leeds reached the semi-finals of the Champions League in 2001 but fell to the same team that had confounded them in the Cup Winners' Cup in 1980, Valencia. Signings of Robbie Keane and Robbie Fowler suggested that the future of the white roses would continue to be rosy, but defeat at the hands of Cardiff City in the FA Cup, and a further decline in fortunes thereafter, saw O'Leary leave Leeds in the summer of 2002, after months of dispute over his severance pay.

O'Leary became Aston Villa manager on 20 May 2003, signing a three-year deal, and at first it seemed that he had learnt from his managerial mistakes, particularly his propensity at Leeds to overspend. Nonetheless, he fell out of favour with the fans after verbally abusing the 'fickle' supporters for booing their own players during Villa's hard-fought defeat of Wycombe Wanderers in a League Cup game. Aston Villa were now playing football that was either dreary or dire, and O'Leary's manner had lost him the respect of the players, backroom staff and, most definitely, the fans, who would routinely appear at matches to unfurl banners directed at O'Leary, bearing the words 'WE'RE NOT FICKLE, WE JUST DON'T LIKE YOU'. 'David O'Leary's appalling football had led to the club's worst Premiership season,' concluded the magazine *When Saturday Comes*. 'His constant talking-down of the club had destroyed morale.'[41] It goes to show that the old adage – that superb players make for bad managers – might, unfortunately for O'Leary, be true.

NIALL QUINN

> To this day I still think that hurling is my favourite sport. I think it is a
> far better game than Gaelic football or soccer. . . . Given the choice
> between a World Cup final and a Munster final, I would choose a
> Munster final any day of the week.
>
> NIALL QUINN, CHAIRMAN OF SUNDERLAND FC[42]

Niall Quinn is one of the most recognised sporting figures not only in
Ireland, but in England too. The first football match I ever attended,
twenty years ago, was an Arsenal game against Southampton, in which
Quinn, then a struggling émigré, scored the only goal for the north
London club. Today he owns an English football club – Sunderland. He
is perhaps symbolic of the way in which the Irish have taken to football,
and are even perhaps coming to take *over* English football. The fact that,
soon after appointing himself as manager, Sunderland were left rooted to
the bottom of the Championship (after having been ignominiously relegated from the Premiership and knocked out of the League Cup by lowly
Bury) does of course detract from his achievements somewhat. But by
retaining his position as chairman, and bringing in as manager Roy Keane,
who has since lifted the club, Quinn has shown that he is not the naive
enthusiast that many had assumed – or feared – him to be.

An all-round sportsman, Quinn was a promising hurler as a youth,
being a member of the Dublin minor hurling side which played Galway
in the All-Ireland final of 1983, and he was also considered to be a promising Australian Rules footballer, so much so that he was offered a contract to play the game down under.[43] He came from a hurling family – his
father hailed from Tipperary – and, like Kevin Moran before him, Gaelic
games always meant more to him at an emotional level than soccer. Even
towards the end of his playing days, in 2002, he wrote: 'In a moment I'd
trade these last nineteen days of soccer for a chance to score the winning
point in a Munster final one sunny day in Thurles, me wearing the blue
and yellow of Tipperary and watching the poppy-red jerseys of Cork wilt
around me as the ball sails over.'[44]

But despite his proficiency with the stick and his promise with the oval ball, the round ball became his vocation. He played for Manortown before deciding to try to make a living across the water. He moved to London to have a trial with Fulham, then run by Malcolm 'Supermac' Macdonald. He was soon playing in the reserves, but after one game against QPR's reserves he was called in by the famous Geordie. 'Son,' Macdonald said, 'you've got no future in football. Go home, get yourself a good education. Forget about this life. I wanted to call you in here to tell it to you straight. Man to man. See, there's two ways of doing this. There's the polite way and there's the truthful way. I'll give it to you the truthful way, son. As long as you have a hole in your arse, you will never make a footballer.' He handed Quinn a signed football and said: 'Here's a souvenir of your time in football.'[45]

Dejected, Quinn returned home, and went back to school – and to GAA. Further bad news came when he was on the losing side in the 1983 minor final. 'I went back to school and settled down for the grey life of study, followed by the Leaving Certificate and then a dose of the real world,' he recalled. Some days later, however, he received a visit from Arsenal scout Billy Darby. 'I'm sorry,' Darby announced. 'I've been waiting till you got the hurling out of the way before I came to ask.'

'What?' Quinn replied.

'Would you like to go to Arsenal for a trial?'[46]

Despite his desire to return to minor football and hurling, and his forthcoming exams, Quinn decided to move to London. Soon he was playing for the Arsenal under-18 side. Fearing that he would fail as a soccer apprentice again, he used the experience to have a bit of fun, clowning around with Charlie Nicholas, continually whacking the ball at the Scotsman. At the end of the trial, the youth development coach, Steve Burtenshaw, pulled him over. 'Go home,' he said, 'and get yourself sorted because we will be offering you a contract to come over to play for Arsenal.'[47]

But Quinn failed to secure a first-team place by the end of the 1985–86 season. He was about to go on loan, but providence intervened when both Tony Woodcock and Paul Mariner picked up injuries, and Quinn was drafted in as a replacement. He heard the news as he emerged from Finsbury Park tube station to buy the Irish newspapers. 'HURLING STAR TO MAKE DEBUT' read a headline in the *Irish Independent*. In a dream start against Liverpool, he set up Charlie Nicholas for a goal and then scored himself.

Yet Niall Quinn was never the regular for Arsenal that O'Leary had been, and would continue to be. In the 1987–88 season, he made only six league debuts. During the following championship campaign, he watched most games from the substitutes' bench, playing only when Alan Smith was injured. Like many footballers with idle feet, he filled in periods of boredom by playing golf, gambling and, in his own words, 'drinking myself silly'.[48]

His agent, Michael Kennedy, finally managed to secure a transfer for Quinn, to Manchester City. City's manager, Howard Kendall, had been impressed with Quinn's footballing capacity, particularly his ball control, but was also well aware of his capacity for drink. After a day of golf and an evening of drinking, Quinn returned home one night to find four messages on his answering machine.

The first, left at about 7 PM, said: 'Hi, Niall. Howard Kendall at Manchester City here. Just calling for a chat about you coming to City. Give us a call when you get in.'

The second, 9.30 PM: 'Hello again, Niall. Howard Kendall here. Still hoping for a chat. They tell me you like going out so I imagine you might be late. Call me. Thanks.'

The third, 11.45 PM: 'Niall, I know now you are most certainly in a pub somewhere, but I'd appreciate a call immediately.'

The fourth, past midnight: 'Look, you big pisshead, I've been calling all night. If you don't bloody ring me . . .'[49]

Quinn scored again on his debut as Manchester City hosted Chelsea in March 1990. In the season's eight remaining matches, he netted three times, his efforts helping rescue City from relegation. His performances in those closing days earned him a place in the international squad that went to Italy for the World Cup that year. Having started on the bench, he came on to score against Holland.

In 1996, after falling out of favour at Maine Road, he moved to Sunderland, where he not only enjoyed his most successful playing days but also established himself as a cult hero on Wearside. After starting slowly, owing to a knee injury, he went on to establish an effective partnership with Kevin Phillips, scoring twenty-one goals in the club's record-breaking First Division–title-winning 1998–99 season. He donated the entire proceeds of his testimonial game against the Republic in 2002 to children's hospitals in Sunderland and Dublin. Such is his status at

Sunderland that, when it emerged that he was in the process of taking control of the club, supporters had planned to stage a 'St Niall's Day' to entice him back.[50]

A regular television pundit, Quinn has always been popular in England, for his cheery and relaxed demeanour as much as for his footballing achievements. Indeed, he is relaxed to the point of being soporific. 'Niall sleeps more than anyone I've ever known,' says his former international team-mate and room-mate Tony Cascarino. 'I joke sometimes that rooming with him is like rooming with a big baby. "Right, Niall, I'll change your nappy and give you your bottle and put you down and then feed you again first thing in the morning." '[51] Quinn is admired for his intelligence, writing a sports column for the *Guardian* (his newspaper of choice since going to England). He is not immune from making the odd malapropism, however – 'It's the sort of goal that makes the hair stand on your shoulders' – while his erudition can test some people's patience. After Quinn made a suggestion to Mick McCarthy during an international match, McCarthy noted that 'anyone who uses the word "quintessentially" during a half-time talk is talking crap' – in his quintessentially Yorkshire manner.[52] More caustically, when he had been told that Quinn had donated the £1 million proceeds of his testimonial to children's charities in Sunderland and Dublin, Roy Keane's reaction was simply: 'Mother-f—king-Teresa'[53]

Like any Irishman in England, Quinn has been the subject of casual abuse on account of his birthplace. In one home game for Man City against Sheffield Wednesday, shortly before the 1994 World Cup, having chested the ball, he went to turn but his studs stuck in the ground, prompting him to take a tumble. An opposition player leant over and called him a 'dopey Irish f—ker', causing the referee Dermot Gallagher to chastise the Wednesday player: 'Less of the dopey Irish stuff, son.'[54] Such offensive fare, while not excusable, is the norm on the field and in the heat of play, when players will use any means necessary to wind up their opponents.

Nonetheless, Quinn's ready smile, made him an easy target for gentle mocking. In 1992, in his days at Man City, he was on a pre-season tour in Italy when he was spotted by travelling City fans at a disco. Amused by how high he had tied up his trousers to his waist, they broke into song, to the same tune as "Ere we go, 'ere we go, 'ere we go': 'Niall Quinn's disco pants are the best/ They go up from his arse to his chest/ They are better than Adam and the Ants/ Niall Quinn's disco pants.'[55] The ditty was subsequently adopted by Sunderland fans, and has been adopted by fans of other teams for their favourite players. In a survey carried out in July 2003, it was voted the funniest terrace chant of all time.[56]

Although dogged by persistent knee injuries, Quinn continued playing until the age of thirty-seven, retiring in 2003. His increasingly frequent periods out of the game towards the end, gave him the chance to spend time with his family, and with his horses. Indeed, his equestrian pursuits started out as a hobby during these hiatus periods; he has since established a number of syndicates in Ireland and England.

Having retired from the game, he was adamant that he wanted to remain involved with football, particularly with Sunderland, and he established the Drumaville Consortium of wealthy Irish businessman. In June 2006, the consortium announced its intention to buy a controlling stake in the Wearside club. This was subsequently achieved, with Quinn returning to Wearside on 12 August, a day duly dubbed 'St Niall's Day' by Sunderland supporters.

Quinn convinced his fellow investors that the club, with its 49,000-capacity stadium and passionate fans, had massive potential. His introduction to football ownership was sobering, however. His decision to adopt the role of manager as well as chairman was a product of necessity. 'We weren't able to appoint a manager four weeks ago, so I stepped into the breach to try and help, but obviously it's not been successful,' he said on 22 August, the night Sunderland went out to the lowest-placed club in the Football League, losing 2–0 to Bury. The result prompted Sunderland supporters to boo their own players and chant: 'What a load of rubbish.'[57]

Since Quinn has sacked himself as manager, Sunderland have lifted themselves up from the bottom of the Championship – mesmerised, one can only presume, by the appearance of Roy Keane, who, at the time of writing, is unbeaten as chief of the Black Cats.

6

ULSTER SAYS 'YES'

Whereas the southern Irish are seen as amiable (if sometimes un-
dependable), intelligent, amusing and full of the joys of life, the
Unionists ... are seen as gloomy, stupid, bigoted and boring. They aren't
fun, you see. They produce comparatively few eminent pop singers,
hairdressers, television cooks, homosexual dress designers, rubbish
artists and esteemed fun people in general.

PETER SIMPLE, THE *DAILY TELEGRAPH,* 1997[1]

the most stubborn, dreary, anachronistic, unlovable group of men in
European politics

MAX HASTINGS ON ULSTER UNIONISTS, 1997[2]

To say that Ulster Protestants have a bit of an image problem is something of a statement of the obvious. Ask your average Englishman to
name any famous Ulster Protestants, and most will reply: Ian Paisley,
David Trimble and George Best. Perhaps some would throw in television
presenters such as Gloria Hunniford or Colin Murray – but this would be
a stretch. Most would assume comedian Frank Carson is a Protestant
because of his name, but he isn't. And then there's that boxing commentator, Jim Neilly.

Generally, Ulster Protestants are a people about whom outsiders
know little – and want to know even less. Unfortunately, particularly in
the Republic and in England, perceptions of Ulster Protestants are largely negative – except for when it comes to footballers, who have been
idolised by generations of English boys, girls, men and women, and have
ensured that that corner of Ireland has not become a place of which
absolutely nothing is revered.

PETER MCPARLAND

I was barely twenty-five yards from the incident at the west end, with the clearest of views. . . . It was the most controversial and, in my opinion, hideous foul in the post-war history of FA Cup finals: an alleged head-on shoulder charge on a goalkeeper which looked like a blatant assault.

PAUL HAYWARD, THE DAILY TELEGRAPH, 20 MAY 2000

He got two goals and a goalkeeper.

ENGLISH FOOTBALL SAYING, 1957

Known as 'Supermac', 'Mighty Mac', 'Peter the Great' and 'Mac Houdini' to the Aston Villa faithful, and as the hero of the 1958 World Cup finals, Peter McParland will forever be known to everyone else as the man who cheated Manchester United out of the 1957 FA Cup final. It is a shame that he is not remembered as Northern Ireland's most accomplished outside-left, but such is the way of posterity.

By the time Con Martin had left Villa in 1956, the Birmingham club had hit a sudden and alarming dip in form. From finishing sixth in 1954–55, they plummetted down the table the following season, avoiding relegation only on goal average. And it wasn't pretty: they had avoided the drop by resorting to a coarse and bruising game. With Stan Lynn and Peter Aldis at the rear, Jimmy Dugdale at centre-half and McParland up front, the rambunctious, vigorous Villains were a stark contrast to the accomplished and polished Busby Babes of Manchester United.

Within minutes of kick-off, however, the uncouth Midlanders took control of the game, passing the ball crisply around the Wembley pitch. After only six minutes, Jackie Sewell crossed into the box: the ball connected with McParland, who from fourteen yards headed towards goal. The United keeper Ray Wood clutched the ball to his chest, but McParland continued on and shoulder-barged the goalie, who, turning his head at the last moment to protect his head, met McParland's shoulder with his own cheekbone.

Both fell to the ground. McParland remembers: 'The ground was spinning round and round in my head, but I managed to continue.'3

Wood fared far worse. He had suffered a fractured cheekbone and was to return, but weakened, only to make up the numbers as an outside right. It was a crueller stroke of luck for United that, just the day before, the FA had announced that it would not support FIFA in the introduction of substitutes. But despite Jackie Blanchflower's heroics, the odds were always going to be against them.

United came back with surprising vigour in the second half: McParland himself was subdued since the collusion, and was booed by United's followers whenever he was in possession of the ball. In the sixty-seventh minute, Villa's Johnny Dixon moved up the right, bending a swift cross in to a rejuvenated McParland, who paced past Duncan Edwards to launch the ball from his head, neatly into the top-right-hand corner of the net.

McParland put Villa in front in the sixty-eighth minute, and scored another five minutes later, in an effort that looked offside. Tommy Taylor netted with six minutes remaining, but Villa's resolve, particularly Jimmy Dugdale's command of the defence, ensured that this would be only a consolation goal. They could not have done it without McParland, who was the best player in the field that afternoon – something that is often forgotten.

McParland came from Newry (where a public park is now named after him) and joined Villa from Dundalk in 1952. His objective from the outset was clear: 'I started out with the ambition of being an international player for my country.'[4] At Villa, his hard-and-fast play on the wing terrorised and flummoxed opposition defenders: in ten years with the club he scored 120 goals in 341 games.

McParland played a crucial role not only in Villa winning the Cup but also in taking them to the final in the first place. In the third-round tie against Luton, he scored with eight minutes remaining, to snatch a draw; he then helped salvage a tie against Burnley with another strike (and scored in the replay victory). Again, he came to the rescue in the semi-final against West Bromwich Albion at St Andrews, twice equalising – his second coming with only six minutes left – to leave the score 2–2. In the replay, McParland set up the only goal of the game to send the team to Wembley. Without McParland, it is highly likely that Villa, rather than securing their first trophy since 1920, would have ended their Cup run of 1957 by going out at the first attempt, in the third round, in January.

In all, the Villains – soon to become, in United's eyes, villains – had rode their luck. Manager Eric Houghton, who had deliberately assembled a side that would play a rough-and-ready game, was unrepentant after the 1957 final: 'There was a chance Wood could be charged over the line. It was accidental that their faces met. I'm proud of him.'[4a] The referee, Frank Coultas, explained why he did not send off the Ulsterman: 'It was clumsy, but with no foul intent. If Wood had not gone down, I would not have given a foul.' It was not the last time that an Irishman would be involved in a shoulder-barged goal at Wembley, as we will see. McParland himself tried to explain, though not excuse, his action, and was more sympathetic towards Ray Wood: 'I had just missed an easy chance. I was angry and I charged him as hard as I could. . . . I felt sorry for him because I wouldn't have liked to have been playing in a Cup final and been carried off.'[5] McParland and Wood eventually became friends, and at a dinner to celebrate the fortieth anniversary of the final, he appeared on stage and stood behind McParland – with an ice bucket on his head for mock protection.[6]

While his place in English soccer history is of dubious provenance, his record as an international for Northern Ireland is free of ambiguity. He was a component of the World Cup side that, along with that of 1982, is most fondly remembered by Northern Ireland fans. Along with Wales (England had fallen at the group stage), the Irishmen made it to the semi-finals in Sweden in 1958. They had beaten Czechoslovakia in their opening tie but were beaten by Argentina. After drawing 2–2 with West Germany in a game that McParland, who scored both goals, believed they should have won, they faced the Czechoslovaks once again in the group play-off. Two goals, again, from McParland ensured that Northern Ireland would take on France in the last eight. Yet, with Northern Ireland reduced through injuries to only only around six fully fit players, and with no reserves, they stood little chance against the mighty French. They duly crashed out 4–0.

No effort on McParland's part could stop Villa sliding down the table when the domestic season resumed that season, and in 1959 they were relegated. McParland remained loyal to the club and helped them to bounce straight back up in 1960, scoring twenty-two of his goals. He went on to win a League Cup winner's medal in the competition's inaugural year of 1960–61.

To the horror of Aston Villa supporters, in 1962 Peter moved to nearby Wolverhampton Wanderers. He later moved to Plymouth Argyle, then played in America, Kuwait and Libya before returning home to manage Glentoran. He was an active campaigner for the abolition of the maximum wage for footballers in England in 1961, although he has watched with interest how far the pendulum has swung the other way now, with footballers receiving 'telephone number' salaries: 'I don't find it sickening that they earn so much. I just think "good luck to them" as it really sets them up for life. They ought to think of the boys of the past, who helped them to get that. . . . Still, I feel there is a day of reckoning when admission prices become too high for the ordinary bloke on the street. Only the elite will be able to afford it. It's a sad situation.'[7] It is a sentiment with which even those loyal, longtime supporters of Manchester United, who despair of the invasion of the infamous 'prawn sandwich', would undoubtedly agree.

HARRY GREGG

It felt like the top of my head had been sliced off. I couldn't feel my seat.
I didn't know if I was dead or alive.

HARRY GREGG[8]

Harry Gregg, another Ulsterman, is regarded by fans of Manchester
United as one of the club's finest goalkeepers – indeed, many United supporters regard him as the best keeper in United's history. He was brave on
the pitch: newspaper photographs of him during his heyday in the 1950s
invariably show him making insane dashes, and throwing himself to the
feet of opposing attackers.

If Gregg was courageous on the pitch, he was even more so off it.
Gregg was one of the heroes of the Munich disaster of February 1958,
when he returned twice to the burning wreckage, first to rescue a baby,
and a second time to rescue the infant's pregnant mother. Yet despite his
feats on the pitch, he never won a trophy with United.

Gregg came from the Derry village of Tobermore, and always harboured dreams of playing professional soccer. He used to practise for
hours on his own. 'Every night with my brothers I would do a series of
exercises – forty press-ups, forty sit-ups, and never smoked or drank. I
was obsessed with being a professional,' he recalls.[9] He played for
Northern Ireland schoolboys and was a youth international before
becoming a full international.

So besotted was he with the game that he used to break into the
ground of Coleraine FC to watch matches, even reserve games. On one
occasion, when Coleraine's reserves were playing Linfield's reserves, he
was caught in the act. But rather than have him ejected or prosecuted, Jim
White, the Coleraine manager, who knew Gregg, asked him to play in
goal. Gregg played in borrowed boots, let in four goals, and never played
for or heard from Coleraine again. Paradoxically, Linfield were impressed,
and a few weeks after the encounter they came knocking at his door.

He thereafter moved to Doncaster Rovers, where he began to make
an impression on his English opponents on account of his confrontational attitude on the pitch and his sportsmanlike demeanour after the
whistle had blown. A young Brian Clough remembered a game between

Doncaster and Middlesbrough at Ayrsome Park, when Clough was getting the better of the keeper. 'I'd stuck a couple past him and he was frantic,' recalled the future Nottingham Forest manager. 'He charged out to the edge of the penalty area, foaming at the mouth, and screamed at me, "You come anywhere near this box again and you'll not get out alive." He'd completely lost it, couldn't take it, but his Irish charm was never far below the surface, and after the game his was the first arm to be draped around my shoulder, in friendship as we left the pitch.'[10]

Such performances brought Gregg to the attention of Manchester United, who, in December 1957, plagued by injury and suffering a consequent severe drop in form, signed Gregg for £23,500, making him the most expensive goalkeeper in the world. He made his debut on 21 December, in a 1–0 victory against Luton Town. He went on to turn out in four First Division games within the space of a week over the holiday period. After his gritty performance against Manchester City on 28 December, a local paper asked: 'Have United bought a goalie or an attacking centre-half?'[11]

The Red Devils had by December 1957 recorded seven defeats – more than they had suffered in the whole of the 1956–57 season – but by the New Year, Gregg's ability and conspicuous confidence had helped to halt the decline. As his team-mate Bobby Charlton recalled: 'Harry seemed huge and enormously strong. His handling was better than anything I had ever seen, and he gave us all a feeling that nothing could get by him.'[12]

But on 6 February 1958, disaster struck at Munich. The team had celebrated the result with a banquet, and Harry stayed up all night playing poker with some of his team-mates. Gregg had taken the lion's share of the winnings and joked to his fellow players that he would allow them to get some of their losses back on the plane home the next day.

In Belgrade the following morning, he boarded BEA flight 609 and was given a two-seater to himself. Bobby Charlton and David Pegg were in front of him, and in a six-seater berth diagonally across from him were his poker-playing chums: Roger Byrne, John Berry, Liam Whelan, Ray Wood and Jackie Blanchflower. Directly across from him sat the wife of a Yugoslav diplomat and her baby. They stopped off at Munich to refuel, where it was snowing heavily. At five to three, the plane launched down the runway; its wheels then locked and it began spinning, before coming to a standstill. The passengers were asked to disembark, and they returned to the terminal. When they returned to the aircraft, Bobby Charlton and David Pegg, nervous about the situation, decided to sit at the back of the plane. The plane began its attempt at take-off, only to come to a halt again when someone pointed out that Alf Clarke, a journalist for the *Manchester Evening Chronicle,* was missing.

At 15.03, the aircraft made its way down the runway for a third time, reaching 117 mph and throwing brown slush up against the windows. The adverse weather conditions meant that it failed to become airborne and overshot the runway. Its port wing slammed into a house, causing the craft to spin violently into another building. The undercarriage and tail had been torn off. Only the failure of the fuselage to explode meant that the collisions did not end in carnage.

Gregg remembers 'Tearing. Ripping. Then darkness. No screaming, no crying, just darkness.'[13] Dazed, he slowly lifted his head, and noticed light coming from a hole. He clambered towards it, where below him he saw United's chief team coach, Bert Whalley, lying dead. Greg kicked his way out of the fuselage and jumped out onto the runway.

The rear part of the aircraft had hit a petrol dump, and the captain of the plane, James Thain, was frantically running around with a fire extinguisher urging people to get as far away from the wreckage as possible. 'Run, you idiot, run! It's going to explode!' he shouted at the Ulsterman. Gregg saw five others running away, to which he issued his own exclamation: 'Come back, you bastards, there's people still alive!'[14] Then he heard a baby crying. He dashed back into the aircraft to retrieve the toddler, and returned for the baby's mother – Mrs Lukic, the pregnant wife of the Yugoslav air attaché in London. He then came across Albert Scanlon with a gash in his head, and blood coming from his eyes and nose. He crawled over the rubble, where he found Charlton and Dennis Viollet, and dragged them from the wreckage across the snow. He saw Matt Busby cradling his stomach in agony, and Jackie Blanchflower in a pool of water with tears running down his face. Blanchflower's right arm was hanging off him, so Gregg took off his tie and put it around the stump. Lying across Blanchflower was Byrne, dead.[15] Dead too was Liam 'Billy' Whelan.

More tragedy was to follow when, following a long illness, Gregg's wife died just over a year after Munich – a disaster he has rarely spoken about since. Perhaps it is the Ulster Protestant in him, or perhaps he was just of his time – belonging to a generation who thought it normal to deal with tragedies with fortitude and quiet stoicism. By all accounts, he is not-traumatised by the affair. In the London *Times* in 1983, Peter Ball wrote: 'Gregg's reluctance to recall Munich yet again was understandable, but however much he decries the analogy, the image of John Wayne or Red Adair . . . is irresistible when one talks about Gregg. In the words of Eamon Dunphy, who knew Gregg at Old Trafford: "If Harry had been in the Falklands he would have been a Colonel H. He's that type, which doesn't normally appeal to us weedy intellectuals, but Harry has this wonderful humanity about him and there is no malice in him." '16

It was to Gregg's great sadness that, from the 1960s, a younger generation began to taunt United with the song: 'Who's that lying on the runway' and another chant directed at him. As he recalls: 'I could barely hear it at first . . . but then as it got louder I understood what they were chanting. "You should have died at Munich . . . You should have died at Munich." '17

Gregg displayed his stoicism once more by turning out for Manchester United a mere thirteen days after the disaster. In an FA Cup encounter against Sheffield Wednesday at Old Trafford, seventeen United players, including the dead, were missing – ten of them internationals – alongside that of his fellow survivor, Bill Foulkes, Gregg's name was the only familiar one, and the only name written down on the programme team-sheet. The rest were left blank, with the sixty thousand crowd in attendance asked to pencil in the collection of reserves, juniors and recently signed imports as their names were announced over the public-address system prior to kick-off.

United won that game 3–0 and made an unexpected run in the Cup that year, beating West Bromwich Albion and Fulham on the way to the final – and with much goodwill from the public. The 1958 final was an event of high emotion, with most of the English public hoping that United would triumph. But their opponents, Bolton Wanderers, were not going to bow to sentiment, especially having lost out to Blackpool so famously in the 'Matthews Final' of 1953. Bolton's Nat Lofthouse put one past Gregg after only three minutes. In the fifty-fifth minute, Gregg saved from Bolton's Dennis Stevens, but as the keeper came to collect the ball on his own goal line, Lofthouse made a dash and ended up barging both Gregg and the ball into the net with a shoulder charge. For the second Cup final in a row, Manchester United had conceded a goal thanks to an elephant-like charge from an opponent, yet whereas in 1957 it had been an Ulsterman, Peter McParland, who was the sinner, this time it was an Ulsterman who was sinned against. Even in the days when such rough treatment of goalkeepers was a familiar sight, it was considered highly controversial. Yet in typically gentlemanly fashion, Gregg and Lofthouse never fell out over the affair, with the English international later admitting that it was a foul and that the goal should not have been given.

Further disappointment came in 1963 when Gregg missed out on the FA Cup final owing to a shoulder injury. United went on to beat Leicester City 3–1, and Gregg made it clear that he was not happy about his omission from the final. During a tour of Italy shortly afterwards, his capricious team-mate John Giles, who had earned a Cup medal, took it upon himself to wind up his compatriot in a hotel bar. Gregg flipped, and soon after room-mates Giles and Shay Brennan had gone upstairs 'Harry came clattering down the corridor crying for John's blood,' as Nobby Stiles remembers. John and Shay had anticipated Gregg's reaction and had pushed a board across their door. 'I want that bastard Giles!' Gregg cried. He smashed through a panel of the door before returning to his own room, which he shared with Stiles, still 'bellowing his frustration'.[18] Nobby Stiles says Gregg has 'a wild, big heart'. Indeed, Gregg, through his friendship with Stiles, may have played his own part in helping England to win the World Cup. While the two were playing cards, the Ulsterman noticed that Stiles was placing the wrong cards. Gregg told Matt Busby, who finally convinced Stiles that a simple way to treat his acute short-sightedness was to use contact lenses. Stiles followed this advice, and wore contact lenses on the pitch – to great effect.[197]

Injury would plague him further, and he missed out on the 1964–65 season, thus missing out on a title-winning medal. In September 1966, Busby bought Chelsea's goalkeeper, Alex Stepney, with the aim of gradually replacing an ageing Gregg, although many believe that he was far from past his best: at the age of thirty-four he was hardly at retirement age for a First Division goalkeeper. The Old Trafford faithful agreed, and would chant his name when he didn't appear. 'I have to say I got great pleasure out of sitting down near the Boss and [hearing] the crowd shout from the Stretford End "We want Gregg!",' the man himself recalls. 'That kind of support, especially the Stretford End, was very important.'[20]

Such adulation was warranted, as Gregg had performed heroics in the 1958 World Cup finals in Sweden, in which Northern Ireland had unexpectedly reached the quarter-finals, where their team spirit saw them match the holders, West Germany, 2–2, and knock out Czechoslovakia, the 6–1 conquerors of Argentina. Gregg was also one of the heroes of United's spectacular 5–1 demolition of Benfica in March 1966.

Subsequent spells at Swansea and Crewe proved inauspicious, and he later managed Shrewsbury. In the assessment of one Manchester United biographer, Gregg 'remains the yardstick by which all United custodians are judged and it will be a momentous day when, finally, one matches him in every respect. Harry Gregg was a superb entertainer blessed with courage, pride and character in ample measure. But when it came to the luck of the Irish, his was nearly all bad.'[21] If, as it is said, Brian Clough was the best coach never to have managed England, and Brazil in 1982 were the best team never to have won the World Cup, then it could equally be argued that Harry Gregg was the best goalkeeper never to have won a trophy with Manchester United.

It's no use. I have got to realise I can never play again.

JACKIE BLANCHFLOWER, DAILY MAIL, 20 SEPTEMBER 1958

Jackie Blanchflower was a gifted centre-half for Manchester United, one of the 'Busby Babes', but his life was overshadowed in two ways: one prosaic, the other tragic. He was forever overshadowed by his older, more ambitious brother, Danny, who was a more complete and more celebrated footballer. And not only was he inferior to Danny – he never got the chance to prove that he could better him.

Along with Harry Gregg, Jackie was one of the survivors of Munich, but unlike Gregg, in some senses Jackie never really 'survived' the crash. Six months after the disaster, he was still walking with a limp. He had sustained six broken ribs in the crash and had fractured his right arm; he also had kidney damage, shock and internal injuries, and acute injuries to his pelvis. While the pelvis injury hurt him the most, his broken arm had the greatest effect on his playing, as it completely upset his sense of balance. Six months after the disaster of February 1958, having struggled to regain his fitness, Jackie Blanchflower decided to end his footballing career. To the end of his days he had trouble with his back and his right elbow, with the result that he preferred to shake hands with his left hand.[22]

Yet Jackie eventually recovered, and he would go on to be a celebrated after-dinner speaker. If anything, Jackie was known as a more jovial, ebullient and humorous character than his brother Danny, who was often solemn. And if Danny was celebrated as a passer and playmaker, Jackie was a consummate all-rounder.

Peter McParland's Aston Villa may have triumphed in the FA Cup final of 1957, but Jackie Blanchflower proved to be awkward opposition that day. After McParland's sixth-minute challenge on Ray Wood had left the Manchester United goalkeeper helplessly concussed, Jackie stepped in to assume the rule of goalie, and displayed some excellent, acrobatic goalkeeping skills, keeping out Villa until the interval – but it was not enough. Liam 'Billy' Whelan was forced to drop back to centre-half, leaving the forward line unbalanced. United had been on for the League and Cup double, and it is said that, had Wood remained in the game, it could have been theirs.

Under such circumstances, the fact that United succumbed by only two goals to one was heroic in itself. As the *Daily Telegraph* wrote: 'Jackie Blanchflower went in goal – and played a blinder!'[23] United reorganised in midfield, but they and Blanchflower could not contain McParland, who scored two goals in the second half. The Villa defence, which conceded a consolation goal from Tommy Taylor with seven minutes to go, was nonetheless too resilient.

Twice League winners on the trot, Manchester United seemed destined for even greater things. Jackie was one of the nine club members who survived Munich. He later recalled his feeling of foreboding as the pilot twice failed to clear the runway. The passengers were told to disembark and return to the airport lounge. 'But in five minutes we were told we could board the plane again,' Jackie remembered. 'As we mounted the steps we could feel the tension. . . . I swear that if one man had had the courage to be a coward, not one of us would have embarked. Once again the plane sped along the runway, and I think every man knew it was take-off or crash.'[24]

Within a matter of seconds, the airliner was a twisted wreck amid the slush of the runway. Jackie had passed out during the crash, and when he came to, he saw the sight of a giant gash in the cabin ceiling, with snow blowing in his face. He spent many weeks in hospital, and awoke from his coma to find a Franciscan monk saying the last rites over him.[25]

Jackie Blanchflower thereafter struggled to regain his fitness, but after six months he decided that he could not continue playing football. He was never the same man, physically and mentally. In June 1959, after a long conversation with Danny in his Manchester home (Spurs were playing at United that weekend), he vowed to stop playing football. Munich had affected Jackie not only physically, but mentally, too. 'He was not the same tousle-haired younger brother who adopted a superior tone and called me kid,' Danny remembered. 'The worry of the thing had taken the charm out of his voice and the twinkle out of his eye.'[26]

John 'Jackie' Blanchflower, a native of Belfast, had played for Pitt Street Mission Club and Boyland Football Club before joining Manchester United in 1949 as an amateur. He made his professional debut in 1951 against Liverpool. He also represented Northern Ireland on twelve occasions. Blanchflower was considered by some as an equal to Duncan Edwards in midfield and Tommy Taylor in attack,[27] both of whom perished at Munich.

First as a right half, and then as an inside-forward, Jackie Blanchflower gained a warranted reputation as a promiscuous goalscorer – hitting the back of the net on twenty-four occasions during United's 1955–56 championship season. He was moved to centre-half in 1956–57. Yet Munich had effectively ended his career, and Jackie spent many years rueing his fortunes, before flowering again as an after-dinner speaker and raconteur of some note. He subsequently became a bookmaker, publican, accountant, paint-storage manager and plumber. He married the singer Jean Parker, and the late Tommy Taylor was best man at the wedding.

Jackie Blanchflower lived in Cheshire, and died in 1998. Shortly before his death, he remarked: 'Life has been full of ups and downs, but without pathos there can be no comedy. The bitterness goes eventually and you start remembering the good times. I loved it at United. From this distance, even going through the accident was worth it for those years at Old Trafford. . . . I feel happy and at ease now.'[28]

DANNY BLANCHFLOWER

An almost unknown Belfast electrician is being hailed by English managers as an international star of tomorrow. Several have even described him as one of the finest wing-halves they have ever seen. The boy they're all talking about is Danny Blanchflower of Glentoran.

THE DAILY MIRROR, 7 AUGUST 1947

As one of Belfast's most famous unknown electricians, Danny Blanchflower turned out to be one of England's greatest footballers. A teetotal, beer barrel–chested Ulsterman with oaks for legs – albeit short ones – Blanchflower was a visionary playmaker for Tottenham Hotspur, guiding the north London side to the League and Cup double in 1961. Blanchflower, a scheming wing-half, gifted passer of the ball and natural leader, was known as the 'thinking man's footballer' – he wrote a column for the august *New Statesman* magazine – and was famous for his curious aphorisms and maxims. While footballers are not generally renowned for their intelligence, Blanchflower was not only clever, but *very* clever: a sagacious character, student of science, and friend of philosophers who had a way with words that lead him frequently to be dubbed 'the Oscar Wilde of Windsor Park'.

On the pitch, he epitomised something which Spurs pride themselves on: he played the beautiful game beautifully, much in the way Glenn Hoddle would go on to do for Tottenham in the 1980s. 'Football is not really about winning,' he would say, 'it's about doing things in style.' While the club's official history book may be guilty of hyperbole in calling him 'a midfielder probably without parallel in the twentieth century',[29] the Ulsterman was, as a character, without parallel – certainly in England.

His mother was also an individual. She played women's soccer in Belfast as a centre-forward in the 1920s at a time when the ladies' game enjoyed tremendous popularity: finals game could muster crowds of twenty thousand. Mrs Blanchflower played in one such final herself, and was the coach of his youth team in east Belfast, where Danny's brother Jackie played alongside Bill Bingham; Bingham himself lived only a street away from the Blanchflowers' home in Bloomfield, a suburb of the city.

He attended a local college of technology, where he studied to become an electrician, and went on to St Andrews University in Scotland, where he read maths, physics and applied kinematics. Nevertheless, he is not the only brainy Northern Ireland international to have played in England. In later years, Iain Dowie, who appeared for Northern Ireland fifty-six times, claims to have used his qualification in aeronautical engineering on the bench: 'My degree allows me to be logical; maybe the algebraic approach makes me analytical.'[30]

Danny had undertaken his degree as training for his role in the RAF, which he had joined in 1944, and he was sent to Canada for aircrew training. By the time he had completed his studies, the Second World War had ended. He returned to Glentoran, for which he had previously played, but now as a professional, for a fee of £3 per game.

In 1948, he moved across the water to be signed by Barnsley, and then went to Aston Villa. At Birmingham, he developed his game both technically and physically, but Villa in the 1950s were in a rut, perpetually ending campaigns in mid-table mediocrity. He felt that both clubs were hampered by complacency and stuck in the past. He later remarked: 'I had a certain affection for Villa . . . but the club had grown fat and lazy on its old tradition, and the decay was eating at the once-solid foundations.'[31] At Barnsley, for instance, he was reprimanded for training with the ball; it was received wisdom in English football at the time that training should never involve using a ball, as this would leave the players 'hungry' for it on match day. Only after they humiliatingly succumbed to Hungary in 1953 did the English come to concur with Danny's prescient – but manifestly obvious – philosophy that honing one's ball skills before a game might be a good idea.

Unhappy at Villa, he took an interest when Arsenal and Tottenham started making approaches to the Birmingham club about securing his services. Arsenal's manager, Tom Whittaker, made the first move, coming up to Villa Park to meet the Ulsterman, but a bidding war between the two clubs saw Spurs gain his talents. Whittaker was the keener, but when the bidding stakes rose to £30,000, Arsenal's directors issued an interdict, saying that they were simply not prepared to pay such a high fee for a wing-half.

Instead, Tottenham's Arthur Rowe took him to White Hart Lane in 1954. 'I wanted to be part of something progressive: to belong to a club that was striving to achieve something; a club that thought in terms of good constructive football; a club that was keen and vital.'[32] Rowe had certainly made progress, with his 'push and run' tactics – a precursor to 'total football', in which players could move into different positions with greater fluidity – having won Spurs their first league title in 1950–51. As Danny was attracted to Rowe's intelligence and capacity to innovate, so Rowe recognised that Blanchflower's brains were as vital as his brawn. Towards the end of Danny's first full season at Spurs, Rowe commented: 'Great as has been his influence as a player, I rate his psychological effect on our boys even greater.'[33]

But Rowe left Spurs in 1955, and opposition sides soon became wise to Tottenham's unorthodox tactics. As a result, Blanchflower's initial five years with Spurs were barren, as the team meandered around the mid-reaches of the First Division. At an individual level, however, Blanchflower bloomed, establishing a promising relationship with inside-forward Tommy Harmer, a relationship that the sports journalist Brian Glanville has called 'telepathic': 'There could scarcely have been two more sharply contrasted figures. Though both had enormous technical talent, and what the Italians call a "vision of the game", Harmer did it all by instinct, while Blanchflower, besides the natural good instincts of a fine player, had his ratiocinating intelligence as well. . . . Yet they combined marvellously, each perfectly understanding the needs and intentions of the other, and they set up some famous victories' – including one which brought ten goals against Everton.[34]

Blanchflower did not always see eye to eye with Rowe's replacement, Jimmy Anderson, who felt that he had displayed a lack of respect by taking tactical matters into his own hands in an FA Cup semi-final when Blanchflower ordered Spurs's centre-half, Morris Norman, upfield. He was stripped of his captaincy and was even briefly dropped at the end of the 1955–56 season, with the official line from the club being that he was unfit. This was of course a nonsense. 'I turned up at White Hart Lane all ready to go,' Blanchflower recalled. 'I thought the lads were kidding when they told me.'[35] For the remainder of the decade, he refused to resume his captaincy.

If he did not see eye to eye with Anderson, over the ensuing years Blanchflower came to endear himself to the English public, mainly for his combination of pragmatism and romanticism. As he put it: 'Football is not really about winning, or goals, or saves, or supporters, it's about glory. It's about doing things in style, doing them with a flourish; it's about going out to beat the other lot, not waiting for them to die of boredom; it's about dreaming of the glory that the Double brought.'[36] One of his best-known aphorisms was the one he issued before a game in the 1958 World Cup: 'We're going to equalise before the other team scores.'[37] Some of his opinions were bizarre, others mocking. As he presented the Spurs team to the Duchess of Kent before the 1961 FA Cup final against Leicester City, the Duchess observed that Tottenham had placed the names of their players on their backs.

'Tell me,' said the Duchess, 'why is it that the other team have their names on the backs of their tracksuits while your team do not?'

'Well, you see, ma'am', said Danny, 'we all know each other.'[38]

He could be cutting, too, describing the acerbic chairman of Burnley, Bob Lord, as 'a self-made man who worships his creator.'[39]

The English press certainly warmed to the Irishman. 'Besides his polished play, Blanchflower has a fluent pen. He can write well, and like most Irishmen he has a ready wit,' announced the *Evening News* in August 1955.[40] On Blanchflower's signing to Tottenham, the *Daily Express* swooned over his 'curling locks and dawn-breaking grin',[41] while the *News Chronicle* referred to this 'thirty-year-old dressing-room Disraeli'.[42] Even as recently as July 2006, he still had the capacity to inspire affection among the English tabloid press. Cursing the petulance, egotism and childishness of England team members in the World Cup, the *Daily Mail*'s Richard Littlejohn asked: 'What would Blanchflower's generation make of this vapid bunch of extravagantly rewarded nancy boys?'[43]

For all his appeal off the field, Blanchflower had yet to secure any silverware with Spurs, but the appointment of Bill Nicholson as manager in October 1958 was eventually to change that — and make history, too. Nicholson was a traditional no-nonsense Yorkshireman, in contrast to Blanchflower the Corinthian aesthete, but the former was devoid of egotism and saw in Blanchflower a natural leader, and consequently gave him free reign on the pitch, and even in the dressing room, where Danny was allowed to give pre-match warm-up talks. Blanchflower also struck up a fine partnership with another opposite: Dave Mackay, a fierce, muscular Scotsman who came to be the brawn to Danny's brain, as it were.

Nicholson built his Spurs side around Nicholson, with Mackay and

John White in chief supporting roles, and at the outset of the 1960–61 season Spurs began with an run of eleven wins on the trot; by Christmas they had dropped only one point in sixteen games (in a draw against Manchester City). Such was the size of the lead they came to command that by the new year, bookmakers were refusing to take any more bets on Tottenham winning the title. There were wobbly moments in the beginning of 1961: the team lost away to their title rivals Sheffield Wednesday and let slip a 4–0 lead at home to Burnley. Nonetheless, they secured the silverware with three games in hand, at home to Sheffield Wednesday on 17 April.

Of course, Tottenham were not a one-man band: Bobby Smith and Les Allen were prolific up front, scoring fifty-one goals between them; Cliff Jones and Terry Dyson dominated on the wing; and Bill Brown was a safe pair of hands between the sticks. But Danny's leadership skills, and his intelligent crosses into the penalty area, were crucial.

That year Spurs had also reached the FA Cup final, where, in an encounter against Leicester, they were ninety minutes away from what had so narrowly eluded Manchester United in 1948, West Bromwich Albion in 1954, United again in 1957, and indeed every team in the twentieth century: a League and Cup double. Such previous form had convinced many commentators that it simply 'couldn't be done'. Blanchflower would not countenance such pessimism. Three years earlier, on a flight home from the World Cup finals in Sweden, he prophesied: 'It's going to be done. And Spurs will be the team to do it.'[44] In the final itself, Leicester initially threatened to prove wrong such a prognostication, but the wind was taken out of their sails when Les Allen collided with the Leicester right-back, Len Chalmers. With Leicester's strategy thrown out of kilter, Spurs took the lead in the sixty-ninth minute through Bobby Smith, and then Leicester conceded another. Before the game, Blanchflower had issued another of his maxims, to the journalist David Miller: 'It appears that we appear to be in control.'[45] And so it proved. Blanchflower consolidated this achievement by helping his team win the FA Cup again in 1962, this time against Burnley. In the League, only a surprise challenge from eventual title winners Ipswich Town prevented a second double, as Spurs came a narrow third.

The following year, Danny helped Spurs make English footballing history when the London club became the first British side to win a

175

European trophy. Now aged thirty-seven, recovering from a cartilage operation and looking 'little more athletic than Eric Morecambe',[46] he took Spurs to the European Cup Winners' Cup final in 1963. In Rotterdam, they faced Atletico Madrid. Blanchflower, realising that this would be the last big game of his career, was fired up – so much so that he took it upon himself to interrupt Bill Nicholson's pre-match pep talk.

The gaffer had been giving a rather pedestrian and mechanical address in the dressing room when Danny jumped to his feet: 'Hang on a minute, boss. What is all this? Can you imagine their team talk next door?' he interjected. 'For heaven's sake, boss. You're making them sound like world beaters. They're not world beaters, but we are. I say forget them. Let's concentrate on our own strengths as a team. . . . We are strong. We are the stronger. More skilful. More devastating in attack. More uncompromising and creative in midfield. More impenetrable in defence. We are the team that is going to win the Cup!' Such zeal inspired the players; one of Blanchflower's team-mates that day, Jimmy Greaves, has concluded: 'What Danny had to say in the dressing room prior to the final won us the Cup.'[47] The final result: 5–1.

While he could be outspoken on most matters, Blanchflower was essentially a private man. His eloquence was regarded by some as 'a smoke-screen, to protect the inner personality.'[48] In 1977, a *Sunday Times* profile concluded: 'The closer you get to Danny Blanchflower, the harder it becomes to describe him. There is the garrulous public figure, alert, imaginative and witty, who was once described by his brother, Jackie, as having not merely kissed the Blarney Stone but swallowed it! There is also an intense, moderately religious, private man.'[49]

His ability to cross cultural and class divides, to write for both the *New Statesman* and the *Sunday Express,* to excel at the quintessentially 'everyman' sport yet avidly read F. Scott Fitzgerald and befriend the philosopher A. J. Ayer – author of the seminal 1936 work *Language, Truth, and Logic* - intrigued the media. In January 1961, he invited Ayer, a Spurs fan, to come down to 'meet the boys' at White Hart Lane – where, as the *Sunday Times* noted, 'there was no monopoly of language, truth and logic by either side.'[50] This thinking man's footballer often flummoxed those who merely wanted to talk about tactics, goals and results. Following one game at Windsor Park, he was approached by a reporter who wanted to know what Danny thought of the then up-and-coming George Best. His reply was: 'George makes a greater appeal to the senses than Tommy Finney or Stanley Matthews did. His movements are quicker, lighter, more balletic. George offers grander surprises to the mind and the eye. He has ice in his veins, warmth in his heart and timing and balance on his feet.' The reporter, greatly agitated, peered up from his notebook and wearily asked: 'Yeah, yeah, but how do you rate George as a player, Danny?'[51] As Frank Keating of the *Guardian* later concluded: 'When he talks, he never uses full stops, only commas. You cannot squeeze a word past his ear post.'[52]

Like that other maverick of English soccer, Brian Clough, Blanchflower's outspokenness, ambition, eccentricity and even egocentricity were sources of fascination. Thus, a month later, in February 1961, he became the target of a popular British television show. When approached by Eamonn Andrews, who announced: 'Danny Blanchflower, this is your life', the footballer replied simply 'Oh no it isn't' and made a swift departure. 'He ran very fast. He was out of the studio in seconds,' recalled his fellow countryman Andrews.[53] Danny is one of a tiny number of celebrities to have refused to appear on *This Is Your Life,* and he was respectfully apologetic about the matter: 'I'm sorry if I rather upset things, but I just did not want to be on the programme. There is no specific reason.'[54]

Blanchflower retired in 1964, vowing never to return to the game, exasperated by it, convinced that it had been taken over by uncultured money men who cared little for their players. There was talk of him returning to Spurs in a managerial capacity, but the board at White Hart Lane feared he would challenge their authority.[55] In 1978, he did return to the game, to manage the Northern Ireland side, before being appointed Chelsea manager on a 'short-term basis' in the 1978–79 season, at a time when the London club was in severe financial difficulties and facing relegation to the Second Division. Within hours of his appointment, Chelsea were thrashed 7–2 by Middlesbrough. Although he liked most of the people at Chelsea, Blanchflower was unhappy working for such a troubled club, one beset by boardroom scheming. 'Sometimes I felt I was working for MI5,' he said. 'The place seemed inhabited by Smiley's people.'[56] He endeared himself to the players, too, but they did not always understand him. Said one senior player: 'He is fascinating to listen to but we're never quite sure what he's trying to say.'[57] In his nine months at the club, Blanchflower was unable to prevent what had looked likely from the started of the season: Chelsea finished rock-bottom of the First Division and were relegated.

Twice Footballer of the Year, inducted into the English Football Hall of Fame – and also captain of Northern Ireland in their first win at Wembley in 1957, and in their triumph over Italy in 1958 to qualify for that year's World Cup – Danny Blanchflower had glorious days as a player. His later years were, however, tragic. His second wife Avrielle died in 1981 after a fall. He went on to develop Alzheimer's – a cruel fate for a man of such mental ability and verbal dexterity. 'He played the game as a musician plays a musical instrument – with wit and flair,'[58] said the Reverend Dick Woods, the vicar at Blanchflower's funeral in December 1993, where the man was appropriately remembered with the tune 'Danny Boy'.

JIMMY MCILROY

I looked at him with my child-like innocence and said, 'But I'm a Protestant.'

JIMMY MCILROY, OF BURNLEY,
TO JIMMY SCOULAR, OF PORTSMOUTH

While most Irish footballers have made their name at large, glamorous clubs that still command support throughout Ireland, Jimmy McIlroy played for a side that few in Ireland today would consider adopting as their English side. Yet in the early 1960s Burnley, champions of the First Division in 1959–60, were a side to be reckoned with. McIlroy was integral in helping them once more become a great English side, before they – like so many other clubs from northern industrial towns – fell into obscurity and mediocrity.

McIlroy was similar in many ways to Danny Blanchflower, in that his game relied on his wits, patience and timing – although, owing to his slim physique, dark hair and film-star looks, he cut a more dashing figure than Blanchflower. Playing on the right, he was graceful, but he could also be mischievous; in a three-year spell with Burnley, he had helped the Lancastrians win the First Division title and the FA Cup, and in 1961–62 he was part of the side that came so close to emulating Tottenham's double feat of the previous season.

Born in 1931, he had come to England from Lambeg, a village outside Belfast, and from a footballing family. His father Harry had played for Distillery, his uncle Willy for Portadown, and although young Jimmy was apprenticed as a bricklayer, he harboured ambitions to become a soccer professional. Like Best and Whiteside, McIlroy honed his skills as a boy by practising with a tennis ball, and at the age of ten he was playing for his school team alongside youngsters who were far older than him. He played for Glentoran before being signed in 1950 by Burnley.

To begin with, his time at Burnley was uneventful, as the Turf Moor side spent the majority of the 1950s in mid-table, neither exciting their fans with pushes for the title nor agitating them with battles against relegation. But the five-foot-nine-inch Ulsterman soon established a rewarding partnership with Jimmy Adamson. 'Play football and enjoy your game', said manager Harry Potts before each encounter. The Lancastrians went on to secure the title by stealth, having never led the table until their last game, when they beat Manchester City on the final day of the season.

It was the first time Burnley had won the First Division since 1921, and with McIlroy they looked like repeating the feat. With five games remaining at the end of the 1961–62 season, they headed the table with two games in hand and with a superior goal average over their closest rivals, Ipswich Town. But they were chasing the Cup, too: exhausted by a fixture pile-up, their form collapsed, leaving Ipswich to take the honours. Deflated by surrendering the title in such spectacular fashion, they surrendered 3–1 to Spurs (and Blanchflower) in the Cup final. McIlroy was one of the few Burnley players who distinguished himself at Wembley that day – unsurprisingly, as he had that year been runner-up Footballer of the Year, behind his team-mate Jimmy Adamson.

An international who had played in the famous 2–1 win over Italy, and who is still Burnley's most-capped player, McIlroy, with Danny Blanchflower and Billy Bingham, formed an impressive triangle on the field. McIlroy settled easily in the Lancashire town. 'From the moment I arrived in Burnley all those years ago, I felt at home,' he remembers. 'Maybe it was because I came from an small Ulster village to a comparatively small town with an eighty thousand population and the most friendly of people.'[59] Indeed, he settled in Burnley and still lives there, playing golf, writing for the *Lancashire Evening Telegraph* and painting watercolours.

As an Irishman, however, he did come across the odd difficulty in his adopted country from time to time, and on the rare occasion that opponents took exception to his background, such prejudice was comically misplaced. There was one clash with Portsmouth's Jimmy Scoular, one of the most-feared players of the era. 'I was going up the wing when Jimmy hit me. I went over the grass verge and over a little railing into the crowd,' McIlroy remembers. 'Jimmy sidled up to me and said: "Listen, you little Irish Fenian bastard, that's nothing to what I'll do to you next time." And I looked at him with my child-like innocence and said: "But I'm a Protestant", and he said, "Oh God, son, did I hurt you?" For the rest of my career, he never tackled me again. In fact, I am certain he guided me past him.'[60]

Following personal disagreements, and in a move that shocked the supporters, Burnley's 'self-made' chairman, Bob Lord, transferred Jimmy McIlroy to Stoke City in 1963 for a derisory £25,000. Playing alongside Stanley Matthews, McIlroy helped the Potteries side to the Second Division title that year, and to the League Cup final. He was briefly chief coach at Stoke City, and more briefly still at Bolton Wanderers – a team he managed for sixteen days in August 1970.

McIlroy currently belongs to an unusual elite. Alongside Bill Shankly (of Liverpool), Billy Wright (Wolverhampton Wanderers), Brian Clough (Nottingham Forest), Jackie Milburn (Newcastle United) and Tommy Finney (Preston), he has his name emblazoned on a stand in a stadium in England. In 1999, after Turf Moor was rebuilt, one end was re-christened 'The Jimmy McIlroy Stand' in honour of one of Burnley's best-loved sons. 'When they informed me, I was stunned,' he said upon the announcement, declaring that it must have made him 'the first Irishman to be speechless.'[61]

GEORGE BEST

George Best,
Superstar,
Walks like a woman,
And he wears a bra.

TERRACE CHANT, C. 1971

A pied piper in one sense, he was an elusive pimpernel in another. He
was a Leonardo da Vinci who wantonly threw away his paint brushes
and his genius. Yet he was generous, a lost child who loved to do tricks.
One of these was to drop a penny piece on the toe of his shoe, then
flick it up into his breast pocket. He never failed.

GEOFFREY GREEN, 1985[62]

This urge to drink, to be generous, has something childish about it, it is
like the furtive cigarette-smoking of those who vomit as furtively as they
smoke – and the final scene, when the policeman appears at the door on
the dot of eight, the final scene is pure barbarism: pale, grim seventeen-
year-olds hide somewhere in the barn and fill themselves up with beer
and whisky, playing the senseless rules of the game of manhood.

HEINRICH BÖLL, IRISH JOURNAL (1957)[63]

If Danny Blanchflower was very much of his *town* – serious, private, care-
ful with words – George Best was very much of his *time*. Best's trademark
shaggy mane, sideburns and rock-star lifestyle and profile reflected not
only the climate of the swinging sixties but the transformation of the
game itself. The abolition of the maximum wage in 1961 had had a two-
fold effect. It spelt the end for the clubs from smaller towns, who could
no longer compete against the financial muscle and lure of the bright
lights of the big-city clubs such as Liverpool, Everton, Manchester City,
Arsenal, Chelsea and Manchester United. The likes of Blackpool,
Wolverhampton Wanderers, Preston North End and Burnley, big sides of
the 1950s, now have only memories.

Secondly, it meant that, rather than earning no more than £20 a week, players were often taking home more than five times that figure, and thus could afford to start living like rock stars. With his handsome appearance and the twinkle in his eye, Best could have passed for a rock star. But he also had the addictive personality of a rock star – a wild, self-destructive streak that saw him squander his talent and go to an early grave. Indeed, his looks were partly his undoing, as he himself recognised, as they led him into the arms of many a beautiful woman. 'If I'd been ugly,' he once said, 'you'd never have heard of Pelé.'[64] It is often said that 1963 signalled the beginning of the 1960s, but it was a significant year in other ways too: British Labour Party leader Hugh Gaitskell's death led to his replacement by Harold Wilson, who would dominate British politics for the next dozen years; the Profumo Affair; the election of the liberal pontiff Pope John XXIII; the assassination of President Kennedy; Martin Luther King declaring his 'dream'; and George Best, truly an Irish and British cultural icon of that decade, signing for Manchester United.

George Best came into his element in the mid-to-late-1960s, becoming one of the greatest players in British football history on account of his superlative dribbling, courage, acceleration, inventiveness and dexterity. He was at the heart of United's three-pronged attack, alongside Law and Charlton, a triumvirate that helped United win the League and European Cup (even though Best did not get on with the serious-minded and fussy Charlton, once throwing an egg at a picture of him in a pub). But just when he seemed to be approaching the height of his powers, his career began to go badly off the rails. By 1971, his disappearing acts were becoming more frequent and lengthy, he was constantly womanising and drinking, and he put on weight and lost a great deal of pace. Perhaps frustrated by his failure to shine as an international – there were no Laws or Charltons eligible to play for Northern Ireland – or perhaps succumbing to the same demons as his mother, drink was becoming not his servant but his master. He was not only losing interest in playing the game but losing the will to win: when he did turn up to play, he did so seemingly to show off, perpetually hogging the ball. When he finally decided he was bored of Manchester United, he went to Fulham, where he entertained crowds but seemingly had no great desire to achieve. Then came severe alcoholism, wasteful sojourns to play soccer in America, brief periods in Edinburgh and Bournemouth, bankruptcy, imprisonment, a liver transplant and, in November 2005, death.

George Best's mother was something of a sportswoman in her own time, having represented Ireland at hockey – before becoming an alcoholic. Young George had originally been recommended to Leeds United, but their scout was not impressed with what he saw during one of Best's early performances, even leaving the game before half-time. Manchester United's Belfast scout was decidedly more impressed. 'I think I've found you a genius', he told Matt Busby by phone.[65]

The fifteen-year-old was offered a two-week trial. He sailed to Liverpool and went by train to Manchester with his schoolboy friend Eric McMordie. The two got lost on the way to Old Trafford, ending up some way from the ground. 'When he eventually arrived, he entered a world of boarding houses, landladies, homesickness and tearful nights. Like any lost child, he quickly returned home,' writes Colm Keane, pointing out that, while the Irishman's success in England was unique, his initial failure to adapt was typical of his countrymen's experience in those years.[66]

Acutely homesick, the pair returned home after only two days. McMordie would return to England, to play for Middlesbrough, and Busby, having telephoned Best's father, persuaded George to do likewise. The Manchester United manager organised work for George as an office boy near Old Trafford, and also arranged lodgings for the Belfast boy, who was now placed in the care of a kindly landlady. He signed professional for the club on his seventeenth birthday: 22 May 1963.

'I wanted to play,' Best remembers. 'Players today moan about the number of games but, when you're young, you can't play enough.'[67] Soon he was playing both in the youth team (more than fifty thousand fans saw him play in the 1964 FA Youth Cup semi-final against Manchester City) and the first team (he made his First Division debut against West Bromwich Albion in September 1963). At five feet eight inches, and weighing only ten stone, the youthful Best did not have an imposing physical presence, particularly in an age when muscularity and speed were the most valued characteristics in English football, but his agility, pace and audacity, and his ability to beat taller men to headers, more than compensated for his slight physique. Beginning as a winger, he was equally happy on the left or right, but he could make the midfield his own too.

He perplexed burly opposition players with his impish stops and starts, veering one way and then the other, outraging international stars and delighting the Old Trafford and Windsor Park faithful for his sheer, brilliant impudence. The teenager was soon playing for Northern Ireland, although, owing to his unreliability, he would win only thirty-seven international caps and, owing to his nationality, would never appear in a World Cup finals. (The Troubles put paid to any move towards reconciliation between the FAI and the IFA, and the creation of a single Ireland team.)

In his first full season, 1964–65, ten goals by Best had helped Manchester United to the League title on the slimmest of margins: they beat Leeds by 0.686 of a goal, in the days before the Football League realised that deciding championships by goal difference, rather than goal average, was a far more understandable and sensible way of separating winners from also-rans. But it was his performance against Benfica in March 1966 in the European Cup, in which Best netted twice in the first ten minutes – just after Eusebio had received his European Footballer of the Year award – that brought him to the world's attention. United, having travelled to Portugal with a 3–2 lead for what was presumed to be an exercise in damage limitation, trounced the opposition 5–1. Best's sixth-minute header, provided by Tony Dunne's free-kick, was followed by David Herd heading on from Ulsterman Harry Gregg, to lay the ball in Best's path. 'This was our finest hour,' said Busby, echoing Churchill.

This wasn't the only allusion made as a consequence of that result. Best's performance at the Stadium of Light had him labelled by the British press as 'the new Stanley Matthews', while the Portuguese media Christened him 'El Beatle' on account of his swarthy features and tousled hairstyle, which resembled George Harrison's. His changing appearance and character would mirror that of the Beatles and others of his generation: the intelligent, charming, amusing and cheeky boy was transformed by the end of the decade into a serious, moustachioed superstar, replete with sideburns, multiple girlfriends, arguments with his colleagues – and substance addiction. He had become an honorary rock star, particularly for people in more conservative countries. 'I remember when we had to go abroad, to places like Albania or Russia, I was like a freak show,' Best later recalled. 'They'd never seen anything like it. All these mad clothes, big multi-coloured shirts with the big lapels and high-heeled boots, and hair twice as long as they'd ever seen before.'[68]

United could not follow up their European success in Lisbon in 1965–66: Best's absence from a semi-final game against Partizan Belgrade saw them unexpectedly going out to the Yugoslavs. But he helped the team regain the First Division title in 1967, scoring ten more goals in the process. United were almost unbeatable at home and remained undefeated from 16 December, with Best getting himself on the scoresheet in the 6–1 hammering of West Ham United's own World Cup–winning triumvirate of Bobby Moore, Geoff Hurst and Martin Peters in May 1967. The following year, Best surpassed himself, scoring twenty-eight goals in forty-one League games, being voted English and European Footballer of the Year, and forming part of the first English team to win the European Cup.

At the final against Benfica at Wembley on 29 May, with the game poised at 1–1, it looked as though the Portuguese might exact revenge for their previous heavy defeat. Only seconds remained when Eusebio broke through the United defence, with just goalkeeper Alex Stepney to beat. Busby turned his back, awaiting the inevitable. But Eusebio hesitated, then blasted the ball from too-close range, leaving Stepney to effect a last-gasp save. If Tony Dunne was exhausted, Best still had a spring in his step, and in the third minute of extra-time he took off on a twenty-five-yard run, to-ing-and-fro-ing past the defence before sidestepping the opposition goalie and running the ball into the net. Brian Kidd and Bobby Charlton both also scored, to give United a 4–1 win.

By the turn of the decade, Best was scoring spectacular solo efforts, including one for Northern Ireland against England in 1970, and against the same opposition the following year, when, at Windsor Park, Gordon Banks pitched the ball in the air in preparation for a kick, only for Best to make contact with the ball, flick it over the keeper and head it into the net. Banks protested, and Best's effort was disallowed – the referee adjudging the Irishman to be guilty of dangerous play. Then there was his goal against Sheffield United, the same year, when he took the ball on the right flank, dashed diagonally past countless Sheffield opposition, and thrusting the ball past the keeper.

Paradoxically, the increasing frequency of Best's solo efforts augured badly, indicating that Best was becoming detached from his team-mates and consumed by his own genius. He had appointed a secretary and opened two boutiques, and his on-field swagger hinted at his increasing complacency. Geoffrey Green of the London *Times* remembers Best's worrying lack of nerves at the turn of the decade. 'Once, before a big European Cup tie, he was calmly drinking Bovril with me at a crowded bar under the Old Trafford stands while other players, already changed, were anxiously living out the last tense moments before the kick-off in the dressing room. With only twenty minutes to the whistle, he had to be reminded that he was playing and still unchanged. Whereupon he departed, to perform in a kind of radiance, destroying the opposition as he has done so often.'[69]

Best had been sent off while playing for Northern Ireland for throwing mud at the referee in a clash against Scotland. In 1970, having scored six times in an FA Cup win at Northampton, he was suspended for bringing the game into disrepute, and in January 1971 he arrived ninety minutes late for an appearance before the FA Disciplinary Commission. Four days later, having missed the train to London again, he didn't show up for United's game at Chelsea and instead spent the weekend with Sinead Cusack. He was suspended for a fortnight, and a year later was dropped from the team on account of his chronic absenteeism. He was told to leave his Cheshire mansion and move into lodgings near Old Trafford.

His genius was, paradoxically, coming to infuriate his fellow United players. He had 'stopped playing as a winner', remembers Dunne. 'George took to beating the same man ten times. The crowds loved it. But by this time you looked across and Denis had made about five runs – Bobby's made four – nothing's happened. Kiddo's [Brian Kidd] made runs – nothing happened.' His team-mates implored: 'George, for f—k sake give them the ball!', to which Denis Law added: 'Give him a f—king ball of his own!'[70]

Best, while he realised that he was playing selfishly, also felt that his ageing team were not up to the challenge, and felt that it was his duty to do most of the work. 'My goals became all-important, because others weren't scoring them so frequently,' he said. 'Instead of revolving around me, the team now depended on me and I lacked the maturity to handle it. I began to drink more heavily, and on the field my list of bookings grew longer as my temper grew shorter.' He was also fed up of being on the losing side after ninety minutes, something he had never been used to: 'I'm still sure it was the thought of playing in a bad team, of not winning anything, of not having a chance to play in Europe that drove me to it.'[71]

In May 1972, he took a plane to Spain, announcing that he had had enough of football. He did make a brief comeback, but neither Wilf McGuinness nor Frank O'Farrell could bring him under control. Tommy

Docherty was less forgiving of his unreliability, and less tolerant about constantly reading tabloid stories of his drinking and womanising. After the two clashed, Best played his last game for Manchester United, versus Queen's Park Rangers, on New Year's Day 1974.

Best would try to make light of his affliction, joking: 'I've stopped drinking, but only while I'm asleep', or: 'In 1969, I gave up women and alcohol – it was the worst twenty minutes of my life.' But the reality was not so amusing. 'When he is boozing he is the most deplorable, obnoxious, sarcastic, ignorant, horrible piece of rubbish,' said his second wife, Alex Best.[72] 'When I did drink it was worse than before I stopped,' he confessed. 'I was cancelling work. I was not turning up for things. I was letting friends down. I was letting family down. It was a total nightmare.'[73]

Best went on to play some games for Stockport County and then went to California, where he turned out for the Los Angeles Aztecs. In the autumn of 1976, he returned to England, where he spent two seasons with Second Division Fulham. Although his pace had almost completely gone, he still had skill and flair. In total, his post-Manchester career saw him play for eleven clubs, including Cork Celtic, Hibernian, the Fort Lauderdale Strikers, the San Jose Earthquakes and Bournemouth. He made his last appearance for Northern Ireland in 1977, against Holland. Such was the esteem in which he was held that there was even talk of brining him back for the 1982 World Cup finals, but he was by now a shambolic figure.

His recurring drinking caused him to go into bankruptcy and led to the failure of his first marriage. His acts of public drunkenness – in 1984 he was convicted of drink-driving and assaulting a policeman, leading him to spend Christmas in jail; in 1990 he appeared clearly inebriated on BBC's *Wogan* show; eight months later he assaulted a man in a London pub – earned him sympathy, particularly from the many women who tried to rescue him from himself, but they also elicited cruelty. A small section of Manchester City's supporters would sing, to the tune of 'She'll Be Coming Round the Mountain':

> Would you like a Newcy Brown, Georgie Best?
> Would you like a Newcy Brown, Georgie Best?
> Would you like a Newcy Brown
> 'Cos you'll soon be six foot down
> Would you like a Newcy Brown, Georgie Best?[74]

By the mid-1990s, Best had become a successful after-dinner speaker, and a pundit on Sky Sports, but he continued to suffer from ill-health, and not even a liver transplant in 2002, and Antabuse tablets being sewn into his stomach, could curtail his drinking. While the women in his life had tried to stop him, it was a sad irony that it was his fans who, having worshipped Best, were helping him to an early grave, insisting on buying him a pint when he walked into their pub.

It would be trite to say that Best's life ended tragically, but it is worth repeating a truism about him: George Best had an ability to do what few have done in Ulster, to become a hero to both Catholics and Protestants – as the multitude who turned up for his funeral in November 2005 attest. Irish funerals, are of course, notorious for their black humour, and it was thus no surprise that, as Frank O'Farrell made his way to pay his respects, he couldn't help wondering to himself whether Best's body would actually be present: 'Will he show up? Because he had a habit of not showing up when he was expected.'[75]

DEREK DOUGAN

Throughout my career I have been called a rebel, a show-off, a belliger-
ent non-conformist, a trouble-maker and a few unrepeatable names
usually prefaced with the tag 'Irish', which is supposed to explain, if not
absolve, everything.

DEREK DOUGAN, 1969[76]

Ian Paisley is a man of the cloth but there is no way he will get within a
thousand miles of the Pearly Gates. He is a geriatric and Trimble is a
bigot.

DEREK DOUGAN, 1997[77]

Frequently dubbed the 'Arthur Scargill of Football' for his bruising, outspoken manner, Derek 'Doog' Dougan was, after George Best, the best-
known Ulster footballer in England in the 1960s and 1970s, a lanky, dashing, always-challenging centre-forward for Wolverhampton Wanderers.
He was also famously forthright, both as chairman of the Professional
Footballers' Association and, in particular, when it came to his persistent
advocating of an all-Ireland football team. This did not endear him to the
IFA or the inhabitants of Belfast's more hardened loyalist areas – the
areas from which he himself had emerged.

In eighteen years playing in the Football League, Dougan scored 222
goals, including 95 for Wolves, for whom he played from 1967 to 1976.
He consolidated his national profile as a television pundit thereafter.
Television brought him spectacularly to public attention in the first place:
his hat-trick on his home debut for Wolves against Hull City was broadcast to the nation in March 1967 on *Match of the Day,* at a time when the
two match highlights it featured was the only football coverage aficionados of the game could see on a weekly basis.

Born in 1938, Derek Dougan was raised in Newtownards Road, east
Belfast, but like his father (a shipyard worker, like Best's), the young
Dougan wanted nothing to do with the Orange Order. 'I will never, never
wear the sash,' he said in 1997.[78] Unlike many of his generation who grew
up in this loyalist heartland, Dougan was taken to the 'Free State' as a boy,

making his first trip to Dublin at the age of fifteen, and going with his mother on shopping trips to Dundalk and Monaghan. He made many friends here, becoming convinced that the Papist south was not a vipers' nest of theocracy and priestcraft.

Dougan played for a short time with Distillery before joining First Division Portsmouth in 1957, having already been honoured for Northern Ireland at schoolboy, youth and amateur levels, playing as a wing-half or central defender. He started playing as a striker at Pompey. During his first season there, he netted nine times in thirty-three League appearances, and after Portsmouth were relegated at the end of the 1958–59 season, Dougan moved to First Division Blackburn Rovers, a team he would help take to the 1960 FA Cup final, only for Rovers to lose 3–0 to Wolves. After spells at Aston Villa, Peterborough United and Leicester, this wandering Ulsterman found the team with which he would finally settle, Wolverhampton Wanderers, making the move to Molineux in 1967.

If 'the Doog' stood out at Blackburn for his militaristic, shaven head, at Wolves it was for his goal-scoring proficiency. During his first season there, Wolves were promoted back to the First Division. Dougan was the team's top scorer in the following two seasons, with seventeen and fourteen goals, and would help the Black Country outfit win the League Cup in 1974. He emulated the hat-trick on his debut against Hull City with another three goals in a UEFA Cup tie against Academica of Portugal in the 1971–72 season, becoming the first and only Wolves player to have scored a hat-trick in Europe. That was his most glorious season: he netted twenty-four goals, and the early 1970s are still the last time Wolves were a force in English football. Another of his many hat-tricks saw him put three past his old club Villa.

Dougan's success was in large measure a result of his partnership with John Richards, but Dougan's pace, acceleration and heading ability also stood to him. 'I developed a technique in the air that no other centre-forward in history was able to develop,' he later said. 'My timing was unique. But what I had to back me up was this amazing speed.'[79]

In his entire career, 'the Doog' scored 222 goals in 546 matches, with his combative approach seeing him accumulate numerous wounds, including damage to his back, and he collected more than two hundred stitches. Although many of these injuries were sustained far away from the football pitch, he thought that taking risks on the field of play was intrinsic to his footballing philosophy: 'I had this attitude that if only one person in a crowd of forty thousand left the ground saying, "Yeh that Dougan is a bit special, a bit of an entertainer", I had delivered on my mandate.'[80] At the end of the 1974–75 season, owing to back problems, Dougan announced his retirement as a player.

Derek Dougan had travelled with Northern Ireland to the 1958 World Cup finals, the youngest member of the squad. He won forty-three caps for Northern Ireland, and later became captain, before falling foul of the IFA. In the summer of 1973, he had decided to make a gesture of peace – just as the rest of Ireland seemed to be on the brink of all-out war. After a telephone call from Johnny Giles, and then one from Louis Kilcoyne, a recognised FIFA football agent, Dougan came up with the idea of fielding an all-Ireland team to play the world champions, Brazil, at Lansdowne Road.

In a later interview with the *Irish Times,* Dougan recalls making the suggestion to the Association: 'I put the idea of north and south coming together to play Brazil at a meeting in London with the two senior officials of the IFA – Harry Cavan, the president, and Billy Drennan, the secretary, a gentleman and a far-sighted administrator. My hands were wet with the sweat of nervous tension. Here, I thought, we were talking about history in the making . . . . Then came the moment I will remember for the rest of my life. Mr Cavan received the news as if a bomb had hit him. In the face of what was for me a great moment in my footballing life, I was confronted by a cold stony silence. Harry Cavan informed me tersely that he would put the matter to the IFA. Billy Drennan, much more enthusiastic, told me that he would keep me posted about developments. But I never heard from either again. I had been captain of the Northern Ireland team for the previous four years, but after that meeting I never played again. And I never played again because Cavan told the manager, Terry Neill, never to pick me.'[81]

Undeterred, Dougan led a contingent down from the north – a contingent that included Pat Jennings, Alan Hunter, Martin O'Neill and Bryan Hamilton – to play alongside their southern counterparts. Dougan scored twice in front of forty thousand people and a television audience, and the all-Ireland team almost beat the Brazilians. 'To this day, I meet people in Belfast, Newry and God-knows-where who tell me "Yeh, I was there the day Ireland came from 4–1 down and nearly beat Brazil." '[82]

The unfortunate incidents of the next year made Dougan appreciate that, while the many of his people back home were feeling less Irish all the time, and were increasingly calling themselves British, he was not viewed in the same way in England. 'I was ashamed that people purporting to act on behalf of Irish people, including me, should perpetrate such an outrage and massacre innocent people. But I was saddened, too, by the reaction of some English people,' he said of his reaction to the 1974 Birmingham bombings. 'All sorts of people with an Irish accent were forced to endure a period in England which can only have come from the Dark Ages. It seemed to those across the water that everyone from Ireland, north or south, was fair game for physical abuse, intimidation, harassment, [and] rejection in pubs and restaurants.'[83]

There were happier times off the field in the 1970s, when Dougan became one of the inaugural members of the first television football panel. He joined Malcolm Allison, Paddy Crerand, Brian Clough and Bob McNab for ITV's studio coverage of the 1970 World Cup. The panellists were not sent to Mexico but were instead put up in a hotel in Hendon, ferried to and from the studio for a month, and paid £500 each for their services. The idea of having commentators issuing punditry from home, rather than live from the game, had been instigated by ITV television producer John Bromley. There was some initial concern from an assistant, who told Bromley about the size of Allison's expenses bill, which included Cuban cigars, champagne and fine wines, but such was the programme's success that he signed Allison's bill himself and ordered that, for the duration of the competition, each member be woken with a glass of champagne.[84] Dougan enjoyed a lively career as a pundit, and Bromley's format has since been much copied, to the extent that a World Cup does not seem complete without Mark Lawrenson and Martin O'Neill on the BBC, and John Giles and Eamon Dunphy on RTÉ, and Saturday afternoons are not the same without Sky Sports' Jeff Stelling and colleagues relaying scores and opinions, and exchanging jokes and insults.

By 1972, Dougan had already expressed his unease with mainstream unionism in his autobiography, *The Sash He Never Wore,* and he has continued to rail against unionism's main political and spiritual leaders. In July 1997, he remarked: 'Our politicians have betrayed us. During the general election they had nothing to say about the health service, about unemployment, the plight of the old, our place in Europe. They talk about just one thing – the Union. That's all the people get and the result is that green is getting greener and orange is getting deeper. But the Troubles are big money for some people and they have a vested interest in preventing peace.'[85]

Dougan later returned to football, to manage Kettering Town, and became chief executive at Wolves in 1982. The latter was an unhappy, brief re-association, in which he lost much of the regard in which he had been held in the city. In 1984 the club was relegated to the Second Division, in 1985 they were relegated again, and once more in 1986, matching Bristol City's record of dropping from England's top division to its fourth in only three calendar years.

He went on to run a company that represents the interests of former professional footballers and then ventured into politics, standing as an independent against the DUP's Peter Robinson in the 1997 British general election. He garnered only five hundred votes but retains an interest in politics: in June 2006 he joined the UK Independence Party, an organisation dedicated to withdrawing Britain from the European Union. 'I do not support political union where we are dictated to by Brussels,' he said. 'The EU is a one-way street towards European government.'[86]

His criticism of the Union of Great Britain with Northern Ireland, meanwhile, has met with disapproval in some quarters. East Belfast has celebrated the feats of its footballing sons in England with a mural on the Woodstock Road depicting Best, Blanchflower, Sammy McIlroy and Dougan, but early in 2005 Dougan's picture was defaced after he reiterated his belief that there should be an all-Ireland soccer team.[87] But he remains an adamant proponent of the idea, not just because he is not averse to north and south becoming a single political state one day but rather so that Ireland, the team that gave Brazil a run for their money in 1973, could potentially become a great soccer nation. 'When Pat Jennings, the last of the truly great players in the North, retired, I went on record as saying that Northern Ireland were finished. And the Republic's performance against Iceland [0–0 at home in 1996], the worst in living memory, proves that they are now into the same scenario. Singly, neither of them may ever again reach the finals of a major competition in my lifetime. But by pooling resources, they have at least a chance.'[88]

TERRY NEILL

I feel that the people running football in Northern Ireland are not providing a structure for them to develop properly. I'm very proud of my Ulster heritage. But it's a small province and it can produce very insular thinking.

TERRY NEILL, 2005[89]

He is immaculately dressed, smooth-talking – the epitome of the Irishman who not only touched and kissed the Blarney Stone but swallowed it!

THE SUN, 2000[90]

Terry Neill has the unusual distinction that, whereas many people have fled from Northern Ireland to England because of violence, he recently fled from England back to Ulster – because of the violence in London. Neill, an Ulsterman who has managed rivals Tottenham and Arsenal, spent forty-two years living in the English capital, where he had built a restaurant business, before being attacked in a dark street in the early part of 2001. He was punched and kicked to the ground and left unconscious and bleeding on the footpath; two hours later, two passers-by came to his rescue. The provocation for this attack? As Neill explained: 'They came out of nowhere. I heard someone shout: "Arsenal bastard!" I looked round and I got smacked in the face. That's the last I remember.'[91]

It is ironic, even perverse, that Neill, having left a part of the world where being the wrong religion in the wrong place can result in an assault – or worse – was the victim of north London's acute soccer rivalry. But it has been this way for some time. Pat Jennings made the transition from White Hart Lane to Highbury, but as he was pushed rather than jumped, Spurs fans never held much of a grudge towards him. George Graham, the manager who went the other direction, fared less well, while Tottenham defender Sol Campbell's move to Arsenal prompted death threats.

Although Neill rescued Tottenham from relegation in the 1974–75 season – his objective when he was appointed Spurs boss – he was never particularly popular there. If truth be told, he was never a favourite with the players at Arsenal; although he brought them FA Cup victory in 1979, he came very close to denying them even that. With Arsenal enjoying a 2–0 lead with five minutes to go, Neill complacently brought off David Price, replacing him with Steve Walford, and in the process disrupted the Gunners' defence – a defence that was then rocked by goals from Gordon McQueen and Sammy McIlroy of Manchester United. It took Liam Brady's exploitation of United's now-nervy defence to secure the Cup. It was perhaps a fitting end to the campaign: Arsenal had made hard work of the competition from the outset, struggling during five matches, and 540 minutes, of play to overcome Jack Charlton's Sheffield Wednesday of the Third Division in the third round.

Such relative unpopularity would not worry Terry Neill. He is a consummate professional, a workaholic and family man who did not go into football to win friends but to succeed. And in the end, he did that with Arsenal, a team that had not won a major trophy for ten years. 'I've had the cars, I've had the houses, I've had the parties and everything money could buy,' he reflected after leaving London. 'And while I always appreciated all of it, it was never really that important to me. I'd been taught by my parents about what was important and that stuck with me – family, friends, honesty and hard work.'[92]

Neill, who went on to captain Northern Ireland at the tender age of twenty-one, and made fifty-nine appearances for his country, was initially discouraged from taking up the game. He attended Bangor Grammar School, a rugby school where soccer was frowned upon. But he had played for his local youth side, the Boys Brigade team, and turned out for Bangor FC well before he went to secondary school. His refusal to desist from switching allegiance to rugby was to his physical cost. 'I got caned every Monday morning by Randall Clarke, the headmaster, for not turning up for rugby matches. I explained that I couldn't let my team down and accepted my punishment as just one of those things.' The headmaster eventually realised that such chastisement was not having the desired effect, and after six weeks of physical punishment he called young Terence into his office again: every Monday from then on they would have a cup of tea and a chat. 'We both had to save face and we never told anyone about the tea. Randall became a great friend of mine in later years and we used to laugh about the battle we had when I was a kid.'[93]

Neill left his home town to join Arsenal as a seventeen-year-old aspiring wing-half, to begin an on-and-off association with the club that would last four decades. He immediately impressed Arsenal manager George Swindin, who gave the teenager his debut in December 1960 against Wednesday, and he duly scored in that game, which ended in a one-all draw. He was thereafter played at wing-half or as a centre-half utility player, and when Billy Wright took over from Swindin at the helm, the former Wolves manager made Neill, a forward-pushing, tough-yet-clean Ulsterman, the youngest captain in the club's history.

The player was a regular for the Gooners until the 1969–70 season, when an influx of new talent (which would go on to rescue Arsenal from the doldrums of the sixties and make them one of the most accomplished sides of the seventies) pushed him to the sidelines. Arsenal's nondescript decade during Neill's time as a player there meant that he only picked up one medal with them – a runners-up medal in the 1968 League Cup final, when a single goal gave Leeds United victory. If Arsenal were humbled that year, in next year's League Cup they were positively embarrassed, losing in the final to Third Division Swindon Town. In fact, the only decoration Neill achieved during his playing days with Arsenal was winning, with fellow defender Ian Ure, BBC's *Quizball* panel game.[94]

Neill had come from a reserved family not given to open displays of affection, and while his father was immensely proud of his son, he did not want to show it. For years, Neill's da, Billy, would travel alone to watch his son play at Old Trafford, Anfield and Highbury, but never told him that he was there. 'The only reason I found out,' remembers Neill, 'was that one day [former Wales international] Mel Charles spotted him at the entrance and told me my dad was outside. I went out and there he was standing looking a bit embarrassed. He said: "I just fancied coming over to see you play, son." That was just his way. We've never been an emotional family but we always knew we were loved.'[95] Neill made the people of Northern Ireland even prouder when in 1972 at Wembley he scored the winning goal against England, and until September 2005 he was still the last Northern Irishman to do so.

His affection for his family, and the manner in which they have remained the most important thing in his life, manifested themselves during his time with Tottenham. After serving his apprenticeship as player-manager of Hull City of the Second Division, he was surprisingly brought to White Hart Lane as a replacement for Bill Nicholson, who had resigned under a cloud in 1974, lamenting the bad behaviour and lack of respect now customarily displayed by professional footballers. 'If I fail,' Neill remarked, 'I've got a wonderful wife and two beautiful daughters to go back to.'[96] Like his fellow Ulsterman, who made his mark at Spurs, Neill possessed enthusiasm, even if he did not display comparable erudition, and his unfussy approach was deemed the tonic the Londoners needed. Spurs had begun the 1974–75 season in dire fashion, rooted to the bottom of the table by 13 September, having taken only two points from their first six league games. Neill brought mixed results – first recovery, then a slump in the New Year – but Spurs did at least finishing fourth from bottom, escaping relegation by a single point.

For the next campaign, tight finances at the club and the manager's desire to streamline the team saw the squad reduced from thirty-one professionals to twenty-six, but the club's acute, and now infamous, parsimony during that period finally saw Neill reach the end of his tether. The breaking point came in the close season of 1976. On 25 April that year, the team was about to embark on a tour to Australia and the Pacific, and Neill had promised a seat on the coach to Heathrow Airport to the only fan travelling with the group, a seventy-eight-year-old retired bookmaker and devoted Spurs supporter called Fred Rhye, who had missed just three Tottenham games in the last forty years. He had also been the only fan to have a place in the club's official car park. But Tottenham chairman Sydney Wale chose this moment to embarrass both Neill – whom Wale, a cautious man, had always regarded as a tempestuous figure – and Mr Rhye, telling the pensioner that he would have to make his way to the airport by alternative means. Wale said that he did this for insurance reasons, and also claimed that he was looking out for the old man's health.

After the team won all nine matches in that tour, Neill suggested that, as a reward, some of his players and backroom staff should be given a bonus from the proceeds of the tour. Again, Wale put a stop to this. A fortnight after returning to England on 25 May, Neill handed in his resignation. To add further insult, Wale only accepted the resignation on 30 June because he didn't want to cut short his holiday. 'They didn't take me seriously,' remembers Neill. 'I was treated like a naughty schoolboy who didn't know how lucky I was.'[97] Within a month, Neill was in the saddle at his old club Arsenal, as its youngest-ever manager; within a year, Tottenham had been relegated.

One of Neill's first acts at the Gunners was to sign Malcolm Macdonald for £333,333: the former Newcastle player scored thirty goals in his first season. He bought Pat Jennings from Tottenham to replace Jimmy Rimmer, and encouraged Brady, O'Leary and Stapleton. As a result, Arsenal made three Cup final appearances in a row between 1978 and 1980; their win in 1979 gave Arsenal fans their only source of cheer in the League or FA Cup in the long hiatus between the League wins of 1971 and 1989.

The FA Cup win of 1979 refused to impress Neill's own children, however. When he brought the trophy home, his daughters, Tara, age eight, and Abigail, six, were suitably unimpressed. 'I sat them down in the lounge and gathered them close. The Cup was sitting on the table. In a hushed voice I said: "Girls, this is what it's all about." They looked at me like I was stupid and said: "Oh Daddy, that's a dirty old thing." Then Tara grabbed the Cup and the pair of them ran next door and threw it around the swimming pool. I was speechless. Then I just laughed. It's only a game after all and my two girls realised that more than I did.'[98] (Others were more seriously unimpressed by ensuing events. In 1983, almost fifty years since they had humbled Arsenal in the FA Cup, Walsall beat them again, this time in the League Cup.)

Charlie Nicholas had been signed with much fanfare that summer but by November had scored in just one game. Neill blamed the players: 'They don't seem to know what it is to hunger for goals and glory. On some days I think they just want to pick up their money and go home. But I'll tell you now; we'll finish in the top six again this season. Whether or not I'll be around to see it is another matter.'[99] They did manager to finish sixth, and Neill was not there to see it.

Players and commentators were unhappy with what they regarded as Neill's poor man-management skills. Liam Brady had made 307 appearances for the club from 1973 to 1980, but he was soon on his way, as was Frank Stapleton, to Old Trafford. 'At one stage players were forming a queue outside his office to present transfer requests,' said Brady of Neill, soon after his departure to Juventus. 'I was one of those players. I'd had enough. Far from improving the atmosphere at Highbury, it seemed Neill made it worse. In some ways it was not his fault. But we felt he failed to grasp the importance of being straight with his staff.'[100]

Neill remains a dapper character, and modest as regards his achievements, even the 1972 win over England. Even when he was dismissed in December 1983, he displayed characteristic composure. 'I'd already packed up my desk. It was no problem. I knew the score and I accepted it,' he remembers. 'In fact I ended up comforting the chairman. He hadn't slept the night before because he felt bad about sacking me.'[101]

*

Ulster will fight and Ulster will be right.

TRUE PREDICTION MADE IN THE WRONG SPIRIT

The names above represent the tip of the iceberg: many more have emerged from Ulster to establish their own 'plantation' in England.

Were it not for Pat Jennings's consistency and reliability between the sticks for Northern Ireland, Willie McFaul, Newcastle United's goalkeeper of the 1960s, would have earned greater recognition. Between 1966 and 1975, he was a rock for the Magpies, aiding them on their march to Europe, despite being only five foot ten. 'It is debatable whether there's a better goalkeeper in the country,' said Bill Shankly of him in 1969.[102]

His fellow Ulsterman, Alf McMichael, who held the record for the highest number of appearances for Newcastle, was regarded by Stanley Matthews as 'one of the best left-backs I have ever played against.'[103] Like McFaul, destiny did not favour him, though: he missed out on two of the club's three FA Cup final appearances in the 1950s – in 1951, after he broke his wrist in training, and in 1955, when he had ligament trouble. McMichael is one of only seven players to have played in more than four hundred matches for Newcastle United; he made the less enviable record of netting an own goal after only thirty-two seconds against West Bromwich Albion in 1951.

There is Manchester United's Sammy McIlroy, who scored the last-minute equaliser against Arsenal in the 1979 FA Cup final, going past O'Leary and the luckless Steve Walford to give the Red Devils false hope. 'You look at the equalising goal and you think, were are back at 2–2, and I honestly thought, looking at them, that they had gone. They were shocked, absolutely bewildered and we had many a chance to stop Brady making the run. But that is the type of team we were. We didn't have the type of nasty streak in us when we should have brought Brady down,' remembers McIlroy of that day.[104] He had previously experienced defeat in the final against Southampton in 1976, having been relegated with United in 1974, and he became a regular in the Sexton years, for the team he had supported as a boy in Belfast. He was not to feature in Big Ron's era, however, and left in style, scoring a hat-trick against Wolves on 3 October, the day United had signed his replacement, Bryan Robson.

Shortly after him came Norman Whiteside, the child prodigy whose career ended as prematurely as it had begun. The United and Everton man set the record as the youngest player to appear in the World Cup finals (in 1982, aged seventeen years, forty-two days) and the youngest scorer in an FA Cup final (in 1983, aged eighteen years, nineteen days), but a persistent knee injury put him out of the game at the age of twenty-seven. By the age of seven, he had been netting for the Boys' Brigade team, frequently scoring ten or more goals in a match. He was Manchester United's salvation in the 1985 final after Moran's dismissal: he received a pass from Mark Hughes, then slid to the right wing and into the area, fooled Pat van der Hauwe with a step over, and then curled a shot past Neville Southall. He has since qualified as a chiropodist at Salford University.

The full-back Mal Donaghy made a record ninety-one appearances for Northern Ireland, a record surpassed only by Pat Jennings. The Luton, Chelsea and Manchester United player appeared in defence for Northern Ireland alongside John McClelland, who himself went on to win the League with Leeds in 1992, as well as later breaking his leg in three places. Billy Hamilton, a Northern Ireland international of the late 1970s and early 1980s who played for Burnley, QPR and Oxford, sustained a serious knee injury, like Whiteside. (Hamilton's near-namesake, Billy Bingham, having reached the FA Cup final with Luton in 1959, went on to win the league title with Everton four years later.)

Then there was Gerry 'the Judge' Armstrong of Tottenham and Watford, who terrorised the Spanish defence in the 1982 World Cup before scoring against them to give the Irish a famous 1–0 victory over the hosts. Having beaten them, he joined them – signing for Real Mallorca within a year of that victory. He went on to put the ball in the net, against Valencia, in the same goal in which he had scored against the national side.

Special mention should go to Arsenal's two jokers: Steve Morrow, who broke his collarbone after falling off the shoulders of Tony Adams while celebrating the League Cup final triumph over Sheffield Wednesday in 1993, and Sammy Nelson, who, having been taunted by fans for scoring an own goal against Coventry City on 3 April 1979, celebrated scoring in the correct net by pulling down his shorts and exposing his backside to the crowd. He was fined £750 and banned for two games.

And these are just the more conspicuous northern Protestants, among many who have come to England to ply their wares. Many of them play in England today, and many more will no doubt do so in the future. While the English media has a tendency to caricature these people as Bible-bashing, lambeg drum–thumping, noisy blockheads, they have shown that Ulster Protestants can have fun too.

7

Talkin' 'Bout the Second (and Third) Generation

[Arthur] Griffith, usually so stolid and unemotional, lost his patience. He rose, like a sleeping lion roused, and declared: 'Before this proceeds any further I want to say that President de Valera made a statement – a generous Irishman's statement – and I replied. I will not reply to any Englishman in this Dail.' 'What has my nationality got to do with it?' asked the ultra-rational Erskine Childers. Banging the table furiously, Griffith repeated, 'I will not reply to any damned Englishman in this assembly.'

FROM *ERSKINE CHILDERS* BY JIM RING, 1996[1]

MAN WHO'S 1/16TH IRISH PROUD OF HIS IRISH HERITAGE
KENOSHA, WI
Despite being just 1/16th Irish, Dennis Kroeger, a 27-year-old marketing manager whose great-great-grandmother hailed from County Cork, is fiercely proud of his Irish ancestry.
Jessica Kroeger, 23, is mystified by her older brother's identification with the Irish people. 'I have no idea where he got this whole Irish fixation from,' Jessica said. 'I mean, Dad's mostly German and Mom's some kind of European mongrel. He never gave a shit about it in high school, but at some point in college it just suddenly kicked in.'
Said Padraig O'Riordan of the Hibernian-American League in Boston: 'He probably doesn't realize that what he's really telling the world is that he's desperate for an identity.'

THE *ONION* (AMERICAN SATIRICAL MAGAZINE), 22 MAY 2002

Those of us who, like myself, are second-generation Irishmen, having been raised and reared in England by at least one Irish parent, are perpetually asked: 'What do you feel, English or Irish?' It is of course a question for which there is no pleasing answer – much like being asked by the head of the Mafia if you find his sister attractive. If you answer that you feel English, 'thoroughbred' Englishmen will deride you as an arriviste Paddy trying to fit in and disguise your bog-trotting ancestry, while an Irishman may insult you as an Uncle Tom denying your cultural roots. If, on the other hand, you reply that you feel Irish, both the Englishman and the Irishman will laugh at you for being a 'Plastic Paddy'.

For this reason, second- and third-generation Irish footballers who have made it in England often receive a great deal of stick on both sides of the water. Their 'neither/nor' status renders them vulnerable to questions as to the state of their mental health, or charges of being mercenary. This is why the English press was particularly affronted by Ireland's win against England in 1988: English- and Scottish-born players brought about the defeat against their native land. (It has to be said that, while mocking the Irish for appropriating foreigners as their own, the English see no contradiction in appropriating South African cricketers (Kevin Pietersen) and Canadian footballers (Owen Hargreaves) and tennis players (Greg Rudeski) as their own.)

Similarly, this is why Roy Keane eventually lost his temper in Saipan in 2002, saying what everybody had been privately thinking – that Mick McCarthy was not really an Irishman. McCarthy, whose father was from Waterford, and who captained Ireland at the 1990 World Cup, has protested: 'I have an emotional tie with Ireland that'll never be broken. I've just got the wrong accent!'[2] But Keane disagreed in Japan, and was reported in the *Guardian* as having said: 'Who the f—k do you think you are, having meetings about me? You were a crap player, you are a crap manager. The only reason I have any dealings with you is that somehow you are manager of my country and you're not even Irish, you English c—t. You can stick up your bollocks.'[3]

While Keane's assessment of McCarthy's playing career is somewhat unfounded, and the Corkman's grasp of the human anatomy certainly in need of correction, who is to say that his judgment on McCarthy's ethnicity was unfair or untrue? Certainly, in the wake of the affair, Kevin Myers thought that much of the Irish nation was in denial, avoiding the proverbial elephant in the room: 'Virtually all comment in Ireland is predicated on the charming falsehood that McCarthy is an Irishman. He is not. He's a Yorkshireman, born and bred,' wrote Myers in June 2002. 'Even when some newspapers incorrectly reported that Keane had called McCarthy "an English c—t", there was some considerable outrage in Ireland at the alleged slur on the purity of McCarthy's "Irishness", as if his home town of Barnsley were on the Ring of Kerry.'[4]

This is not by any means new in Anglo-Irish history. Sean MacStiofain, the first Chief of Staff of the Provisional IRA, was Christened 'John Stephenson' and brought up in east London by an Irish father and a mother he believed to be Irish. During the early 1970s, the British press constantly referred to him disparagingly by his original name. 'Mad corporal John Stephenson,' wrote the *Evening News*'s John Evans in November 1972[5]; 'MacStiofain's much-publicised Irish birthright is largely a self-delusion born out of the fantasies of his boyhood and adolescence' added the *Sunday Telegraph*[6]; while Bernard Levin of the London *Times* concluded: 'Does not the evidence already suggest that Stephenson is a perfectly ordinary psychopath, who calls himself Sean MacStiofain, or some such rubbish, in order the better to be an Irish patriot, instead of what he is, an English homicidal maniac.'[7] Unsurprisingly, when MacStiofain surrendered his hunger strike of 1972, disgracing the IRA, he too came to be referred to in Republican publications as 'John Stephenson'.[8] A similar fate had visited Erskine Childers, the Anglo-Irish author of *Riddle of the Sands* (1903), who first betrayed England by siding with Ireland in the War of Independence, and then betrayed the Irish Free State by siding with the Republicans in the Civil War – an Englishman executed by a Free State firing squad.

It may seem flippant to put Mick McCarthy in the same bracket as Childers and MacStiofain, but McCarthy, like so many Hiberno-English footballers, has had the tag of 'Plastic Paddy' affixed to him for years. It doesn't help, of course, that McCarthy is a perfect caricature of a Yorkshireman: a wry, straight-talking northerner given to semi-serious, semi-self-mocking aphorisms, a man who says what he likes and likes what he says: 'We just have to crush Chelsea next week now we're on a roll' uttered the Sunderland manager in January 2006, as the side was free-falling its way to the Championship. 'You can't buy talent like that. And even if you could, it would cost you a lot of money', he has said of Robbie Keane; in response to Sunderland beating Middlesbrough in September 2005, their first Premiership victory since December 2002, he declared: 'It wasn't a monkey on my back, it was Planet of the Apes.'[9] While there are those who cast aspersions on the 'Irishness' of second-generation Irish players, it is fitting that so many descendents of emigrants have succeeded for Ireland, in that 'Ireland' should perhaps best be viewed not as a country but as a nation that, through its diaspora, extends beyond national boundaries. Some of us over here in England like to feel we are Irish; some like to feel we are English; others choose, on grounds of expediency, to become technically Irish. What is not in dispute is the achievements made by some of those who, whatever their justification, have put on a green shirt at international level and made their mark with English clubs.

SHAY BRENNAN

Shay Brennan appears on a chat show with Julio Iglesias. Presenter Anne Diamond
asks the Spaniard the meaning of the world 'mañana'.
'It means maybe the job will be done tomorrow, maybe the next day,
maybe the day after that. Perhaps next week, next month. Who cares?'
Diamond turns to Brennan to ask him if the Irish have an equivalent to 'mañana'.
'No. In Ireland we don't have a word to describe that degree of
urgency.'[10]

Shay Brennan, a Manchester lad born to a mother from Carlow, was
always proud of his Irish roots, and like John Carey, also of Manchester
United, was a versatile footballer: he usually played at right full-back but
was able, when necessity demanded, to move to the forefront of the
attack. He joined United at an early age, turning professional with the
club in April 1955, and went on to become the first 'non-Irishman' to play
for Ireland in 1965, after FIFA decided at a congress meeting in Tokyo
the previous year that players could qualify for the country of their ancestry.

The Hiberno-Englishman's debut for United came with the team's
most difficult fixture ever, the FA Cup tie against Sheffield Wednesday,
played just thirteen days after the Munich Disaster. In an atmosphere
charged with emotion, Brennan, playing on the right wing, scored twice
to secure an unhappy 3–1 win. He won the league with United in 1965
and 1967, and the European Cup in 1968, and was much loved by his
team-mates for his happy demeanour and laid-back disposition, and especially his mickey-taking.

Nobby Stiles, a life-long friend of Brennan's, remembers Shay's run-
ins with Matt Busby's assistant, Jimmy Murphy, a 'nuts and bolts man. He
certainly wanted a bolted defence, and down the years he used to scream
at my friend Shay Brennan when he regularly ignored instructions to boot
the ball into the stand and give his defensive colleagues time to re-group
when the pressure was on. Shay knew Jimmy hated the way he would just
knock it over the touchline rather than follow the order to put it in the
"f—king sixty-sixth row of the stand" but he kept doing it. It was a little

quirk in Shay's nature, and it made him one of the few players ever to risk the anger of Jimmy Murphy.'[11]

On Brennan's death, from heart failure on 9 June 2000, at the age of sixty-three, Wilf McGuinness reflected that everyone at United regarded him as the 'Dean Martin' of football because 'he was so laid back, he never had to push himself. . . . He was the most popular player at Old Trafford.'[12]

TERRY MANCINI

It was a great honour to be selected and I lined up on the side of the pitch, desperate to get playing. All the pre-match ceremony seemed to go on forever, and then the music started playing and it went on and on, and I turned to Don Givens and said, 'For f—k's sake, their national anthem goes on a bit', and he said, 'That's ours, Terry.' I didn't have a clue!

TERRY MANCINI, DALYMOUNT PARK, 1973[13]

Terry Mancini's failure to tell the difference between the Polish national anthem and 'The Soldiers' Song' has become the stuff of folklore. Such is the degree to which it has been repeated in bar saloons, with different versions of which country's anthem he was confusing the Irish anthem with – Romanian, Hungarian, Czech; take your pick – that many now take the story to be a tall tale. For your punter in an East End boozer in London, the anecdote supports the notion that the Irish football authorities are so desperate to recruit talent that they will resort to recruiting a second-rate Anglo-Italian boy; for an Irishman propping up a bar in Dublin, the yarn confirms what many Irishmen think of Englishmen in general and Cockneys in particular: that they are an ignorant, philistine lot.

Mancini did actually utter those words, and while his surname came through his mother's family, he had an Irish father, who died when Mancini was only seven, and he only realised he could represent his paternal homeland after a chance conversation with fellow QPR player Don Givens. Although his debut is remembered for his brief conversation with Givens, the part he played in beating the Poles 1–0 is less well recalled. The result was a particular source for celebration in that Poland only a few days earlier had humbled England, their 1–1 draw at Wembley denying England a place in the 1974 World Cup finals.

The name of the Irishman Mancini is repeated in reference to another, lesser-known but even more curious occurrence. During the end of QPR's 1972–73 Second Division promotion campaign, the prankster Mancini, otherwise bald-headed, ran out for the last game of the season at Loftus Road sporting one of his wife's wigs. Those in attendance were bemused – though not alarmed, this being the early 1970s – as to the identity of this stranger, before he theatrically removed the hairpiece – to the delight of the fans. Mancini caused an even bigger stir when, seeking a transfer, Rangers put a £15,000 price tag on his head. When Arsenal, somewhat surprisingly, came in with an offer, QPR chairman Jim Gregory upped the asking price to £45,000. Mancini, unhappy at a gesture that had made a possible move more difficult, exacted revenge by once more making a spectacle of himself at Loftus Road: 'As I walked off the pitch, I looked up into the South Africa Road Stand and Jim Gregory is sitting there with his arms over the railings looking down at me. So I turned around, dropped my shorts and wiggled my arse at him. Unfortunately, the BBC cameras were there, and consequently Jimmy Hill had me on *Match of the Day*, asking me why I had done it.'[14]

Mancini was fined £150 and banned for two games, but his actions that day have since been the inspiration for high art. The poet Pete Goulding composed the tribute 'Terry Mancini's Arse':

> What on earth were his thoughts
> When he bent down and dropped his shorts?
> Did this Cockney centre-back
> Decide to do it for the crack?
> Though many there did darkly speak
> Of balding Terry's massive cheek.

JASON MCATEER

'One hundred and eighty!'

JASON MCATEER, SEEKING TO CATCH JIMMY WHITE'S ATTENTION
AT A DUBLIN NIGHTCLUB[15]

Scouser Jason McAteer isn't known as 'Trigger' for nothing: he is also the man who, it is said, wanted a takeaway pizza cut into four, not eight, slices, because he hadn't the appetite for eight.[16] But McAteer's public persona as a loveable simpleton belies his football acumen, as displayed at Bolton, Liverpool, Blackburn and Sunderland, and for Ireland. His limitless enthusiasm when playing for the Republic made him a crowd favourite at Lansdowne Road, particularly following his goal against Holland, which took Ireland to the 2002 World Cup finals.

McAteer is often cherished as a childlike cheeky-chappy, fond of practical jokes – such as, in February 2002, unloading a tray of water on Niall Quinn in a television interview, before stripping down to his underpants – but this disguises his characteristic Liverpudlian thick hide. He is not fussed by Roy Keane's reproaches: 'I've got a lot of respect for Roy, although he's a miserable bastard – and you can write that.'[17] It also masks his serious side: with Ireland, he was effective either in a central or a wide position, and after Sunderland he has gone on to manage Tranmere.

KEVIN SHEEDY

'Ole, ole, Sheedy saves the day'

T-SHIRT, 1990

Kevin Sheedy, of Everton and Ireland, was born in Buith Wells, Wales, and is still held in regard for the goal he scored against England in Italia 90 to seal Ireland's 1–1 draw with the old enemy. Born in 1959, the left-winger was not renowned for his pace but, like his adopted Merseysider Ronnie Whelan, he could be devastating with his passing, and like Staunton, also on the other side of the city of Liverpool, he was a master of set-pieces.

As his team-mate with the Blues, Andy Gray, notes: 'The two wingers Kevin Sheedy and Trevor Steven were superb. You'd struggle to name a better pairing. They both had skill on the ball and great delivery. Long before Beckham came along, Sheeds was a master of direct free-kicks. Between them in the Championship season they scored thirty goals. An unbelievable record.'[18]

'Sheeds' started his career with Hereford United, just across the Welsh border, and had a brief spell with Liverpool, making two League appearances for them before moving on to join the Toffees for £100,000 in 1982. He made 327 appearances as a midfielder, netting ninety-seven times, and was part of the Everton outfit that took the FA Cup in 1984, the League in 1985 and 1987 and the European Cup Winners' Cup in 1985. The later part of his time at Goodison Park was marred by recurrent injury, and in 1992 he was given a free transfer, joining Newcastle and then Blackpool.

MARK LAWRENSON

'Ireland will give 99 percent, everything they've got.'

MARK LAWRENSON[19]

As one of Liverpool's victorious, moustachioed team of the 1980s, Mark Lawrenson is known to today's generation of football fans as BBC's lugubrious talking head: that one on the telly on Saturday lunchtimes with hangdog features, who seems always to pronounce solemnly on x team's promising future, or prognosticates y team's impending disaster, a man who, even when attempting to heap praise on a team, does so in a deflated, dispirited and almost exasperated manner.

Lawrenson's sepulchral comportment as a pundit is a far cry from Lawrenson the player for Liverpool: a tall, strong dynamo on the park who could outpace most opposing forwards, and a ready challenger in the air – or, in the words of an official guide to Liverpool's greatest players, the 'finest and cleanest recovery tackler in the country, stretching out a long, willowy leg to reclaim the ball from the attacker's toe before calmly rising to touch the ball on to Hansen or bring it away from the danger zone himself.'[20]

The Preston man, whose mother was born in Ireland, added beauty to brawn: he was a neat and elegant central defender who, owing to his versatility was employed for his mother's country as a midfielder by Giles, Hand and Charlton. At Liverpool, he won nine major medals, including the 1984 European Cup, and was ever-present in the Reds' 1985–86 double success.

JOHN ALDRIDGE

John Aldridge or Tony Cascarino were as Irish as the Tower of London, but it was possible for our imaginations to accept them as Irishmen-of-convenience, in a way which wouldn't really be possible with a Russian or a German.

KEVIN MYERS

Scouser John Aldridge, an Ian Rush replacement and facial impersonator, played for Oxford United, Liverpool, Real Sociedad and Tranmere, and on sixty-nine occasions for Ireland. For the Republic, he is probably most fondly remembered for his touchline tantrum in the World Cup finals of 1994, when officials procrastinated as he sought to come on to replace Tommy Coyne with Ireland trailing 2–0 to Mexico. The officials were duly met with a ripe riposte: they had explained to them in fluent Anglo-Saxon why he should be permitted on to the field .

His responsibility, to replace an outgoing Ian Rush in the 1987–88 season, might have inspired terror in a lesser man, but he scored twenty-six goals that season to bring Liverpool – who had ended the previous campaign with nothing – the League trophy, by a handsome nine-point margin.

ANDY TOWNSEND

'South London.'

ANDY TOWNSEND, ON BBC's *QUESTION OF SPORT*,
AFTER BEING ASKED WHICH PART OF IRELAND HE CAME FROM

Chelsea and Ireland's combative and industrious midfielder Andy Townsend, who was born in Maidstone in Kent, was, like McGrath and Staunton, another Irish international who came into his element at Aston Villa. Townsend was outstanding in Villa's 1994 League Cup win over Manchester United, and went on to captain the Republic during the 1994 World Cup.

Townsend – who is somewhat confusingly named, as he actually looks and sounds like Roger Daltry, not The Who's chief axeman – has since carved out a niche for himself as a pundit on ITV, where his repertoire of phrases and interjections has become legendary: 'Let me tell you . . . I tell you what, Gabby . . . The goalkeeper had absolutely no chance whatsoever . . . Not a prayer . . . Nonetheless, nonetheless . . . Full marks to . . . I've got to say . . . Vitally important . . . That cross was delivered, literally, on a plate.'

Townsend has also been the victim of threats from the far right in Britain. In May 1999, the neo-Nazi group Combat 18 made telephone calls to the FAI, advising Roy Keane, Denis Irwin, Andy Townsend and Tony Cascarino to 'Go home to the Irish bogs'[21] – proving once again that what fascists lack in intelligence they make up for in ignorance.

TONY CASCARINO

How can a man called Tony Cascarino play football for the Republic of Ireland? Good question. Ask the punters at Stamford Bridge and they'll say, 'Well, 'e wasn't going to play for Italy, now, was he?'

TONY CASCARINO, 2001[22]

Tony Cascarino is perhaps Ireland's most famous non-Irish Irishman, a Kentish hairdresser with an Italian name. The Millwall and Chelsea footballer's mother was called Theresa O'Malley, the youngest of four daughters born to Agnes and Michael Joseph O'Malley of Westport, who had emigrated to London.

Young Tony had always felt closer to his mother's side of the family than to his father's. 'I grew up with a strong sense of "Irishness",' he recalls, but he nonetheless followed the England football team, even going to Spain in 1982 to cheer the lads on. 'I'd supported England as a boy; England was my team, the land of my birth.'[23] It was only by accident that he realised that he could realise an ambition to appear on the international stage: in 1985, while Cascarino was at Gillingham, he talked to Seamus McDonagh, the Republic's No 1, on loan from Notts County, about the matter. McDonagh said that he would speak to Eoin Hand about the matter; only weeks later, Cascarino was invited to come over to play in an Irish testimonial game for Jimmy Holmes against a Glenn Hoddle selection at Dalymount. It was Cascarino's first-ever visit to the Emerald Isle, and his performance that day led to him being named in the squad for the next Ireland World Cup qualifier game, against Switzerland. It was the first of eighty-eight appearances for 'his' country.

Cascarino, like many other Irish internationals, had travelled with a British passport – even to Argentina after 1982 – but when FIFA changed the rules in 1996, requiring players to hold passports of the country foe which they played, it emerged that Cascarino wasn't even eligible for an Irish passport. He was told by his mother that Michael O'Malley was not his biological grandfather; thus Cascarino had not a drop of Irish blood in him.

*

Who put the ball in the England net? I did.

RAY HOUGHTON, ON RETURNING TO DUBLIN IN 1988

Alas, there's no room left to mention Ray Houghton, because he's Scottish, and because he *did that thing*.

8

CHANGED UTTERLY?

More people know where Ireland is today than ever before.

JACK CHARLTON, AFTER EURO 88

So what does it all mean? What is the significance of the manner in which Ireland has taken soccer to its bosom? There are many ways of interpretating this phenomenon, both positive and negative. On a sporting level, the achievements of Ireland's footballers in England – from Carey to Keane – is something Irish soccer aficionados should herald purely from a sporting point of view. On a cultural and patriotic level, it is also a source of celebration for those who perceive these sportsmen's feats as being comparable to Yeats's and Joyce's subversive achievements – taking on an English medium and bettering their former masters at it. Yet it is also important to reflect that this story is paradoxically, and simultaneously, one to lament.

The fact that so many young men were forced to flee Ireland to emigrate to England in the 1950s and 1960s, owing to the establishment's cultural insularity and economic mismanagement, is well documented, as is the fact that the migrants often ended up on the lower rungs of English society. I still see many of these old men in the pubs of west London: they still miss the auld country, but at the same time resent with equal feeling the men who forced them to leave it. And the footballers who did so, pushed even harder by a GAA that lost some of its best talents to soccer because of its unwillingness to permit members also to enjoy this foreign sport, are among this number.

That fact is that (we can say this, admittedly, with the benefit of hindsight) soccer was never a threat to Gaelic games: in fact, it could have worked to their benefit. During the 1990s – when television audiences for soccer matches were among the highest for any sports fixture (witness the 1.7 million who watched Ireland v. Norway in 1994, the 1.5 million for Ireland v. England in 1990, and the 1.3 million for Ireland v. England in 1991) soccer truly became a national sport. As Eoghan Corry has noted of these years: 'The penetration of soccer into people's lives was on a par with Uruguary, traditionally the most soccer-mad country per head of population in the world.'[1] But during that time, interest in Gaelic games has not withered but increased. It is not just the sheer number of people who now follow games, or the quadrupling of media coverage of the GAA since 1991,[2] but the way in which Gaelic is now perceived. Gaelic games have lost much of the stigma they once held, and are no longer caricatured by liberal middle-class Ireland and the Dublin 4 set as pursuits for culchies, crypto-republicans or fanatical Church-goers.

In *GAA, The Glory Years of Hurling and Football* (2005), Ronnie Bellew pointed out that the fact that *Hot Press* can devote a radio advert to its coverage of Gaelic games in July 2004 signifies a substantial cultural shift in the country. 'Fifteen years ago,' writes Bellew, 'the notion of *Hot Press* devoting its front cover to the championship and hiring the voice of the GAA to promote the magazine would have been as unthinkable as Bono being asked to sit in as the expert analyst for the All-Ireland hurling final commentary. In the 1980s and the early 1990s, *Hot Press* – the unofficial voice of alternative Ireland – was usually fairly hostile towards the GAA. Its sports columnists delighted in humorously gratuitous attacks on 'bogball' (Gaelic football) and 'stickfighting' (hurling). . . . 'Bogball' and 'stick-fighting' weren't just unfashionable; they were, in the eyes of the *Hot Press* commentators and others, bound up with religious repression, gombeen politics, straight-laced Gaelgeoirs, and the plain people of Ireland who ate their dinners in the middle of the day.'[3]

In a way, the GAA's fear that soccer would usurp Gaelic football and hurling mirrored the concerns of those who predicted in the 1920s that cinema would be the death knell for theatre, and for those who prophesied in the 1950s that television would see the end of cinema. These new mediums, far from killing off their predecessor, actually aroused in the public consciousness a further appetite for storytelling. Likewise, the internet has not killed off books but encouraged a thirst for learning, as well as making it – via Amazon and other online booksellers – much easier to get hold of books.

Similarly, too, soccer's ascent in Ireland has not posed a fatal threat to Gaelic but has stimulated the appetite for competitive team sports; people have become more accustomed to reading about, hearing about, and watching on television Ireland's sporting adventures, which, since the Charlton years, have become national occasions. Prior to Euro 88 or Italia 90, those who shunned Gaelic and had the opportunity to see two or three Five Nations rugby games at Lansdowne Road a year never realised the dramatic allure that sport had: theatre without a script. The nation, and non-sporting types, became enthralled by the country's feats on the field, and all the emotions that are manifest in football: the tragedy and delight, the hubris and personal conflict, and the shattered – and realised – dreams.

Certainly, the joy the Irish now derive from football, and the joy Irish footballers have given English spectators, is to be celebrated. But England's gain has been Ireland's loss not merely on account of the number of citizens it haemorrhaged from the 1940s to the 1980s, but also in terms of the effect it has had on the football leagues of Ireland themselves. Soccer players who want to make it will go to England to do so, attracted in the last fifty years by the high wages, the large crowds, the prestige and the glamour. Paddy Coad remains the only Irish player of note who never left the country. In contrast to the English League's glory days of the 1960s and 1970s, and its renaissance since the early 1990s, the Eircom League and Irish League have remained in perpetual ill-health, attendances in the south often struggling to reach four figures, with such neglected stadiums as Tolka Park and Richmond Park standing as a visible embodiment of the parlous state of domestic league football. The Bosman ruling has ensured that this flight of Irish talent will continue, with English clubs continuing to poach the cream of Irish soccer from the country's domestic sides. To compound this – and indeed as a result of it – instead of supporting their local team, many Irish people prefer to follow the English and Scottish League teams, making fortnightly pilgrimages to Anfield, Old Trafford or Parkhead.

I recall a bizarre incident in 2002 on a ferry from Holyhead to Dublin Port, when, on a Saturday evening, Irish fans of Liverpool and Manchester United happened to be travelling back on the same ship. They took up rival camps in the bar, and after having consumed enough alcohol, began exchanging derogatory chants: 'In your Liverpool slums/

In your Liverpool slums/ You look in the dustbin for something to eat/ You find a dead cat and you think it's a treat/ In your Liverpool slums'; 'Who the f—k are Man United', etc. Here were two sets of Irish people insulting each other in the name of protecting the pride of two English teams, making derogatory references to places where none of them had ever lived: truly football-inspired aggression for a postmodern age.

And just as England has taken Ireland's best, it has given it its worst, another one of its famous gifts to the world: football hooliganism and loutishness. I may have adopted one of the rougher sides to support in Ireland, Shamrock Rovers, but it was disheartening, having been to half a dozen games, to see many of their fans having adopted the uniform, and all the worst mannerisms, of their English counterparts: the Burberry caps, the threatening wanker gestures, the mafioso-esque single finger drawn across the throat, the borrowed chants.

One might say that this is all part of the rough and tumble of footballing banter, but such hostility can boil over. In September 2003, the Dublin edition of the *Sunday Times* reported numerous arrests by Gardaí relating to football violence, mainly involving fans of Shamrock Rovers, Bohemians and St Pats, along with those from Dundalk and Cork City. Shamrock Rovers were expelled from Richmond Park following their supporters' behaviour on one occasion, and there was an attack on Bohs supporters on 1 September.[4] This summer, Rovers and Bohs fans clashed again in a 'mini riot' in Middle Gardiner Street, where a contingent of thirty Shamrock Rovers fans threw bricks, bottles, batons and even a beer keg at their rivals.[5]

It could also be argued that the support lent to the likes of Man United, Liverpool and Chelsea, whose replica kits can be seen throughout the island, is symptomatic of a wider Anglicisation of Irish society. The failure to keep Ireland free of foreign games mirrors the failure to re-Gaelicise the country. Ireland is culturally more similar to England than it was in 1922. Just as the Irish have taken up the English game, they no longer read the *Irish Press*, but the *Sun* and the *Mirror*; Quinnsworth has become Tesco Ireland; Walkers crisps rival Tayto; pharmaceuticals now come from Boots, and music from Virgin and HMV; entertainment comes in the form of Coronation Street and EastEnders — and of course live soccer from Sky.

But who's to say that this is not a two-way street. In England today one of the principal airline carriers, bearing a harp on its tail-fin, is

Michael O'Leary's Ryanair; Bulmers has had spectacular success this year with rocketing sales of its cider (known in Britain as Magners); Dara O Briain, Patrick Kielty and Graham Norton continue to prosper for the same reason that Dave Allen, Frank Carson and Terry Wogan did before them, by making English people laugh with a quintessentially Irish form of humour; Tony O'Reilly owns daily newspapers; in May, Setanta broke Sky's monopoly of the Premier League's live coverage; and Sunderland football club is owned by an Irishman and its team run by another one.

Many contend that Ireland's embrace of soccer signals the coming to modernity of a country that no longer wants to dance at the crossroads. This is partly true, but the alarm over the Nice Treaty being rejected, or Dana's election to the European Parliament in 1999 on a platform of what might be called traditional Irish family values, or the fact that many foreign immigrants are often the subject of abuse or resentment, seems to indicate that many want their 'old country' back.

Yet in the end, the fact that the Irish learnt to play and beat the English at their own game does not prove that they have attained some form of revenge on the English, or that, by adopting the English game and English ways, they have succumbed to the overbearing Anglicisation that the Gaelic League always resisted, or that Ireland has become a 'modern' country. Most of all, it shows that Ireland has just become a normal country, whose people, like the English, the Italians, the Argentinians, and people elsewhere around the world, see football as a metaphor for life, with each important international victory an occasion for national celebrations and a sense of togetherness, and each vital defeat a source of introspection and recriminations, with such setbacks deemed to stand for the country's woes and its supposed fall from a halcyon age.

The difference is that, whereas in Euro 88 Ireland was delighted with heroic failure, Ireland today wants more. Like England, or any other country that takes pride in itself, it wants to be the best. That's what Jackie Carey wanted, what George Best wanted, what Roy Keane sought, what so many Irishmen and women sought. So next time Eamon Dunphy has one of his turns on television, just remember, he'll be having a tantrum for precisely the right reason.

BIBLIOGRAPHY

Barrett, Norman, *The Daily Telegraph Football Chronicle*, 3rd edition, Carlton Books, Dubai (1999)

Bellew, Ronnie, *GAA, The Glory Years of Hurling and Football*, Hodder Headline Ireland, Dublin (2005)

Bishop, Patrick and Eamonn Mallie, *The Provisional IRA*, Corgi, London (1996)

Böll, Heinrich, *Irish Journal* (1957) [*Irisches Tagebuch*, trans. Leila Vennewitz, Secker & Warburg, London 1983]

Bremner, Jack, *Shit Ground No Fans, It's by far the greatest football songbook the world has ever seen*, Bantam Press, London (2004)

Butler, Bryan, *The Official Illustrated History of the FA Cup*, Headline, London (1996)

Cate, Curtis, *Friedrich Nietzsche*, Random House, London (2002)

Charlton, Jack, with Peter Byrne, *Jack Charlton, The Autobiography*, Partridge, London (1996)

Clough, Brian with John Sadler, *Cloughie, Walking on Water, My Life*, Headline Book Publishing (2003)

Crick, Michael, *The Boss, The Many Sides of Alex Ferguson*, Simon & Schuster, London (2002)

Corry, Eoghan, *The Nation Holds Its Breath, Great Irish Soccer Quotations*, Hodder Headline Ireland, Dublin (2006)

Doherty, Richard, *Irish Men and Women in the Second World War*, Four Courts Press, Dublin (1999)

Dunphy, Eamon, *Only a Game? The Diary of a Professional Footballer* (2nd edition), Penguin, London (1986)

Foster, Stephen, *The Book of Lists: Football*, Canongate, Edinburgh (2006)

Glanville, Brian, *Football Memories,* Virgin, London (1999)

Gray, Andy, *Gray Matters,* Macmillan, London (2004)

Greaves, Jimmy, with Les Scott, *Greavsie, The Autobiography,* Time Warner Books, London (2003)

Hamilton, Ian (ed), *The Faber Book of Soccer,* Faber and Faber, London (1992)

Hildred, Stafford and Tim Ewbank, *Keano, Portrait of a Hero,* John Blake Publishing, London (2004)

Holt, Nick and Guy Lloyd, *Total Football,* Flame Tree Publishing, London (2005)

────── *Total British Football,* Flame Tree Publishing, London (2006)

Hornby, Nick, *Fever Pitch,* Victor Gollancz, London (1992)

────── (ed), *My Favourite Year, A Collection of New Football Writing,* H. F. G. Witherby, London (1993): 'Republic Is a Beautiful Word, Republic of Ireland 1990' by Roddy Doyle

Houlihan, Con, *More Than a Game: Selected Sporting Essays,* Liberties Press, Dublin (2003)

Joannou, Paul, *The Black 'n' White Alphabet, A Complete Who's Who of Newcastle United FC,* Polar Print Group Ltd, Leicester (1996)

────── *United, The First 100 Years . . . and More, The Official History of Newcastle United FC, 1882 to 2000,* 3rd edition, Polar Print Group Ltd, Leicester (2000)

Keane, Colm, *Ireland's Soccer Top 20,* Mainstream Publishing, Edinburgh (2004)

Keane, Roy with Eamon Dunphy, *Keane, The Autobiography,* Michael Joseph, London (2002)

Kerrigan, Gene, *Never Make a Promise You Can't Break, How to Succeed in Irish Politics,* Gill & Macmillan, Dublin (2002)

Kimmage, Paul, *Full Time, The Secret Life of Tony Cascarino,* Scribner/Townhouse Dublin (2001)

Law, Denis with Bob Harris, *The King,* Bantam Press, London (2003)

L'Estrange, Jonathan, *The Big Book of More Sports Insults,* Weidenfeld & Nicolson, London (2005)

McColl, Graham, *Aston Villa 1874–1998,* Hamlyn, London (1998)

Marples, Morris, *A History of Football,* Secker & Warburg, London (1954)

Moore, Chris, *United Irishmen, Manchester United's Irish Connection,* Mainstream Publishing, Edinburgh (1999)

225

Motson, John, OBE, *Motson's FA Cup Odyssey, The World's Greatest Knockout Competition,* Robson Books, London (2005)

Nawrat, Chris and Steve Hutchings, *The Sunday Times Illustrated History of Football,* Hamlyn, London (1994)

Nietzsche, Friedrich, *The Gay Science* (1887) (trans. Wlater Kaufmann) Random House, New York (1974)

Quinn, Niall, *The Autobiography,* Headline, London (2002)

Ring, Jim, *Erskine Childers,* John Murray publishers, London (1996)

Simpson, Paul, Alan Oliver and Mikey Carr, *Newcastle United, The Top 11 of Everything Toon,* Rough Guides, London (2005)

Soar, Phil and Martin Tyler, *Arsenal 1886–1998,* Reed Consumer Books Ltd, London (1998)

Soar, Phil, *Tottenham Hotspur, The Official Illustrated History 1882–1995,* Hamlyn, London (1995)

Sweeney, Eamonn, *There's Only One Red Army,* New Island Books, Dublin (1997)

Tibballs, Geoff, *Crap Teams,* Michael O'Mara Books, London (2005)

Tomlinson, Ricky, *Football My Arse!* Time Warner Books, London (2006)

Walmsley, David, *Liverpool's Greatest Players . . . The Official Guide,* Headline, London (1997)

Weight, Richard, *Patriots, National Identity in Britain 1940–2000,* Macmillan, London (2002)

West, Ed, *Don't Mention the World Cup,* Summersdale, Chichester (2006)

West, Patrick, 'The Irish in Manchester, 1844–60: A Cultural Analysis', unpublished MA thesis, Manchester (1997)

White, Jim and Andy Mitten, *Manchester United, The Top 11 of Everything Red,* Rough Guides, London (2005)

Winner, David, *Those Feet, An Intimate History of English Football,* Bloomsbury, London (2006)

NOTES

D Tel	Daily Telegraph
E News	Evening News
I Ind	Irish Independent
I Post	Irish Post
I S Mirror	Irish Sunday Mirror
L Eve Standard	London Evening Standard
S Independent	Sunday Independent
S Tribune	Sunday Tribune
S World	Sunday World
Times	The Times (of London)

NOTES TO PROLOGUE, PP11–14

1 *S Tribune* 1/12/02

NOTES TO CHAPTER 1: PP17–20

1 *A History of Football,* Morris Marples, Secker & Warburg, London (1954), 25
2 Marples 1954, 25, 51
3 *English History 1914–1945,* cited in the *Observer* 27/8/06
4 Houlihan, 2003, 14
5 Quoted in the *Times* 23/8/06
Notes to Chapter 2: ppxx–xx
1 Bellew 2005, 321
2 Corry 2006, 124, 250
3 Corry 2006, 250–51
4 Joannou 2000, 159
5 Doherty 1999, 25
6 Weight 2002, 145
7 Houlihan 2003, 69
8 Letter from John Gleeson of Rercross, County Tipperary, to the *I Independent* 10/5/06
9 David Quinn, 25/8/06

NOTES TO CHAPTER 3: PP27–69

1 *S Independent* 19/3/06
2 ibid.

[3] McColl 1998, 57

[4] *S Independent* 19/3/06

[5] *Guardian* 29/5/99

[6] ibid.

[7] ibid.

[8] *S Independent* 19/3/06

[9] *Guardian* 29/5/99

[10] Keane 2004, 18

[11] *S Tribune* 22/2/04

[12] *I Times* 21/2/04

[13] Brack in Hornby (ed.) 1993, 164–65

[14] *Sunderland Echo* 30/3/04

[15] *Northern Echo* 12/5/97

[16] *Irish S Mirror* 25/6/06

[17] Corry 2006, 310

[18] Newsquest Media Group Newspapers 21/9/04

[19] Cited in Winner 2006, 34

[20] *Guardian* 29/4/05

[21] Tomlinson w Giller 2005, 11

[22] Charlton 1996, 115

[23] *Observer* 26/2/84

[24] Keane 2004, 41

[25] Clough w Sadler 2003, 222

[26] *Guardian* 29/4/05

[27] Keane 2004, 45

[28] *Irish Mirror* 1/2/03

[29] *Guardian* 29/4/05

[30] ibid.

[31] Cited in Winner 2006, 22–23

[32] Interview on *qprnet.com* 5/7/04

[33] ibid.

[34] *S Times* (Dublin edition) 31/8/03

[35] Keane 2004, 86

[36] ibid.

[37] Quoted in Corry 2006, 145

[38] Montgomery 2003, 60

[39] Clough 2003, 251

[40] ibid. 245–46

[41] ibid. 245–48
[42] ibid. 255
[43] BBC One, 9/6/06
[44] *Observer* 16/6/02
[45] Keane 2004, 191
[46] Eddie Kelly, *Shoot* December 2003
[47] Keane 2004, 187
[48] *Guardian* 22/4/02
[49] *Shoot* December 2003
[50] See, for instance, http://nominated.homestead.com/BLUESBROTHERS.HTML
[51] http://home.skysports.com/list
[52] *Observer* 16/6/02
[53] Cited in Corry 2006, 31
[54] *Irish Post* 27/5/06
[55] www.leedsfans.org.uk/leeds/players/729.html, logged 30/8/06
[56] *Guardian* 12/11/99
[57] Cited in Holt & Lloyd 2006, 424

NOTES TO CHAPTER 4: PP70–122

[1] Cited in West, P., 1997, 52
[2] *Times* 01/6/06
[3] L *Independent* 24/8/95
[3] *Daily Dispatch* 12/2/49
[4] *Sporting Chronicle* 31/12/49
[5] ibid. 8/6/57
[6] Corry 2006, 297
[7] D *Mail* 15/4/61
[8] Tomlinson 2006, 104
[9] *Times* 3/12/68
[10] *Independent* 24/8/95
[11] S *Times* 2/1/05
[12] I *Times* 31/1/98
[13] *Mirror* 7/2/98
[14] I *Times* 31/1/98
[15] S *Tribune* 1/12/02
[16] I *Times* 31/1/98
[17] Cited in Keane 2004, 30
[18] D *Tel* 9/9/05
[19] Stiles w Lawton 2003, 131

[20] *Guardian* 9/9/05

[21] ibid.

[22] *D Tel* 9/9/06

[23] ibid.

[24] Keane 2004, 36

[25] Sean Ryan, *S Independent* 11/9/05

[26] Cited in Moore 1999, 63

[27] Stiles w Lawton 2003, 83

[28] Keane 2004, 66

[29] Adapted from Keane 2004, 66

[30] Moore 1999, 63

[31] ibid., 70

[32] ibid., 64–5

[33] ibid., 75

[34] Cited in Moore 1999, 72

[35] Law w Harris 2003, 212

[36] *S Times* 4/1/06

[36a] *Sunday Times* 4/1/06

[37] ibid.

[38] ibid., 4/1/06

[39] ibid., 4/1/06

[40] Nawrat & Hutchings 1994, 187

[41] Corry 2006, 237

[42] E West 2006, 23

[43] Moore 1999, 81

[44] ibid., 83

[45] ibid., 92

[46] White & Mitten 2005, 73–74

[47] Crick 2002, 281

[48] *www.fai.ie* logged 11/5/06

[49] Quinn 2002, 85

[50] *Ooh Aah Paul McGrath,* Paul McGrath, Mainstream, 1994, cited in Moore 1999, 101

[51] McColl 1998, 128

[52] *S Independent* 4/2/01

[53] Moore 1999, 100

[54] *S Independent* 11/2/01

[55] Keane 2004, 157

[56] ibid., 158

[57] Cited in *S Independent* 4/2/01

[58] *S Independent* 11/2/01

[59] White & Mitten 2005, 54–55

[60] McGrath 1994, 128.

[61] Cited in Keane 2004, 161

[62] McColl 1998, 150

[63] *S Independent* 18/2/01

[64] *Mirror* 18/4/88

[65] Cited in Keane 2004, 163

[66] *I Independent* 31/1/04

[67] The *People* 18/1/04

[68] *I Independent* 31/1/04

[69] The *People* 18/1/04

[70] Keane w Dunphy 2002, 87

[71] Cited in Corry 2006, 320

[72] Moore 1999, 51

[73] *http://news.bbc.co.uk* 15/8/01

[74] *D Tel* 27/5/99

[75] *www.news.bbc.co.uk* 22/8/01

[76] *www.news.bbc.co.uk* 15/5/04

[77] Moore 1999, 55

[78] *www.gaa.ie* 28/11/04

[79] *www.news.bbc.co.uk* 16/8/00

[80] *The Gay Science* (1882), trans. 1974, 228, original italics

[81] Corry 2006, 175

[82] ibid. 175–76

[83] Keane w Dunphy 2002, 20

[84] Hildred and Ewbank 2004, 251

[85] ibid., 28

[86] ibid., 27

[87] Clough w Sadler 2003, 310, 314

[88] Hildred and Ewbank 2004, 43, 90

[89] ibid., 84-85

[90] ibid., 95

[91] Moore 1999, 125

[92] *D Tel* 24/8/06

[93] Moore 1999, 136

[94] *D Tel* 24/8/06

[95] Keane w Dunphy 2004, 231
[96] *S Telegraph* 30/6/06
[97] Cited in Corry 2006, 177
[98] Clough w Sadler 2003, 309
[99] Barrett 1999, 26
[100] *Guardian* 24/04/03
[101] ibid. 6/5/03
[102] Hildred and Ewbank 2004, 210, 55
[103] Moore 1999, 123
[104] Moore 1999, 131
[105] Corry 2006, 323
[106] Quinn 2002, 151
[107] *Times* 10/8/06

NOTES TO CHAPTER 5: PP123–156

[1] Houlihan 2003, 50
[2] Quoted in Corry 2006, 218
[3] ibid. 93
[4] *D Tel* 19/10/01
[5] ibid.
[6] ibid.
[7] ibid.
[8] ibid.
[9] *I Post* 6/5/06
[10] *S World* 30/6/06
[11] *I Post* 6/5/06
[12] *D Mail* 7/5/85
[13] *L Times* 21/9/83
[14] *D Mail* 7/5/85
[15] *Guardian* 15/4/03
[16] Keane 2004, 101–2
[17] *L Independent* 4/12/86
[18] Holt & Lloyd 2006, 350
[19] *D Tel* 19/4/05
[20] *Guardian* 20/5/05
[21] ibid.
[22] *D Tel* 19/4/05
[23] *Observer* 22/1/78
[24] *D Mirror* 9/12/78

[25] Houlihan 2003, 51
[26] *Observer* 17/2/80
[27] ibid.
[28] Keane 2004, 112
[29] *D Mirror* 9/12/78
[30] Hornby 1992, 120–2
[31] Motson 2005, 59
[32] *Observer* 22/1/78
[33] Moore 1999, 162
[34] Cascarino w Kimmage 2001, 80
[34] Keane 2004, 92
[36] Moore 1999, 158
[37] ibid., 156
[38] ibid., 159
[39] Corry 2006, 147, 211, 260
[40] Keane 2004, 150–1
[41] *When Saturday Comes* Sep 06
[42] In Rafferty (ed.) 1997, 161
[43] *www.fai.ie* logged 11/5/06
[44] Quinn 2002, 16
[45] ibid., 44
[46] ibid., 48
[47] ibid., 49
[48] ibid., 131
[49] ibid., 132
[50] *I Post* 13/5/06
[51] Cascarino w Kimmage 2001, 18
[52] Curry 2006, 29, 233
[53] ibid., 323
[54] Quinn 2002, 188
[55] ibid., 182
[56] *http://news.bbc.co.uk/sport1/hi/funny_old_game/3065009.stm*
[57] *Guardian* 23/8/06

NOTES TO CHAPTER 6: PP157–203

[1] 29/8/97
[2] *L Eve Standard* 8/4/97
[3] McColl 1998, 64
[4] *Evening Mail* (Birmingham) 13/11/99

[4a] *D Tel* 20 May 2000

[5] Cited in *D Tel* 20/5/2000

[6] McColl 1998, 62

[7] *Evening Mail* (Birmingham) 13/11/99

[8] *S Times* 2/1/05

[9] Moore 1999, 17

[10] Clough w Sadler 2003, 106–7

[11] Moore 1999, 21

[12] Miller 1994, 75

[13] *S Times* 2/1/05

[14] ibid.

[15] ibid.

[16] *Times* 4/2/83

[17] Moore 1999, 13

[18] Stiles w Lawton 2003, 114–5.

[19] Stiles w Lawton 2003, 119

[20] Moore 1999, 24

[21] Ivan Ponting, *Manchester United – Player by Player,* quoted in Moore 1999, 24

[22] *D Tel* 4/9/98

[23] Barrett, 93

[24] *Times* 4/9/98

[25] ibid.

[26] *D Tel* 04/09/98

[27] ibid.

[28] *Independent* 4/9/98

[29] Soar 1995, 74

[30] Foster 2006, 272

[31] *D Mail* 13/11/61

[32] ibid.

[33] *D Mail* 18/02/55

[34] Glanville in Hamilton (ed) 1992, 100

[35] ibid, 101

[36] Nawrat and Hutchings 1994, 110

[37] Moore 1999, 22

[38] Tomlinson and Giller 2005, 27

[39] Greaves 168, 190

[40] *E News* 11/8/55

[41] *D Express* 27/9/54

[42] *News Chronicle* 1/10/57

[43] *D Mail* 4/7/06

[44] Nawrat & Hutchings 1994, 110

[45] Barrett 1999, 123

[46] Miller in Barrett 1999, 123

[47] Greaves w Scott 2003, 223–4

[48] *S Times* 12/2/61

[49] *STimes* 24/4/77

[50] *S Times* 29/1/61

[51] Greaves w Scott 2003, 190

[52] *Guardian* 16/12/78

[53] *Evening News & Star* 7/2/61

[54] *D Tel* 7/2/61

[55] Soar 1995, 129

[56] *S Express* 7/6/81

[57] Tibballs 2005, 33

[58] *L E Standard* 16/12/93

[59] *Belfast Telegraph* 24/06/99

[60] *Independent on Sunday* (London) 20/2/05

[61] *Belfast Telegraph* 24/06/99

[62] In Hamilton (ed) 1992, 173

[63] Böll 1957 (trans. 1983), 89

[64] *Guardian* 25/11/05

[65] Holt & Lloyd 2005, 70

[66] Keane 2004, 7

[67] *Guardian* 21/4/01

[68] Cited in Keane 2004, 57

[69] From 'Pardon Me for Living' in Hamilton (ed.) 1992, 175

[70] Moore 1999, 70

[71] *Guardian* 25/11/05

[72] Corry 2006, 99

[73] Keane 2004, 62

[74] Bremner 2004, 133–4

[75] *Sunday Times* 4/1/06

[76] Cited in Corry 2006, 120

[77] *Observer* 13/07/97

[78] ibid.

[79] Keane 2004, 77

[80] *I Times* 7/12/96
[81] ibid.
[82] ibid.
[83] ibid.
[84] *Observer* 3/10/04
[85] *Observer* 13/7/97
[86] *Belfast News Letter* 26/6/06
[87] *Guardian* 13/7/05
[88] *I Times* 07/12/96
[89] *L Evening Standard* 21/3/05
[90] *Sun* 5/6/00
[91] *Mirror* 21/8/01
[92] ibid.
[93] ibid.
[94] Soar and Tyler 1998, 118
[95] *Mirror* 21/8/01
[96] Soar 1995, 129
[97] ibid., 130–1
[98] *Mirror* 21/8/01
[99] Soar and Tyler 1998, 151
[100] *Daily Star* 17/5/80
[101] *Mirror* 21/8/21
[102] Joannou 2000, 314
[103] Joannou 1996, 276
[104] Moore 1999, 108

NOTES TO CHAPTER 7: PP204–218

[1] pp271–2
[2] Cited in the *Guardian* 25/5/02
[3] ibid.
[4] *S Telegraph* 2/6/02
[5] *E News* 29/11/72
[6] 10/09/72
[7] *L Times* 07/09/72
[8] *The Provisional IRA,* Patrick Bishop and Eamonn Mallie, Corgi, London, 1996, 245
[9] Corry 2006, 204, 205, 206
[10] Cited in the *S Mirror* 6/11/00
[11] Stiles w Lawton 2003, 66
[12] *Mirror* 13/6/00

[13] Quoted in *I Examiner* 23/7/05

[14] ibid.

[15] *Guardian* 2/2/02

[16] Tomlinson 2006, 156

[17] *Guardian* 2/2/02

[18] Gray 2004, 108

[19] Corry 2006, 211

[20] Walmsley 1997, 95

[21] *http://news.bbc.co.uk* 7/5/99

[22] Cascarino w Kimmage 2001, 16

[23] ibid., 106

NOTES TO CHAPTER 8: PP219–223

[1] Corry 2006, 26

[2] Bellew 2005, viii

[3] ibid. 2005, xi

[4] *S Times* 14/9/03

[5] *I Independent* 26/8/06

IN FULL FLOOD

FINBARR FLOOD

Frank, insightful and witty memoir of a career spent in professional foot-ball, as managing director of Guinness, and as chairman of the Labour Court and Shelbourne Football Club.

'Finbarr writes in straightforward but touching terms of the poverty of the times . . . [his] insights into the industrial-relations dilemmas of the 1990s are fascinating'

Sunday Independent

'not only an engrossing account of a fascinating and eventful life, but also a valuable insight into the evolution of the Irish economy from a static and tradition-laden monolith into the dynamic Celtic Tiger economy'

Irish Book Review

All author royalties to Our Lady's Hospital for Sick Children, Crumlin
Paperback: €13.99 | ISBN: 1–905483–02–3
Available from all good bookshops and from www.LibertiesPress.com

MORE THAN A GAME

SELECTED SPORTING ESSAYS

CON HOULIHAN

Definitive collection of sports writing – on Gaelic games, soccer and rugby to hare coursing and cricket – by the acknowledged master of the craft.

'The writing is impeccable . . . The pen portraits are little gems . . . Proves that sports journalism, when done well, can be a real art form'

Books Ireland

'A wonderful read, and not just for the sports nuts'

Ireland's Own

Paperback: €14.99 | ISBN: 0–9545335–0–X
Hardback: €25 | ISBN: 0–9545335–1–8
Available from all good bookshops and from www.LibertiesPress.com

A Sporting Eye

Fifty Years of Irish and International Sports Photography

Fionnbar Callanan

'a captivating collection of 150 black-and-white and colour shots, taken all over the world'

Munster Express

'this book, covering sporting events from the 1940s to the present day, will delight sports fans and nostalgists alike'

Irish Times

All author royalties to the Irish Hospice Foundation
Hardback: €25 | ISBN: 0–95483–01–5
Available from all good bookshops and from www.LibertiesPress.com